D0606707

AMERICAN CRAFTS

A SOURCE BOOK FOR THE HOME

AMERICANCRAFTS
A SOURCE BOOK FOR THE HOME

BY KATHERINE PEARSON
▪DESIGN BY KIYOSHI KANAI▪

STEWART, TABORI & CHANG, PUBLISHERS, NEW YORK

Photographs:
Pages 2-3: Stoneware vessel, Richard DeVore. Photo by Breton Littlehales. Page 4: Glass, Michael Glancy. Photo courtesy Heller Gallery. Photo by Gene Dwiggins. Pages 8-9: Teapot, Peter Shire, 1981. Photo courtesy Janus Gallery.

Design: Kiyoshi Kanai
Assistant Designer: Ida Nakano

Library of Congress Cataloging in Publication Data

Pearson, Katherine.
  American Crafts for the home.

  Bibliography: p.
  Includes index.
  1. House furnishings—United States. 2. Handicrafts—United States. I. Title.
TX311.P36 1983   745.593   82-19477
ISBN 0-941434-30-3

Text copyright © 1983 Katherine Pearson
Illustrations copyright © 1983 Stewart, Tabori & Chang Publishers, Inc.
This copyright is held for the benefit of the individual photographers who retain copyright in their individual photographs.

All rights reserved. No part of the contents of this book may be reproduced by any means without the written permission of the publisher. Published in 1983 by Stewart, Tabori & Chang, Publishers, New York, New York.
Distributed by Workman Publishing Company, 1 West 39th Street, New York, New York 10018

TABLE OF CONTENTS

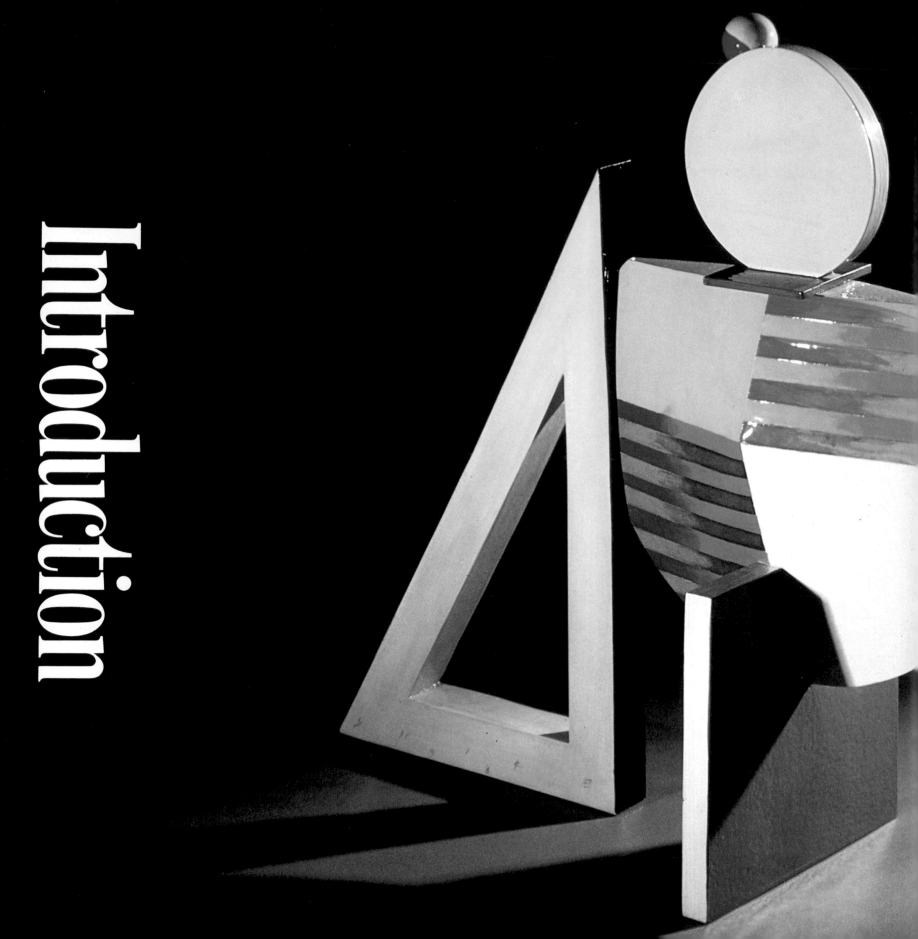

Introduction

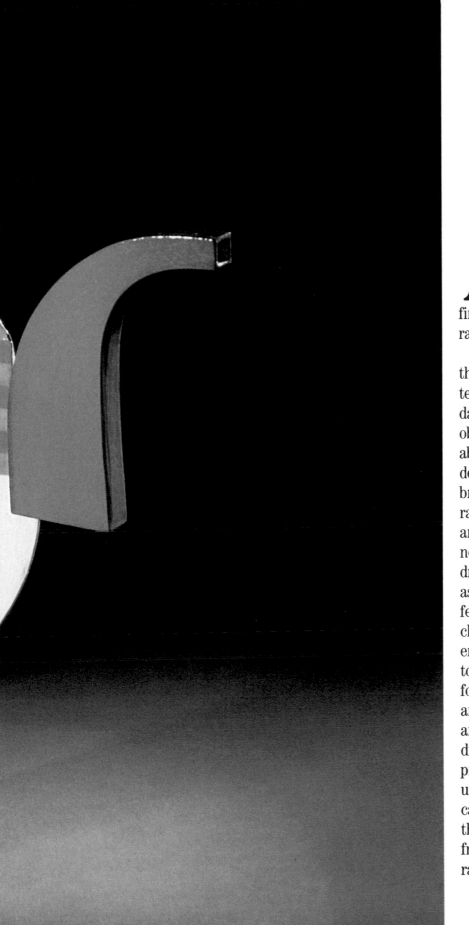

All across America, craftsmen working in clay, fiber, wood, metal, and glass are creating beautiful handmade objects for every room in the home. There are functional objects, decorative ones, and works of fine art that would enrich any interior, whether of contemporary or traditional design.

American Crafts is a source book for the home of some of the most outstanding work currently available. I have attempted to survey the rich diversity of work being created today and to present stimulating ideas for incorporating these objects into your current home setting. Items for the kitchen abound. Ceramic cookware, for example, beautifully decorated to go from oven to table, along with copper pots, brass and forged iron cooking utensils, wooden spoons, spice racks, and chopping blocks are among the items illustrated and described here. For the dining table, you'll discover dinnerware patterns that are sometimes understated, sometimes dramatic, but always distinctive. Handblown glass stemware as well as elegant silver and pewter flatware round out the offerings designed to grace a table setting. With all of these to choose from, you can either start from scratch to create an entirely new table setting, or you can select individual pieces to add a dramatic note to an existing table setting, whether formal or informal. Silver decanters, coffee and tea services, and ceramic teapots are among the other designs—traditional and innovative—that may be called into service or proudly displayed and never used. In all cases, I have attempted to provide information about how the craftsman works, since an understanding of the basic working methods and techniques can help you to evaluate quality. Furthermore, a glossary at the back of the book provides a quick reference to the most frequently used terms, such as stoneware, earthenware, raku, salt glaze, slip decoration, and glaze.

If you are thinking about purchasing a piece of fine furniture, once again you can choose from a wealth of singular furniture designs being handcrafted today. I have chosen to present a broad sampling of this work, which also ranges from the most traditional to the most innovative styles. Pieces include tables, chairs, and desks, as well as, storage items for the bedroom, living room, dining room, or kitchen. And you'll find all of these pieces in a variety of traditional and exotic woods—from ash to zebrawood.

If you already collect fine art, or are ready to begin, I am sure you'll discover objects here too that will tempt you, including ceramic vessels, hanging plates, glass sculptures and vases, tapestries, and quilts. Gift-giving for special occasions need no longer be a chore, nor uninspired. Coiled and woven baskets, turned wooden bowls, perfume bottles, jewelry and valet boxes, and fireplace accessories are among the distinctive gift ideas presented. In addition, should you discover one craftsman whose work you especially admire, I have devoted one chapter to how to proceed with a commission. Most craftsmen welcome the opportunity to create something special for a client and will work closely with you.

Many of the works illustrated in this book were photographed in the homes of young professionals, new and established collectors, and gallery owners. They are just a few of the growing number of Americans who have discovered the unmatched pleasures of buying, owning, using, and displaying contemporary American crafts. These collectors are drawn to crafts for a variety of reasons. Some people particularly value the exceptionally fine craftsmanship typical of the best contemporary crafts—an attention to detail in the execution of each work rarely seen in commercially produced objects. Other people, who wish to personalize their homes or offices, find crafts an excellent way to express their tastes and make their places unique. For many, the craftsmen themselves are part of the appeal. Unlike art movements

centered either on the east or west coasts, craftsmen live and work in every state, giving you the chance to talk with them and know them. Everyone likes to talk about himself and craftsmen are no exception. Because the craftsman sees his work as an extension of himself, you'll find him, in most instances, eager to talk with you. In addition to local craftsmen whose studios you can visit, craft fairs all across the country provide an excellent opportunity to learn directly from the maker. Galleries also encourage exhibiting craftsmen to be on hand for openings, and in the case of major commissions, a gallery director is likely to foster an exchange between the purchaser and the craftsman. With this kind of personal involvement, the piece you bring home, already unique, carries with it the special stories and memories that enhance its personal value. A beginning collector need not be intimidated by the price of contemporary crafts. It is possible to start a collection without a huge investment. Within each category of crafts that I discuss throughout the book, I have endeavored to give you not only price ranges for the best work available, but also a greater appreciation for the considerations a craftsman must make in pricing his work. By describing some of the difficulties encountered by the craftsman, the unpredictable nature of many craft materials, and the skills required to create high quality work, I think you'll have a better understanding of prices.

Although the handmade object certainly has a special status among mass-produced ones, craftsmen have not overly romanticized the work of the hand. They have, in fact, often embraced new technologies in their work. What is more important to the craftsman is the freedom to make personal statements in functional objects. Rather than design safe patterns, objects, or forms that must sell to a mass audience, he concentrates on creating unique statements that appeal to a smaller, more self-confident group.

The remarkable vitality in the crafts movement today has been building since World War II. Prior to that time, craft skills were learned primarily within the family. Using local materials only, both skills and traditional patterns were passed along from one generation to another, much as we see happening still in Appalachian wood carving, splint baskets, cornshuck dolls, and quilt patterns. That picture began to change, however, with the GI bill. With funding available to veterans, college enrollment jumped tremendously, increasing monies available to universities. Art departments could, for the first time, afford to buy wheels, kilns, looms, and metalworking equipment and thereby expand their course offerings beyond the core curriculum in painting and drawing. Of that first generation of craftsmen trained in art schools, most did not set out to become the next great potter, but many who were required to take a course in ceramics found clay to be an appealing medium. Thus hooked, they began to develop skills working with clay while at the same time they absorbed the basic principles of art and design.

To create original work (and therefore scorn derivative work) is one of the cardinal rules of art school training. When craft instruction moved from the family to the university, it was inevitable that the new generation of craftsmen would apply their knowledge and skills to wholly original designs, rather than to the repetition of historic patterns. For the first time in craft media, an attitude toward experimentation was fostered and an emphasis on making a personal statement prevailed. The innovative and individual works we enjoy today are a direct outgrowth of these changes in craft education after World War II.

American Crafts celebrates the work of the leaders as well as some of the outstanding newcomers to the crafts movement. It's an armchair look at some of their best work, meant not as a collector's comprehensive list of the most important craftsmen in America, but rather as a rich sampling of the astounding diversity of work in all the major media. The stunning four-color photographs throughout this book are accompanied by brief descriptions about how things are made, so you can learn how to judge quality for yourself. Ideas for displaying, grouping, and lighting to ensure that each piece is presented to its best advantage are also given. And although special care of handmade objects is the exception rather than the rule, advice is provided on how to care for specific materials that will guarantee generations of use.

Finally and most importantly, as a real source book, *American Crafts* contains two invaluable directories: one listing every craftsman whose work is featured in the book and another listing major galleries across the country where good work may be seen. In the individual listing for each craftsman, you will find information on the type of work he creates, the medium in which work is produced, whether or not commissions are accepted, the price range for most work, and the major galleries in which the craftsman's work can be found. The separate state-by-state listing of galleries tells you at a glance what galleries to visit in your area or when you're on a vacation or business trip.

With this book as introduction and guide, I hope you will explore the world of crafts further, discovering good work on your own. Had American craftsmen not found a ready market for their work among the general public, collectors, and museums, the crafts movement would never have reached the vital, active place it is now in. It is my hope that this book will increase that market while it introduces you to a remarkable new source for unique art work and functional pieces for your home.

Rich color on simple, contemporary forms distinguishes the work of Richard and Sandra Farrell. Pinks, reds, and pastel greens are used on matching dinner plates and salad/dessert plates as well as on companion serving pieces, such as these covered porcelain casseroles. Photo by Joseph Kugielsky.

Ceramic Cookware

Fine cookware and kitchen accessories of clay are being produced today by some of America's most respected craftsmen. Unlike craftsmen of earlier centuries, who made a few simple vessels and tools to suit many purposes, contemporary craftsmen offer the modern cook specialized equipment for today's varied menus and sophisticated tastes.

With a few esoteric exceptions, you'll find that all of the specialized cookware available in gourmet kitchen shops is also available from craftsmen, at a price and performance comparable to the professional quality of equipment sold in those shops. American craftsmen can supply you with kitchen equipment every step of the way—containers for storing dry ingredients; bowls for preparing and mixing; pots and pans for boiling, baking, roasting, broiling, and sautéing. And with the craftsman's beautifully hand-decorated cookware, there's no need to transfer food from one dish to another before serving.

For preparing and cooking food, ceramic utensils run the gamut from mixing bowls, colanders, skillets, open baking and roasting pans to covered casseroles and steamers—all handsome enough for table service. Food storage ceases to be a utilitarian chore when cannisters and spice racks are handsomely, and often playfully, decorated, in hand-painted clay.

Handcrafted cooking equipment grew out of the self-sufficient craftsman's own needs and cooking habits. Thus, utensils and

Left: *Pottery and wood warm Louis and Sandra Grotta's pristine white kitchen. A collection of stoneware cooking pots (most by the late William Wyman) is handsomely displayed within a cabinet niche. The vegetable-filled ceramic bowl is by Craig Easter and the dramatically striped wooden bowl was turned by Bob Stocksdale. The cat's favorite perch is a graceful three-legged stool by Joyce and Edgar Anderson. Photo by Tom Grotta.*

Below: *The term "ovenware" indicates a piece designed for baking. Julie Larson stamps "ovenware" on the back of each of her stoneware pieces, along with the liquid capacity of the dish. Substantial handles make it easy to carry this hefty baking dish—poacher to table or buffet, and its unusual octagonal design and earthy glazes make it a handsome addition to any table. 3½ quart capacity, 3 × 21 × 9". Photo by John Littleton.*

Bottom Left: *The deep coppery glazes that Harriet Cohen achieves in her casseroles are characteristic of the earthy tones of high-fired stoneware. The stoneware basket is by Michael Cohen. Photo by Jonathan Wallen.*

Bottom Right: *This durable stoneware steamer by Jonathan Kaplan and Janet Huling is simple and well-proportioned. Photo by Terry Wild.*

decorative styles available are as varied as the personal preferences and diets of the craftsmen themselves. Their designs are tested and refined through day-to-day use in their own kitchens. For example, new awareness of nutrients lost in prolonged cooking of vegetables prompted potters to modify a clay casserole to create a steamer, which cooks vegetables quickly in very little water, preserving the maximum amount of nutrients. The ubiquitous honey pot was first made for the craftsmen's own use and proliferated as public demand grew. Now you can reap the benefits of the craftsmen's personal freedom in designing cookware.

The greatest variety of functional crafts for the kitchen are made of stoneware, porcelain, or earthenware clays. Cookware made of any of these ceramic materials can be brought from oven to table, but each material has special properties that affect its appearance, its day-to-day use, and its care.

Stoneware

Stoneware is a very rugged, high-fired clay, which quite literally has a stonelike quality—very hard

Below: Tacha Vosburgh's steamer is fashioned after a Yunnan-style Chinese steamer. It should be used on top of a slightly smaller saucepan containing several inches of water. As the water in the saucepan boils, the steam rises through the central chimney of the steamer (visible in the photo) to cook the foods, preserving their flavor, color, and nutrients. Vosburgh has left the exterior of the stoneware un-glazed to contrast with the glazed landscape images on the lids. Rope handles stay cool to the touch. 10" diameter.

Bottom: These covered casseroles by Tyrone Larson are made with matching trivets for oven-to-table convenience. The snug covers and heat-retaining property of the stoneware make them ideal for buffet service. Left, 1 quart casserole, 6½ × 8 × 6½"; right, 2 quart casserole, 8 × 10½ × 8". Photo by John Littleton.

and kind of rough to the touch when unglazed. Stoneware can often be identified by the tiny, dark flecks on its surface after firing. The flecks are iron particles within the clay which rise through the surface and the glaze during the firing process. You can see these flecks, for instance, in the casserole by Jonathan Kaplan and Janet Huling on page 15, a simple, sturdy form that enhances the natural qualities of stoneware. The high-firing (at 1200° C and above) that gives stoneware its strength also mutes bright glaze colors, so stoneware always retains an earthy, warm appearance. That doesn't mean dull, however, as you can see from the rich coppery glazes of Harriet Cohen's casseroles on page 15 and the sophisticated glazing on Julie Larson's baking dish on page 15.

These handsome stoneware dishes also offer superior baking results. Stoneware absorbs heat readily and distributes it evenly for perfectly browned breads and blue-ribbon pie crusts.

If baking bread is your passion, you may have already experienced the unique benefits of stoneware bread pans. When Pierre Franey, writer on food and cooking equip-ment for the New York Times, happened upon a handsome stone-ware bread pan, he praised its even heat distribution, noting that stoneware resulted in a better crust than a black metal pan.

Even if you never bake bread, you can still enjoy the benefits of stoneware in the even heat distri-bution it provides in open baking and roasting dishes, souffle dishes, covered casseroles and steamers, individual soup bowls, and soup tureens. In addition to the stan-dard square and rectangular bak-ing dishes, such as the ones you might use for a batch of brownies or a tasty lasagne, you'll find round and oval alternatives available in a range of sizes to suit your recipes and your guest list.

Stoneware also holds heat for a long time. Thus, cooks experienced with stoneware recommend lowering the oven temperature to 25° F less than the temperature suggested in the recipe. Because of these heat-retaining properties, food stays pleasantly warm in a stoneware serving dish—a boon for second helpings. This also en-ables you to plan hot hors d'oeuvres for your guests that might not be practical otherwise. For example, you might consider serving guests hot soup as they ar-

Below: Frances Lee Heminway produces a complete line of unembellished porcelain dinnerware and table accessories, all finished in a white satin matte glaze with an appealing sheen.

Left: *In this oval baking dish, Mara Superior captures the naiveté of American folk art, but both the simple drawing and the apparent delicacy of the porcelain are deceiving. The hand-built form is thoughtfully designed in high-fired porcelain for reliable strength and performance. Though all of her work is of a similar style, Superior does not repeat a given design in any of her pieces.*

resulting in surprising durability. The refined white casseroles and baking dishes you've seen, embellished with lovely hand decoration, belie the great strength of porcelain. So it's not surprising to discover that craftsmen use porcelain to make almost every form of baking dish, casserole, and steamer. Although porcelain has no real functional advantage over stoneware—the two materials have similar properties—some people prefer the more formal or delicate look that porcelain makes possible. Porcelain is compatible with many different decorations, from the luscious glazes of Sandra and Richard Farrell's casseroles, on pages 12 – 13, and the naive drawings on Mara Superior's baking dish (above) to the unembellished forms of Frances Lee Heminway's bowls (left).

rive instead of traditional hors d'oeuvres. A hefty soup tureen with compatible cups or mugs set out on a quilt-covered table is as inviting as a roaring fire. For more festive celebrations, mulled wine in a tureen would surely welcome guests on a cool winter night. Soup or wine can be heated in the oven right in the tureen, which can then be counted on to keep it all warm—even without a flame underneath.

Porcelain

Porcelain is a white clay body that becomes vitreous, or glasslike in its hardness after firing. Like stoneware, it is fired at a very high temperature (1300°C or above),

Below: Charles B. Nalle has created a series of service pieces in an updated Art Deco style. The slip-cast porcelain set includes soup and salad bowls, a larger serving bowl, tumblers and pitcher. Salad bowl, 4 × 4 × 5". Pitcher, 12 × 6 × 4". Photo by Thomas Stiltz.

Bottom: Thickly rolled rims and fat looped handles create a cohesive design in which each element is appropriate to another. The additional thickness also adds extra strength to the rims of low-fired earthenware casseroles by Stanley Mace Andersen.

Right: Beth Fein's watermelon cup illustrates the intense colors possible with low-fired clays, in this case white earthenware.

Earthenware

The greatest appeal of earthenware is that it can be decorated with bright glaze colors because it is fired at relatively lower temperatures (under 1100°C). For example, the bold orange and green of Stanley Mace Andersen's casseroles, on this page, would not be possible at the higher firing temperature ranges of stoneware and porcelain. The color of earthenware clay body may be either white or a deep terra cotta color. Unlike stoneware and porcelain however, earthenware is highly porous (think how quickly water seeps through the walls of a terra cotta planter); therefore, it must be glazed to hold water for cooking. Unfortunately, the porous clay is more easily chipped than stoneware and porcelain and so it must be handled more carefully in baking and washing.

Flameware

Clay cookware, in general, cannot be used on top of the range. Flameware, however, is a unique clay body, a form of stoneware with a very low rate of thermal expansion, which means that the pot can be used directly on a surface unit, either gas or electric. Cur-

This patty-pan squash, eggplant, and row of spring asparagus are actually trompe l'oeil serving pieces in white earthenware by Barbara Eigen. She develops her own glazes in order to come as close as possible to the color and texture of real pears, pumpkins, cabbages, artichokes, and other fruits and vegetables. Photo by Jim Kiernan.

Below: As a rule, clay cookware cannot be used on top of the range. But Ron Propst's flameware skillet is made from a special clay formula that will not break over the direct heat of electric or gas range-top units. The wooden butter dish and knife by Joe Chasnoff and Judy Azulay are made of solid wild cherry and finished with natural oils and may be used to serve butter or cheese. Photo by Joseph Kugielsky.

Bottom: Beth Changstrom's steamer is decorated with a simple iris pattern. One piece from a coordinated set of dinnerware and serving pieces, this steamer, like other casserole forms, can be taken right to the table for serving. A steamer, meant to be used over a saucepan with water in it, should be heated at the same time as the saucepan; as the water in the saucepan comes to a boil, the clay has time to adjust slowly to the temperature difference.

rently, however, only a few American potters are producing flameware skillets, sauce pans, and butter warmers. Versatile flameware allows you to sear meat or sauté ingredients on top of the range, move the pan to the oven for baking and, if need be, finish the dish under the broiler—all in one pan. You can even prepare your recipe ahead of time and freeze it in flameware, but you must remove it from the freezer and let it thaw for an hour before heating.

Like other clay cookware, flameware is dishwasher-safe. There is a risk that the clay will absorb water if you leave it to soak overnight, however. If flameware has not been allowed to dry completely, the build-up of moisture inside its walls—whether from soaking or recent washing—may cause the piece to crack when reheated.

Oven-to-tableware

Clay pieces intended for cooking are always designed to be attractive enough to double as serving dishes. In commercial terms, they are ''oven-to-tableware.'' No matter what the decorative style of your kitchen or family dinner-

ware, the ceramic items available from craftsmen can complement your table service. You'll find a variety of styles, from the straight-forward warmth and simplicity of stoneware and the brightly glazed hues of earthenware to the exquisite refinements of porcelain.

Think for a moment about the decoration on oven-to-tableware. Most decoration on commercial cookware consists of machine-applied decals. To enjoy the softer effect of hand-painted decoration, one must look to more expensive china, which is usually imported. Lovely as such dishes are, few of us are blessed with them unless we have been fortunate enough to inherit them or receive them as a wedding gift. At a single craft fair, however, you will find many different styles of hand-painted decoration on porcelain, stoneware, and earthenware at prices that are competitive with or lower than imports. The craftsmen who produce these ceramic works draw inspiration from a wide variety of sources—traditional oriental brushstrokes, naive country French figures, and classic floral decoration, as well as stylistic trends reflective of the broader art world. What these dishes have in common is the unmistakable im-

Below: Byron Temple's *distinctively contemporary salt-glazed storage jars draw inspiration from eighteenth-century salt-glazed pottery. In this modern kitchen of stainless steel and laminate, they are framed by Warren Durbin's woven tray. Dan Dustin's spoons are shaped with regard for the natural growth pattern of the wood, making each one unique. Photo by David Arky.*

Right: *The Yellow Cab cookie jar is one of a fleet by Glenn Appleman that includes a Packard Convertible and a Buick Roadmaster. Low-firing of earthenware permits bright glossy colors and the metallic luster glazes that simulate chrome. Photo by David Arky.*

print of the maker's hand.

The uniqueness of the handmade object can impart a special charm to your table. Even one attractively decorated bowl, pot, or pan can lift your usual table setting out of the ordinary. For example, a hand-decorated stoneware or porcelain pie dish is an especially nice substitute for a glass or metal pan. As you serve each guest, the hand-applied decoration of the plate is revealed. Even if you rely on frozen crusts, you can transfer a slightly thawed pie crust to a stoneware plate of standard size. (And when a pie or quiche is presented in a good-looking handmade plate, who would suspect a frozen crust!)

Below Left: *This batter bowl by Michael Cohen has a thumb grip opposite the spout for ease in pouring a heavy batter. Other details, such as a beaded rim and the smooth rim line that becomes a spout, distinguish this form. Cohen's work is represented in the permanent collection of the Museum of Modern Art, New York City. 10" diameter × 7".*

Below Right: *A set of seven stoneware mixing bowls by Tyrone Larson illustrates the impressive control possible with experienced wheel-throwing; these range from the smallest at one cup to the largest at eleven quarts, all of accurate measure. Smallest, 4" diameter × 2". Largest, 14" diameter × 7½". Photo by John Littleton.*

Bottom Left: *Mixing bowls are made for day-to-day tasks, and few clays are more durable for constant use than stoneware. Jonathan Kaplan and Janet Huling opted for stoneware's strength in a set of bowls that have an appealing simplicity and stability. Photo by Terry Wild.*

Bottom Right: *A ceramic colander has greater weight, and therefore greater stability, than one of thin metal. Nadine Gay highlights this advantage with a broad, continuous foot on her white earthenware colander. Substantial handles that stand away from the bowl make the colander easy to hold even with steaming hot spaghetti in it. Photo by Joseph Kugielsky.*

Baking and Serving Dishes

When you are serving a very large crowd, the craftsman's overscaled platters, baking dishes, and bowls may be especially useful. Although restaurant supply houses can provide functional containers in which to prepare large quantities, there's little warmth in serving food in industrial pans. In contrast, big clay pots, steaming hot from the oven, announce a "come and get it" welcome to guests. These great clay baking and serving pieces evoke an image of an abundant sideboard. In addition, the heat-retaining properties of ceramic pots keep the food warm, relieving the host or hostess from constant attention to the buffet.

Storing, Marinating and Mixing

Ceramic vessels are ideally suited for food storage and preparation. The vitreous, or glasslike, glazes on stoneware and porcelain cannisters, spice jars, and cookie jars keep moisture from seeping in, and household pests cannot chew or crawl through ceramic walls and snug-fitting lids. The lip of the container and the underside of the lid are often intentionally left unglazed to diminish chances of chipping and to ensure a tighter fit.

The mottled salt-glazed crocks and jugs, like Byron Temple's, on page 21, continue a long-standing tradition of salt-glazed storage containers, which date from Colonial America. Early salt-glazed crocks held everything from ground meal to fruit. Today's cooks are finding that their contemporary counterparts also preserve dry pasta, teas, and a host of other foods.

Ceramic bowls or pans are excellent for marinating foods, as even acidic foods will not react chemically with the high-fired glazes of clay. There's no danger that food will discolor or absorb an unpleasant taste from the bowl or cooking pan.

Clay mixing bowls, batter bowls, and colanders are heavier than plastic or stainless steel, and there's comforting stability in their weight and their more secure base. And of course, they are often more beautiful. It's a pleasure to mix a bread dough in a handsome stoneware bowl—stainless steel seems cold and institutional in comparison. And a clay colander of fresh garden vegetables makes a handsome still-life in your sink.

Left: *To create a contemporary, somewhat architectural pitcher in white porcelain, Don Williams first throws a large cylinder form on the wheel and then cuts away the space for the handle. Photo by Joseph Kugielsky.*

How to Care for Ceramic Cookware

Most craftsmen recommend confidently that their sturdy clay cookware go right into the dishwasher. Like anything in the dishwasher, however, a ceramic pot may be likely to chip. After many years of dishwashing, the glaze may develop fine lines in an overall crackle pattern. Always ask the craftsman or gallery owner what care is advisable. You may decide that you value the piece enough to wash it each time by hand.

Clay cookware will not tolerate sudden temperature changes without breaking. Although you can take a dish from a hot oven to the table, you cannot safely move a casserole directly from the refrigerator to the oven nor put a hot dish in cold water. To be on the safe side, many potters (and commercial manufacturers) recommend that when cooking in a ceramic pot, you put the prepared dish into a *cold* oven. The cookware then heats slowly as the oven heats. You can't get ahead by preheating empty cookware in the oven; without food or liquid to absorb some of the heat, you risk breakage here, too. Some potters are casual about this precaution, usually because they've gone for years without a mishap in their own kitchens. You should keep in mind this property of ceramics, however, lest you lose a favorite pot.

What to Look for When Buying Ceramic Cookware

When you are evaluating functional cookware, there is no substitute for handling the piece. You can determine the weight and balance of the piece and the comfort of holding it only by picking it up. An understanding of how a pot is made will also give you some help in evaluating ceramic work.

Most functional pottery is formed from a lump of soft, wet clay centered on a rotating disk (the wheel). This method of making pots is commonly referred to as "throwing pots on a wheel." The potter uses only his hands to pull the clay up to form the walls of a bowl. It's harder than it looks! As

Left: *Emphasis is on form in Sarah Bodine's white stoneware cream and sugar set, designs that were refined over several years with special attention to performance in pouring. They create a lovely tabletop still-life paired with a blue-and-white checked porcelain platter by Ted Keller. Photo by David Arky.*

the wheel turns, clay that is not perfectly centered will wobble or undulate and soon collapse. It takes many, many months, even years, of daily practice to master throwing on the wheel. Since a beginner can throw a pot fairly quickly, although it may be poorly formed, you must look for the signs of well-developed skill: uniform thickness, controlled form, and flawless glazing.

One sign of a poorly skilled potter is a bottom-heavy pot. To appreciate the difference, consider the ideal: A piece from an accomplished potter will have walls of uniform thickness, and the bottom will be no thicker than the side walls. It's common for new potters to leave a lot of clay at the bottom, as they lack the long practice required to pull the clay evenly into the walls. A serious student often throws a pot and then slices it in half in order to see if the thickness is uniform. Unfortunately, you will not be able to slice a finished pot in half to measure the thickness of the walls and the bottom, but as you begin to pick up and compare more and more pottery, you will develop a sense of the correct weight in relation to the size of a piece.

The next step, which is tricky

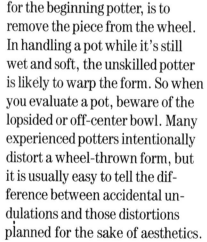

for the beginning potter, is to remove the piece from the wheel. In handling a pot while it's still wet and soft, the unskilled potter is likely to warp the form. So when you evaluate a pot, beware of the lopsided or off-center bowl. Many experienced potters intentionally distort a wheel-thrown form, but it is usually easy to tell the difference between accidental undulations and those distortions planned for the sake of aesthetics.

Careless glazing is perhaps the most obvious sign of a beginner or clumsy worker. If a glaze is applied too thickly, it will accumulate around the foot of the bowl. After firing, the casual potter may attempt to conceal this mistake by grinding the undersurface of the piece smooth. But this ground surface can be easily distinguished from the mark of an experienced potter, who deftly draws a wire through the bottom of the piece to remove it from the wheel, leaving a concentric wire-cut swirl.

Uniform thickness of the glaze,

well-developed color, and an apparent close bonding between the glaze and the clay body are signs of an experienced craftsman. Recognition of these fine qualities comes more easily after comparing the work of many potters with differing levels of experience.

Occasionally, tiny pinholes occur in a glaze as a result of impurities that were trapped in the glaze. Dust in the studio, for example, can cause pinholes. These tiny pinholes, however, are not considered to affect adversely the quality of the piece. A great many pinholes or larger craters, though, are an indication of careless working habits and are particularly objectionable on functional pottery where they might trap food. The potter must also take into account such unpredictable variables as the amount of moisture in the air when glazing. On a rainy or humid day he must mix a heavier glaze, since the glaze will absorb moisture from the air and become thinner even after it is applied to the

clay. In fact, nothing that the potter does is an easily acquired skill. The potter, as well as those who work in fiber, wood, metal, or glass, must put in several years of dedicated practice and experimentation to be able to achieve the professional quality of work that you seek for your home.

This brief overview omits the enormous technical knowledge of clay mixes, glaze chemistry, and firing temperatures that the potter must master in addition to skills of throwing. The more sophisticated your knowledge of ceramics, the better your judgment of any craftsman's work will be. If you spot only one flaw, there may be others that you cannot detect until you begin to use the pot.

In addition to these signs of serious craftsmanship, there are other signs of quality that stem from the functional design of a piece. For instance, when you use any oven-to-tableware, you'll probably be moving among family and guests with a hot serving dish, so the design of the handles on both the lid and the base is especially important. You should be able to grasp the handles securely with protective hot pads. When you pick up a casserole or baking dish before purchasing it, consider the thickness of a hot pad and the added weight and heat when the dish is filled with steaming food. Aesthetically, the handles or knob on a lid should look like they are an integral part of the form and not appendages. A recent trend to overscaled handles on casseroles has produced a few unfortunate pieces in which the handles overpower the form.

The inside contour of any clay cookware also influences the ease with which it can be cleaned. If the side walls are joined to the bottom of a bowl or baking dish in a rounded contour, it will be easier to clean than if the walls and bottom meet at a sharp right angle. No doubt you've experienced this already in commercial cookware. Removing accumulated food and stains is even more difficult under an inverted lip or when a joint connects at less than a right angle.

With the tremendous numbers of professional craftsmen producing cookware, there's no need to settle for anything less than top quality.

If you truly want to learn, ask questions. People love to talk about themselves and their work. Craftsmen are no exception. Their work is highly personal and they are usually delighted to tell you about it. The craftsman's story goes home with you in the piece you choose, becoming a part of the memories and personal connections that add pleasure to your day-to-day kitchen routine.

Most metalsmiths who make knives use a high carbon tool steel, which holds a sharp edge longer than stainless steel. Bob Coogan makes functional kitchen knives, such as this heavy duty cleaver, serviceable little herb chopper, and one-of-a-kind utility knives that are as much fun to look at as they are to use. Photo by David Arky.

Metal Pots, Pans, & Utensils

With the industrial revolution, the independent metalsmith became anonymous, lending his vast knowledge and design talents to a manufacturer's brand name. With the craftsman's assimilation into mass production, we lost not only meticulous handwork, but the highly personal styles that even today allow an art historian to identify work done by a particular craftsman two hundred years ago. Contemporary metalsmiths, once again working independently, have revived both the handwork and the idiosyncrasies of individually wrought styles.

While continuing a tradition of handcrafted copper pots, American craftsmen are also making use of modern technology to cast one-of-a-kind pots in iron and bronze. Blacksmiths forge handsome black iron utensils sturdy enough for years of daily use. And knifemakers are exploring unique knife designs for kitchen, dining, and outdoor use.

Pots and Pans

For the purist, there's no substitute for copper when it comes to making delicate sauces. And even a novice cook appreciates copper cookware for the gleaming warmth and richness it imparts to the kitchen. Now, after a long hiatus, American craftsmen are again hammering sheets of copper into saucepans, omelet pans, dutch ovens, and tea kettles.

Although performance and appearance are reason enough to covet this aristocratic metal, the craftsman's singular design distinguishes his pot even from the *crème de la crème* of copper cookware. Stephen Hyer, for example, has created the ultimate tea kettle, shown on page 29; it is a working steam calliope with

Left: *When not in use, Gina Mowry's handsome copper skillet decorates the mantle of this kitchen fireplace. The long, gracefully curved handle is contoured to a chef's hand and forearm, making it easy to support the 12" diameter, pewter-lined skillet. Photo by David Arky.*

Below: *In order to achieve a new form that will perform better, Curtis LaFollette borrows from industrial technology. His intriguing olive oil can was shaped in copper by a commercial die-forming process and then carefully hand-finished. Photo by Joseph Kugielsky.*

five keys on which you can play lively tunes as the water boils. Also unique are the elegant and contemporary lines of Curtis La-Follette's unusual olive oil can, on this page, a tool for the discriminating cook who is as conscious of good design as he is of prime ingredients.

Forged iron, while at the opposite end of the hierarchy of metals, holds its own among them for its excellent properties of heat conduction. It is also useful for dishes that must be cooked partly on top of the stove and partly in the oven. Gary Noffke, whose iron skillet and copper coffee maker are shown on page 33, is one of the very few metalsmiths producing exceptional cookware in iron today. Another is Jerry Harpster who casts pots of tin-lined bronze, see page 29, also known for good heat conduction.

Like your grandmother's cast-iron skillet, iron pots should be seasoned before use. They must also be dried thoroughly before storage, and occasionally they should be wiped lightly with cooking oil to preserve their seasoning. Although the weight of iron cookware is a drawback, its sturdiness is a plus. Properly cared for, iron pots can last for generations.

Cooking Utensils

Kitchen utensils—spatulas, skimmers or strainers, skewers, and cooking forks—should be out within easy reach of the cook, not squirreled away in drawers. Forged iron utensils from blacksmiths, often highlighted with brass and copper, are worth keeping on display. These utensils come with a matching rack, as the craftsman knows well that you'll want them out for your convenience and for guests' admiring eyes.

Today's blacksmiths don't shoe horses, by the way, and their work rarely has the bulk and heaviness of horseshoes. The new generation of blacksmiths, many of whom have been trained in art schools, achieve surprising fluidity

Left: *The steam outlet of Stephen Hyer's magnificient copper tea kettle is fitted with a miniature keyboard and five musical pipes. When the water boils, tunes can be played on his Original Steam Calliope Teakettle. 8 × 14 × 7". Photo by Joseph Kugielsky.*

Below: *This cast bronze casserole by Jerry Harpster has a wooden handle that is removable for oven cooking. The care of tin-lined bronze pots is much like that of tin-lined copper pots. The handle of Dan Dustin's lilac-wood spoon has slight ridges (created by the wood's natural splitting during carving) that contrast with the bowl's smooth finish. Casserole, 7" diameter. Spoon, 11" length. Photo by Joseph Kugielsky.*

in iron. Their utensils have open, vinelike designs that make them charming to display and less heavy in the cook's hand. In addition to forged black iron, contemporary craftsmen also forge and fabricate stainless steel. Two fine examples are Joseph L. Brandom's set of utensils (right) and David Paul Bacharach's brass and stainless tongs on page 31.

Today's craftsman tends to produce only those things on which he can improve. For instance, a great many specialized tools, such as nutmeg graters, apple corers, and citrus zesters, are now widely available. The craftsman leaves these items to the relatively low-cost production techniques of the factory.

Knives

A handmade kitchen knife is for someone who recognizes and appreciates the feel of a good knife and who wants the very best. Knives available range from herb choppers, small paring and multi-purpose knives to carving sets and hefty cleavers. In addition to kitchen knives, craftsmen make a wealth of distinctive outdoor and hunting knives.

The metalsmith uses a high-

·31· METAL POTS, PANS & UTENSILS

Above: *In a modern interpretation of antique tableware, David Paul Bacharach hammers bronze into lightweight, fluid handles capped off with highly polished and engraved stainless steel. These elaborately decorated vegetable tongs would add elegance to any buffet or seated dinner.*

Below: *The handle and blade of Bryant Clark's graceful herb chopper echo one another in shape. The beautifully contoured walnut handle provides a firm grip for lively chopping. 8 × 8½ × 1¼". Photo by Jonathan Wallen.*

Bottom: *David Boye says of his knives, "The user feels a sort of grace and power which makes everyday tasks more enjoyable." Photo by David Arky.*

Right: *This three-piece coffee steamer was a collaborative effort between metalsmith Gary Noffke, who fabricated the copper steamer, and glass artist Fritz Dreisbach, who made the glass drip cone and jar. Hand-textured surfaces distinguish both the steamer and the square steel skillet. Photo by Joseph Kugielsky.*

carbon tool steel, better quality than is generally available in commercial knives. These knives hold a sharp edge much longer than commercial knives, but do require more care when sharpening is needed. If you are not close enough to return the knife to the maker for periodic sharpening, you may need to commit yourself to learning how to correctly sharpen with a good Arkansas stone.

You will find these handcrafted knives superior in performance, and they should be treated with respect, like any fine tool. The high carbon content does cause these knives to rust, so they should be rinsed and wiped dry immediately after use. Both the dishwasher and prolonged soaking in a sink are damaging to their performance. To preserve their excellent cutting edge, store them in a knife rack when not in use. It is certainly a waste to buy superior quality and then destroy such a knife by letting it get knocked about loose with other utensils in a drawer.

This jewel-like solid wooden bowl with delicate fluting reverses to become a sturdy chopping block (see page 32). Both the chopping block and the wooden nutcracker tongs are made by Bradford Woodworks. Photo by Jonathan Wallen.

Wooden Kitchen Equipment

Woodcarvers produce a wide variety of cooking utensils, rolling pins, pastry boards, cheese boards, chopping blocks, cannisters, spice racks, and knife racks—just for the kitchen. All of these items have merit both in terms of serviceability and decoration. No synthetic material equals the tactile and visual richness of wood, and handwork is far superior to machine work when it comes to enhancing the natural properties of each unique piece of wood.

Below: Bill Kendall carefully matches the end grains of white oak and cherry to form repeating patterns in his cutting and serving board. Layer upon layer of laminated plywood create stripes in a deep salad bowl by Rude Osolnik. The salad set by Dan Dustin was made from a single piece of mountain laurel; the spoon and fork were split apart from each other, and their matched grains can still be seen in the handles. Photo by David Arky.

In wooden pieces made for daily use, craftsmen devote great care to the finish. It is just one of the processes done by hand that distinguishes the craftsman's work from that of the machine. To retain the hand finish and prevent irreparable cracking of the wood, you must not wash wooden objects in the dishwasher or allow them to soak in the sink.

Wooden Spoons

In what may seem an absurd example, compare an inexpensive mass-produced wooden spoon with a hand-carved one. Regardless of the grain pattern of the wood, the shape of a manufactured spoon must conform to the standardized template of the machine, which cuts thousands a day from raw lumber. The straight handle does not feel particularly comfortable in your hand, and the random grain pattern is more likely to become rough and splinter. Ironically, the lack of any finish at all is sometimes touted as imparting a "natural" look.

With this admittedly inexpensive spoon in one hand, hold a craftsman's spoon in the other. The most obvious difference in the handmade spoon is the contoured

shape of the handle, curved to fit securely within a loose fist. A craftsman sensitively examines the raw wood and calculates just where and how to carve the spoon in order to take advantage of the wood's natural grain. It's not unusual for a craftsman to keep a piece of wood around his shop for some time, all the while studying the grain closely before making his first cut.

After shaping and fine-sanding a spoon, the craftsman will spend additional time applying an oil or beeswax finish, which protects and further enhances the beauty of the wood. Needless to say, you'll pay more for the hand-carved spoon, but you'll still be enjoying its beauty and its feel many years later when you've been through several generations of the mass-produced variety.

Craftsmen carve spoons in graduated sizes, slotted spoons, tasting spoons, spoons with flat bottoms for stirring and with long handles to keep your hand away from the heat. Companion utensils carved from the wood include spaghetti servers, spaghetti measures, meat mallets, and salad tongs and bowls.

With the introduction of non-stick surfaces on frying pans,

Left: *In addition to the variety of spoons and other cooking utensils of domestic hardwoods shown here, Barry Gordon also carves left-handed spoons to make life easier for southpaws. The silkscreened tea towel was designed by potter Betty Woodman for the Fabric Workshop. Photo by Joseph Kugielsky.*

Below: William Patrick creates a stylized mountainscape on this doughboard by laminating domestic hardwoods with brilliantly colored imported woods. The companion rolling pin features an inlaid moon and stars. Patrick finishes both pieces with vegetable oil only and recommends rubbing it on periodically to prevent the wood from drying. Photo by Joseph Kugielsky.

wooden spoons and wooden utensils of all kinds became even more useful. Plastic utensils become scorched with use, and metal utensils scratch the nonstick finish, so wood is the best alternative. Another, often overlooked, advantage of wood is that it is quiet, particularly when used with metal bowls and pans (no raucous scraping when you get the last bit of batter out of a stainless bowl).

Pastry Tools

A rolling pin is a very personal thing, and most pastry chefs, amateur or professional, have a preference for a particular shape. Individual likes and dislikes are well satisfied by craftsmen who market both the slim French pin and the traditional American rolling pin with handles.

For the accomplished baker the pastry board is also a sacred piece, never to be roughed up by chopping. But even the cook who never attempts piecrust may be attracted to boards that are decorated with inlaid woods of contrasting colors in abstract patterns or stylized landscapes.

Chopping Blocks and Cheese Boards

Countertop chopping blocks from craftsmen should not be confused with cheese boards. Although a handsome chopping block might be used to serve cheese, a cheese board is designed for serving, not chopping. A generous surface area and a depth of at least one inch distinguish the tough chopping block from a smaller, lightweight cheese board. Chopping blocks vary from massive floor models to substantial countertop pieces.

Laminating many smaller pieces of wood together has several advantages: greater strength, less chance of warping, and less chance of splitting along grain lines. Craftsmen have turned laminating into a decorative advantage as well. By exploiting the natural color and grain line of the wood, the craftsman may juxtapose contrasting colors and grains of wood to create intriguing patterns.

Below: *Rounded forms and a hand-buffed, lacquered finish enhance the unique grain patterns and natural colors of imported woods, such as zebrawood on the far left and padauk on the far right, in salt and pepper shakers by Mitchell Azoff. Tallest, 10" ht.*

Bottom: *These salt and pepper shakers by Ken Jupiter are simple and geometric. He adds detail with a single slim line. Photo by Joseph Kugielsky.*

Right: *This distinctive wooden salad bowl by John Whitehead is turned from Oregon Bigleaf Maple burl. Not all bowls made from burl are suitable for functional use; many burl edges are easily chipped. The brightly printed bandanas are an Italo Scanga design for the Fabric Workshop, a not-for-profit institution that invites leading artists from other media to experiment with printing on fabric. Photo by Joseph Kugielsky.*

Wood benefits from occasional oiling with common vegetable oil. Otherwise, the wood begins to dry and crack, creating a rough working surface. After using wooden spoons, rolling pins, or chopping blocks, wipe them clean with a damp cloth or sponge and dry immediately. This minimal care will preserve the special quality of hand-finished wood.

Pricing Crafts for the Kitchen

Everyone agrees that you can only make an accurate comparison of price when weighing objects of equivalent quality. Today, we have become so heavily dependent on manufactured goods that there is very little in the market to compare with the craftsman's sensitive hand work. But to give you an idea of what to expect of craftsmen's prices, here are some general observations.

If you are an indifferent cook, out of obligation or necessity, chances are that you buy inexpensive utensils either from the grocery store rack or at the local hardware or housewares store. In that case, few craftsmen can match the prices you pay. If, on the other hand, you get real pleasure from a well-designed pot and are accustomed to shopping at specialty kitchen stores or restaurant supply houses, you'll find similar prices and quality from craftsmen.

Some materials are inherently more expensive than others, such as copper and porcelain compared with cast iron and stoneware. Also, the more involved or difficult the execution of a piece, the higher the price. For example, a porcelain pitcher is likely to cost more than the same form made in stoneware. Porcelain has less plasticity than stoneware and is therefore harder to throw on a wheel. The stoneware version can be slightly less expensive because it takes less time to execute and there are fewer losses. The craftsman working in porcelain not only spends more time on one pitcher; he will discard a larger percentage of unsatisfactory pieces. This is not a new idea. The most respected glass house in France, Baccarat, destroys all finished pieces that have bubbles in the glass, and Baccarat prices reflect that standard of excellence. Many craftsmen institute their own discipline of destroying less-than-perfect tries, and they, too, must put a price on quality control.

The mark of the hand and the finely executed hand decoration of the craft object are not available from a manufacturer at any price. Only you can evaluate the pleasure you derive from using a hand-made object. Even if you felt the price was considerable, it takes only one guest who remarks on the piece, complimenting your good taste and individual style, to be reassured that the price was right!

Below: Wendell Castle *laminates wood both for strength and aesthetics, taking advantage of the resulting solid block of wood to carve an organic, tree-like chopping block. Photo by Jim Eager.*

Incorporating Crafts into Your Kitchen Decor

The artistic diversity available from professional craftsmen provides options for many different decorating styles: country, contemporary, or eclectic. The handmade is the essence of the popular country or Colonial kitchen. The work of today's craftsmen recalls the iron and copper pots, salt-glazed jugs, wooden utensils, and basket storage of the open-hearth kitchen. These contemporary pieces, made from traditional materials, offer the best of two worlds: a Colonial look with the advantages of modern performance. Unlike antiques that you might display for a period look, these pots and utensils can be used every day.

Well-designed crafts are also right at home in the clean contemporary kitchen. A hand-thrown casserole with freely applied glaze adds contrast and lively interest to an otherwise streamlined kitchen. Great artists and architects have long known the aesthetic value of playing disparate forms off one another.

If you break down the contemporary style into design elements, you'll find that the kitchen is

Left: *Spices will retain their flavor longer if they are protected from light and moisture, as when stored in wooden spice jars. This set by Knock on Wood comes with a wooden rack that can stand on a counter or be hung on a wall. Photo by Joseph Kugielsky.*

either completely neutral or highlights a few bright colors against a neutral background. The craft work on these pages demonstrates the options within a contemporary color scheme—from cool gray and earthy browns to cobalt blue, brilliant orange, and intense green. Another key element of the contemporary style in kitchens includes a few well-placed pieces of graphic art. Certainly some craftsmen's overscaled pottery, embellished with bold pattern and strong colors, satisfies that requirement handsomely.

If you are like many other American families who simply prefer a cheerful kitchen with color and bright patterns, there's a place for the handmade in your home as well. Pretty pieces decorated with whimsical animals and delightful flowers in rainbow colors of yellow, sky blue, green, and pink are among the painterly styles pursued by some craftsmen. These glaze colors are possible only at relatively low firing temperatures, which means you sacrifice something in the strength and heat resistance of the piece. That's why the more colorful kitchen accessories are usually cannisters, salad and mixing bowls, colanders, and serving

platters, which are not used for cooking in the oven.

In many of today's homes, the kitchen is open to other rooms, making the display of handmade cooking equipment even more important. If your kitchen's interior is visible from your dining room or living room, your handmade cookware assumes a dual role: It becomes both functional and decorative.

Adding handmade cookware to your current supply is not likely to crowd your storage cabinets; distinctive pieces from craftsmen are rarely put away. A round open casserole or platter becomes a platform in which to float a few blossoms, display fresh garden vegetables, apples, or pinecones and nuts, as the seasons change. Large pieces need not be filled; three to five pieces of fruit grouped to one side create a presence just as much as a well-filled bowl. In a similar way, you can unclutter the table or counter by collecting salt and pepper shakers, sugar bowls, honey pots, and other condiments

on a large clay platter. Whether earthy stoneware or delicate hand-painted porcelain, these pieces lack the sterile commercial look that would isolate them as kitchen equipment. These attractive, versatile ceramics can enhance any room of the home until called into service as cookware.

A Practical Start on a Collection

Though you may not think of yourself as a collector, handmade utensils for the kitchen are a good way to begin. The familiarity of a casserole or a baking dish may seem less intimidating than a painting, but the creator has nonetheless drawn upon a sculptor's judgment of form and mass and upon a painter's understanding of color and line.

Fifteen or twenty years ago, one had to do a bit of hunting in scattered craft fairs or local craftsmen's studios to find handmade kitchenware. But today a handmade piece is likely to turn up

anywhere—in the gourmet cooking shop, in prestigious mail-order catalogues, in major department stores, at fine craft galleries and museums. For a concentrated grouping of work by many different craftsmen, survey the craft shops, juried fairs, respected craft guilds, and guild-sponsored fairs.

When you find yourself taken with a craftsman's work, it's easy to rationalize the purchase of something you need for the kitchen. In handling crafts and using them every day, you learn the subtleties of the handmade, and you come to enjoy the comments from family and friends who notice the distinctive design. As your confidence and judgment matures, you will develop a personal style throughout your home with the unique handcrafted objects you buy and use.

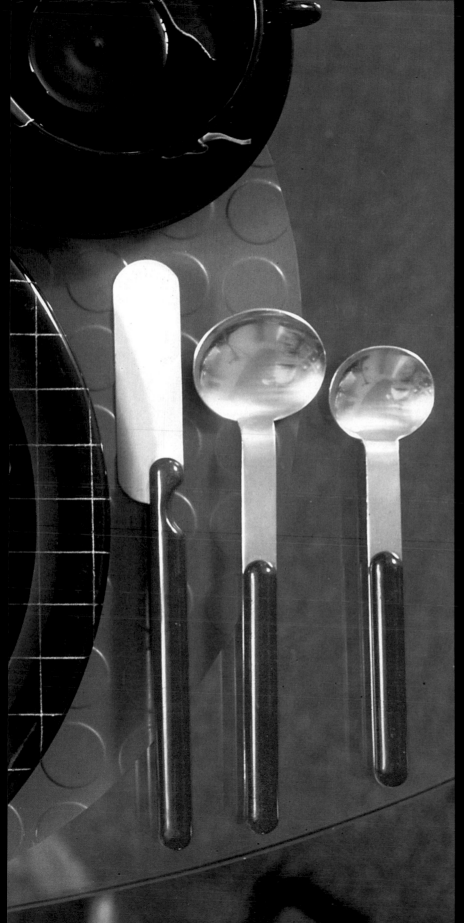

Ceramic Dinnerware

You can set an entire table with handcrafted dinnerware, or you can add distinction to your current table setting by incorporating beautifully handcrafted plates and accessories. Craftsmen provide a rich new source for personalizing your table with pretty pastel settings in porcelain, boldly decorated earthenware patterns, or understated, simple designs in stoneware. The original designs available enliven special occasions and add warmth to family meals.

Preceding Page: Mineo Mizuno's striking dinnerware plate is painted with a
subtle gray grid. Companion pieces
are decorated with paint spatters or
fat green chili peppers. The glossy
black glaze is an elegant, neutral
background for nouvelle cuisine or any
menu for which visual presentation is
important. The large plates are ideal
for buffets. Dinner plates, 11"
diameter. Tablesetting in the home of
Ken Deavers, owner of American
Hand. Photo by Breton Littlehales.

Right and Below: *In her porcelain
tablesetting, Lyn Evans mixes pretty
pastels in repeat patterns that have a
watercolor-like softness. When not in
use, the dinnerware shares an antique
pine hutch with split oak baskets by
Ken and Kathleen Dalton. Photographed in the home of Nancy and
Harvey Leeds. Photo by David Arky.*

To appreciate the individuality inherent in handmade dinnerware, it's helpful to understand the basic forming techniques that distinguish the craftsman's work from commercially manufactured dinnerware, and how the clays used affect the creative process. Essentially, the craftsman employs any or all of three basic techniques: wheel-throwing, hand-building, or slip-casting.

Wheel-throwing

When a perfect spherical form is desired—for soup and salad bowls, round dinner plates, and casseroles—craftsmen generally work on a wheel. A piece takes shape much more quickly on a turning wheel than it does when hand-built. Although it takes a great deal of practice, to the onlooker it appears an effortless motion. In fact, it requires a deft hand. As the clay rotates between his fingers, the potter pulls up a perfectly round, symmetrical form from a wet lump of clay, determining the angle and the height of the walls as he works. The speed of the wheel, which makes it appear so easy, also magnifies any error the potter makes, quickly destroying a

bowl thrown off-center by too firm a pressure on the walls. A round dinner plate is particularly difficult to throw on a wheel, not only because there is less room to maneuver the hand while shaping the form, but also because the plate is more likely to collapse as it approaches a horizontal plane.

Hand-building

When hand-building, the craftsman builds his desired shape either with slabs of clay or with coils. In the slab-forming technique (also called slab-building), the potter rolls out a thin slab of clay, much as you would a pastry dough. With a sharp edge, he cuts shapes from the flat clay. If he's creating a complex form, such as a teapot or a casserole, he must cut the bottom surface, side walls, handles, and other appendages. Using slip (very wet clay) as an adhesive, he affixes the slabs of clay together, literally building a form with slabs. For the innovative craft designer, the advantage of slab-building is that a vessel or a container need not be round; it makes a whole new sculptural direction in functional dinnerware possible. Kaete Brittin Shaw's elongated teapot on page

79 and Peter Shire's cubist, non-functional teapot on page 86 are wonderful examples of innovative, slab-built designs.

Press molding is a hand-building technique in which the potter presses clay into a plaster mold. Using a contoured mold, the potter is able to achieve a consistently shaped concave form that is ideal for a dinner plate with a raised edge or for any other concave form. And consistency of shape and size can be maintained more easily with press molding, which is a decided advantage when trying to make a set of bowls or plates.

Coiling, the oldest of all pottery methods for forming spherical shapes, is still used today. There is an upper limit to the size of a pot that can be thrown on a wheel, but by coiling, a potter can make much larger forms. Today, most craftsmen using the coil technique are reserving it for the construction of nonfunctional vessel forms and for overscaled ceramic sculptures rather than for ceramic dinnerware. The actual technique consists of rolling clay into a long rope shape with the flat, open palm of the hand, and then coiling the rope around and around to form the walls of a vessel.

Below: Dorothy Hafner's *boldly deco-rated porcelain dinnerware sets a dra-matic table. Each intricate pattern is handpainted before firing; this particu-lar pattern is titled Fire Flies, Jelly Beans and Arthur Murray Dance Steps.*

Below: *Matte black glazes inside cups and bowls and on some plates set off the luscious pastels of Phillip Maberry's finely thrown porcelain dinnerware. The cup and bowl, formed as perfect half-spheres, and an in-novative use of color mark this as adventurous work. Photo courtesy of Hadler-Rodriguez Gallery.*

Right: *James D. Makins's understated porcelain setting is arranged here for informal dining. This refined dinner-ware is also appropriate for a formal event with sterling silver flatware and fine white linens. The setting includes dinner and salad plates, small bowls for salad or dessert, stemmed sherbets, wine goblets, and demitasse cups and saucers. Photographed in the home of Ken Deavers, by Breton Littlehales.*

Although the surface may be smoothed with a wooden paddle, some potters prefer to let the coils remain visible in the finished piece, revealing the process by which it was made.

Slip-casting

In slip-casting, liquid clay, known as slip, is poured into a preformed plaster mold. The mold absorbs the water from the clay, leaving a firm clay plate or bowl behind. The craftsman is able to achieve thinner walls through slip-casting than through wheel-throwing or slab-forming and, thus, finds it an especially appropriate technique for forming dinner plates and

bowls. It is, in fact, the forming method used universally by com-mercial manufacturers who desire thin, translucent china plates.

Porcelain

All china, including fine china and bone china, is made of porcelain. The very first porcelains brought into Europe by Marco Polo were known as "china," and the name stuck. Today, however, handmade porcelain dinnerware is generally referred to as porcelain, while commercial porcelain is more often referred to as "china."

Certain qualities make porcelain ideal for dinnerware. Unlike other clays, porcelain is white or slightly gray, allowing a full range of color and decoration on its surface. Its particular density or body makes it possible to achieve a thinner edge on a plate or bowl than is possible with either stoneware or earthenware, contributing to its refined and more formal appearance. Because porcelain can withstand high-temperature firings, it has unusual strength. Its impervious, glasslike surface also does not have to be glazed for use as dinnerware.

Porcelain is used in complete table settings, which may include dinner and salad plates, soup bowls, stemmed sherbet bowls, wine goblets, coffee cups and saucers, and demitasse cups, as well as serving pieces and oven-to-table casseroles.

James D. Makins's elegant unglazed porcelain dinnerware, on this page, is true to the basic qualities of porcelain. It features exceptionally thin edges, a glasslike imperviousness even when unglazed, and the natural gray tint of the clay. Makins exploits all of these characteristics in his work, which varies from shiny white to off-white through subtle gradations of gray to rich matte blacks. He achieves remarkable variations within this seemingly limited pal-

ette, and he also pays close attention to creating beautiful, simple forms.

For other craftsmen, color figures strongly in the decoration of handmade porcelain dinnerware—colors that range from soft pastel washes to pure, bold hues. Using luscious pastel tints on the simplest of plates, Phillip Maberry mixes colors within one place setting and sets off the pastel colors with shiny black glazes on the

inside surface of the cups and bowls (see page 46).

An uninhibited use of color and strong pattern characterizes another group of porcelain artists, Dorothy Hafner and Mineo Mizuno among them. Their designs, shown on pages 46 and 48, are high-styled, adventurous, and meant to be featured on the table of the self-confident pacesetter.

In the decoration of some contemporary porcelain, you can also

find a sensitive interpretation of ancient oriental styles. Catharine Hiersoux's asymmetrical brushstrokes on clear white porcelain plates, on page 50, have a timeless quality that makes her dinnerware compatible with fine old china and crystal.

It's worth noting here a distinction between commercial china and porcelain in the craftsman's hands. The much-admired translucency of commercial china is dependent on the thinness of the plate. Craftsmen, too, are capable of achieving this same wonderfully delicate translucency. However, if an artistic translucent effect is desired, the craftsman would create a form that makes the translucency readily apparent. Molly Cowgill, for example, fashioned a bowl form, see page 127, with standing walls to take advantage of overhead room lighting and general daylight, thereby dramatizing the translucent quality of the porcelain. But since translucency requires a light source behind it, which is not possible on a table, most craftsmen do not concern themselves with designing translucent dinnerware. The bride's test of seeing light through her china plates as a sign of high quality is not a valid test when

Below: Glossy black dinnerware by Mineo Mizuno is set off by fire-engine red napkins and flatware on Ken Deaver's glass dining table. The centerpiece is a grouping of Elsa Rady's delicate porcelain bowls in black, celadon, and oxblood glazes. Photo by Breton Littlehales.

Left: The tablesetting can be varied for another occasion by using Donna Polseno's raku-fired boxes for the salad course with versatile dinner plates by Mineo Mizuno. Photo by Breton Littlehales.

Right: Scott McDowell paints placemats and table to match his porcelain dinnerware inspired by American Indian designs. As is often the case with handmade dinnerware, place settings are of a similar style, but no two are exactly alike. Photo by Edward Claycomb.

evaluating the craftsman's porcelain plate. A lack of translucency by no means reveals a lack of skill or quality.

Museum collections of porcelain urns that date back to the tenth century are enduring evidence of the strength of this clay. You can expect the same durability from your porcelain dinnerware, even though it may look quite fragile. The deceptive strength results from the high temperatures at which porcelain is fired. The higher the temperature, the harder the fired clay. While porcelain and stoneware can withstand a very high temperature, other clays collapse and melt.

Because of its strength, most potters put their own porcelain dinnerware right into the dishwasher. Others contend that the extreme heat of the dishwasher will gradually create crackle lines in the glaze. As with commercial

Left: For formal evenings, Julia Walker mixes antique family crystal with handblown goblets by Steven Maslach. Catharine Hiersoux's elegant porcelain dinnerware also graces the table. Photo by David Arky.

china, dishwasher washing probably will result in wear and tear over time, and you must weigh your time in handwashing against the life of the china. If unglazed porcelain absorbs stains over a long period, it is easily whitened by soaking in water with a little bit of liquid bleach, just as you would clean a porcelain sink.

If decoration is applied over the final glaze, the dinnerware should definitely not be put into the dishwasher. The gradual fading of antique china in the dishwasher, for example, is the result of overglaze decoration. If decoration is applied before the final glaze, it is protected from fading or wearing away, but it is very difficult to tell by looking whether the decoration is overglaze or underglaze. You are safest to follow the potter's recommendation for dishwashing. And when in doubt, wash by hand.

A few decorative glazes should never be put in a dishwasher: luster glazes, which look like metallic gold and silver and are most often used on earthenware, and a pearlized glaze, which looks like mother-of-pearl. Even with care, these iridescent glazes may show wear within your lifetime, particularly if they are on a handle or rim.

Right: *These porcelain dinner plates are particularly well-suited to buffet service; the raised rim helps contain generous portions. And guests won't have a problem remembering which* plate was theirs because Curtis C. Hoard paints a different pattern on each one. Hefty wine goblets are handblown by Jan Zandhuis. *Buffet in the home of Julia and Carter Walker. Photo by David Arky.*

Stoneware

Stoneware is what most people picture when they think of pottery —natural clay colors and muted glazes of deep blue, green, and gray. Both the form and decoration of stoneware dinnerware tend to be restrained and subordinate to the earthy colors and texture of the natural clay.

Subdued glaze colors are a signature of stoneware, an unavoidable effect in the high-temperature firing that gives stoneware its exceptional strength. Although many American craftsmen continue to create simple, unadorned stoneware dinnerware, others have led the way by introducing new decorative styles. Among the most notable is John Glick, whose imprinted patterns and slip decoration has been extremely influential. His elegant stoneware settings, like the one shown on page 53, are in the permanent collection at the Vice President's home in Washington, D.C., where they were used with handblown goblets and fine silver for official dinners under Joan Mondale. When she left the Vice President's official residence, Mrs. Mondale was so pleased with the stoneware pattern that she commissioned another set for her

Below: A strong geometric pattern is softened by seemingly random applications of glazes that recall unconscious doodles. Patrick Loughran contrasts the boldly decorated surface with the rich terra cotta earthenware body. One of the most appealing features of his press-molded dinnerware set is the hefty coffee cup; its generous capacity is easy to support with a comfortable, well-balanced handle. Photo courtesy of American Craft Council, by Mitch Bader.

personal entertaining.

The unaffected simplicity of stoneware is suitable both for family dining and, with appropriate accessories, for special occasions. Stoneware has its attractions both for contemporary-minded hostesses and for traditionalists. Its honest expression of material appeals to modernists, who realize that it can be quite elegant with simple silver patterns and refined stemware. But those who love a more informal, country-style table are also attracted to the rustic strength of stoneware.

All in all, stoneware is a reliable standby. Durable and dishwasher safe, it is hard to beat for constant use and easy care. It offers the same serviceability as its commercial counterparts, but surpasses them in its range of rich, warm glazes, and individualized decoration.

Earthenware

One advantage of earthenware in a table setting is the opportunity to place brighter colors on the table. At the lower temperatures used to fire earthenware, the potter can design with a broad range of lively colors, resulting in bold patterns, such as Patrick Loughran's setting, on this page. Stanley Mace Andersen, whose casseroles are shown on page 18, also produces earthenware dinner sets in the same style as the casseroles.

Fired earthenware may be white or an attractive terra cotta color. White earthenware, used by some potters, may rival porcelain in appearance, but not in performance. The safest test is to ask the craftsman what the clay is, as earthenware requires more careful handling to prevent chipping. If, for some reason, you are still uncertain, there are two tests to distinguish porcelain from white earthenware. Porcelain has a higher ring or pitch when struck compared with earthenware's resonance. If you immerse a plate in water, the porous earthenware will absorb water and darken, whereas the vitreous porcelain will not absorb water.

Earthenware is more easily chipped than any other clay, and so is often used in thicker forms for extra strength. Potters will advise you not to put earthenware in the dishwasher, as you run a great risk of chipping and fading glaze colors.

Choosing Dinnerware for Your Home

Handmade dinnerware settings generally include a dinner plate, a smaller plate and/or bowls, and a drinking vessel. Each piece is versatile, so that an intermediate-size plate may be used for a salad, dessert, or hors d'oeuvres, and a bowl may be used for a small green salad, a fruit dessert, or a cocktail dip. Depending on the formality of the setting, the beverage container may be a cup and saucer, a demitasse cup, a mug, or a clay goblet.

The highly individual quality of handmade dinnerware makes impossible the commercial feature of open stock reordering. Like any one-of-a-kind art object that is damaged or broken, it is irreplaceable. Consider purchasing an extra setting or two to avoid disappointment.

Consider not only how the single place setting looks, but the relation of an entire table setting to your room. Relating the wall color to the setting, or vice versa, is one of the safest ways to insure compatibility, but even that is not foolproof. If you have a large-patterned wallpaper in the dining room, you must be careful to choose dinnerware that will not compete. Solid colors and small prints on the wall are more accepting of pattern in the table setting. It may be worth your while to buy

Left: Long-time collectors of fine American crafts, Louis and Sandra Grotta successfully combine the works of a few craftsmen in their dining room. The table and wooden place plates are by Joyce and Edgar Anderson; the stoneware plates by the late William Wyman, the cups and centerpiece urn by Toshiko Takaezu. Photo by Tom Grotta.

Bottom Left: Shallow shelving backed with deep rust felt is a simple display for Todd Piker's traditional stoneware dinner setting. Photo by Donald Pahl Heiny.

Above: Imprinted patterns and overlapping slip decorations create luxurious surface effects on John Glick's stoneware tablesetting. His rich decorative style has influenced many younger potters. Photo courtesy of American Craft Council, by Mitch Bader.

a single dinner plate from a craftsman to try it out in the room. (If you decide against the pattern, you can always use the odd plate as a serving platter.)

You'll probably be more satisfied if you don't try to jump too far afield from the decorative style of the room itself. For example, if you want to create a more formal setting in a rustic country dining room, a refined stoneware setting with complementary linens and a simple sterling pattern is more appropriate to the room than gilt-edged bone china.

Mixing a few handmade dishes with your existing china is an easy and affordable way to personalize and update your table. Many brides of the sixties were steered to safe gold- and silver-rimmed patterns as their formal service with the advice that they would soon tire of strong pattern or color. Now, many of those brides are finding that they are bored with a safe pattern. Handmade pieces can free a table from that "wedding china" look. It's easy to enliven an evening's menu by introducing the handmade dishes with a new course—to serve soup, salad, dessert, or an after-dinner coffee. And a set of small plates can be used for either salad or

dessert to perk up an otherwise predictable dinner service. Perhaps easiest to incorporate are serving dishes, as you are already accustomed to not having these match the dinner plates. The inherent individuality of hand-decorated plates makes them more difficult to combine with patterned commercial plates. Handmade plates seem most at home

with classic white porcelain or with some of the simple Scandinavian stoneware patterns.

Price Ranges

In commercial china alone, excluding stoneware and earthenware, the price of dinner plates varies considerably—generally, anywhere from $15 to $400. Din-

ner plates from craftsmen fall well within the extremes of this range, being rarely as low and rarely as high. As a rule, handcrafted dinner plates range from $35 to $200.

With such a broad price range for commercial place settings, it is also very difficult to make direct comparisons between craftsmen's settings and comparable commercial patterns. To give you a general idea of what to expect, craftsmen seem to have settled into two levels of pricing. At the lower end, a five-piece place setting for $150 is fairly common. With a few exceptions, the pricing then tends to jump to $300 for a five-piece place setting. Some may even go as high as $600.

There is one important difference when buying handcrafted dinnerware, and that is that you cannot buy, for example, four place settings now with the hope of adding four more in several years. By the time you are ready to purchase additional settings, the craftsman may no longer be producing your style. If your budget is limited, you're better off buying all dinner plates at one time. The dinner plates can be used either with commercial accessories or with another craftsman's work that complements your plates.

Left: *What appears at first to be another handcrafted ceramic tablesetting is a trompe l'oeil tablecloth, designed by John Moore to suggest a well-appointed tablesetting on marble. This silkscreened fabric is produced by the Fabric Workshop. Photo by Joseph Kugielsky.*

Below: *Handmade and commercial dinnerware mix easily in this table setting in the home of collector Jack Lenor Larsen. James D. Makins's white porcelain bowls and creamer, which clearly show the ridges created during wheel-throwing, stand out when placed on oxblood-glazed plates designed by Larsen for Dansk. Refined blue-gray goblets by Tom and Pia Hart add subtle color to the setting. The table achieves further individuality by the inclusion of Fred Woell's small spoon and Chunghi Choo's silver decanter. Photo by David Arky.*

In addition to shaping glass by blowing, the artist may use a thin pair of pincers to pull the glass into delicate, fingerlike appendages. Fritz Dreisbach enhances the handmade character of each of his crystal champagne goblets with such freely formed ornamentation. Photo by John Littleton.

Stemware

Handblown glass goblets, delicate porcelain, hefty stoneware, and luxurious silver and pewter goblets are all available from craftsmen in a wide variety of styles and colors to suit your dining decor. There is graceful stemware suitable for the most formal settings, and full, hardy drinking vessels perfect for informal gatherings.

O f all your choices, hand-blown goblets are the most abundant. Compared with clear glass and cut or faceted, commercially produced stemware, the goblets from today's studio craftsmen are characterized by exquisite colors and more fluid forms. Much of the current work derives inspiration from the finest art glass of the past, including the soft rose colors of Venetian glass, the deep blue and iridescent golds of Art Nouveau glass, and the spiral stem decorations associated with eighteenth-century glassware. But these references to the past are just that. Contemporary stemware is created in a refreshingly spontaneous spirit that beautifully complements today's entertaining styles.

What to Look for When Buying Stemware

Before you choose from all these styles, you'll want to take into consideration two important points: (1) How does the goblet feel in your hand? and (2) How does it feel when raised to your lips? These are the two most critical ways to judge any goblet, no matter what medium or style you prefer.

The first test is to grasp the goblet as if you were about to drink from it. Does it fit comfortably in your hand? Can you hold it around the bowl? How about when you hold it at the stem? Set it down? Does the foot stabilize the goblet, or does it feel a bit shaky? If it's not well balanced, your guests might end up sloshing wine on their clothes or on your rug.

The second test is to examine the lip of the drinking vessel. Run your finger gently around the edge. Is it smooth? Then, with one finger inside the rim and another just on the outside, run them around the edge of the lip to check the thickness. You'll have to be the judge here, but in general, most people prefer a relatively thin lip. This is easiest to achieve with glass, porcelain, or metal. Stoneware goblets tend to be

thicker just because of the clay. If the lip is too thick, it may not be satisfying for serving fine wine. On the other hand, some husky individuals revel in a great, weighty stoneware goblet that makes them feel as if they are really downing a hearty drink. My suspicion is that stoneware goblets are favored by real beer drinkers.

Porcelain goblets, such as Sally Silberberg's on page 63, can be

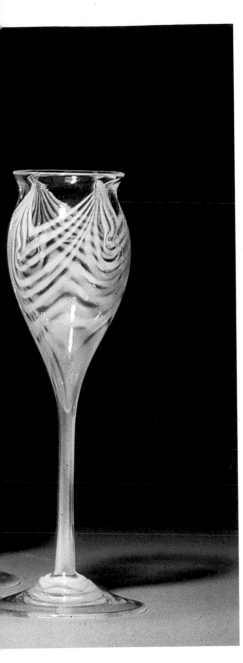

Left: Nancy Freeman's *elegant goblets were selected by Joan Mondale for the Vice President's home, where they were used with handmade ceramic dinnerware for state occasions. To achieve the flowing surface decoration reminiscent of Art Nouveau, Freeman spirals molten colored glass threads around the clear blown-glass forms, then uses a sharp metal pick to pull the parallel lines of colored glass into pointed swags. Goblets 9" ht. Photo by Bob Barrett.*

Below: *Fritz Dreisbach has created ingenious double-ended goblets with colorful latticinio work inside clear glass. When the goblets are turned upside down, the broad bowl for champagne becomes the base for the smaller cognac glass. Photo by John Littleton.*

thrown with a very thin bowl and lip, making the goblet delicate and lightweight. You may be more comfortable with this kind of drinking vessel. Porcelain, in fact, may be worked even thinner than handblown glass goblets.

Metal, too, can be fashioned quite thin. Whether silver or pewter, a gleaming polished metal goblet on the table adds a definite look of pure luxury. Although some people object to drinking from metal, most admire the image of richness it creates. Many metalsmiths make prototype goblets in silver or pewter, for which you may place a special order in whatever quantity or size you need.

Making Handblown Glass Stemware

Although handblown goblets now far outnumber any other stemware made by craftsmen, it has only been within the last twenty years that the independent craftsman has been able to produce handblown glass. The handblown glass we enjoy today is the result of a technical innovation. Until the early 1960s, there wasn't a furnace small enough to be practical for the individual artist nor a glass formula that would melt at the relatively lower temperatures provided by such a small furnace. Therefore all glass production was limited to the factory.

To appreciate how studio glassmaking has affected glass design, compare the studio process with the factory. In commercial glassmaking, an industrial designer conceives and plans a piece and sketches it on the drafting board. Working from the designer's drawing, a team of about five people work together to create the piece. In making a goblet, for in-

Below: This tumbler created by Tom and Pia Hart is designed to fit comfortably in the hand. The lovely fluting on the lower part is ground smooth on the bottom so the glass rests stably on the table. Photo by Jonathan Wallen.

Left: The symmetry of Josh Simpson's goblets is pleasing to the eye and hand, and remarkable in that he blows them "off hand," or without a mold. 9" ht. Photo by David Arky.

Studio artists who blow glass goblets fall roughly into two schools: those who flaunt the handmade quality in loose, free-flowing shapes and, at the opposite extreme, those who control the glass in refined, meticulous forms. Both are appealing.

The looser forms are an intentional strategy to distinguish the studio glass from the scrupulous consistency of mass-produced glass. On the table, freeblown goblets, like those of Fritz Dreisbach on pages 56-57, can relax an otherwise formal setting.

Some craftsmen do blow goblets into molds of their own making in order to achieve a greater degree of similarity among their glasses. A rare few, with years of skill, achieve remarkable consistency of height and shape in freeblown goblets. Freeblown or offhand blowing indicates glass shaped without a mold.

In addition to the fluid, spontaneous goblets available from craftsmen, there are also beautifully colored ones. Color, in the rich tradition of Venetian glass, becomes the important, expressive design element in these glasses. Colors, from pale yellow, pink, blue, and green to deep wine red and cobalt blue form elegant

stance, one person specializes in the bowl, another the stem and foot, and another joins the two, with all work overseen by a team supervisor. To achieve exacting consistency from one piece to the next, each element is blown into a mold. Even though beautiful, high-quality glass is handblown under this system, the sense of the hand may be hard to detect. With the industrial revolution, we began to define quality in terms of machined precision and unerring standards of duplication. Even though handblown glass is still generally considered superior, the handmade character is too often refined out of the final product if it is intended for a mass market.

In studio glass, the craftsman works directly with the material, making each piece a unique, spontaneous response to the hot glass. Unlike clay, which a craftsman molds with his hands, the glass artist must shape hot glass without ever touching it. To see a goblet take form is fascinating. The process is begun in a gesture similar to twisting honey on the end of a spoon, when the craftsman takes a gather of molten glass from the furnace onto the end of the blowpipe. Then, working rapidly, the craftsman blows a bubble within the hot glass and uses simple hand tools to refine the shape, alternately expanding the bubble by blowing through the pipe and returning the glass to the furnace to keep it malleable. From first gather to finished piece, he must keep the glass in constant motion, spinning the blowpipe to prevent the molten glass from being pulled downward by gravity, creating a lopsided form.

When first observing the skilled glassblower at work, you are struck by the speed with which a goblet takes shape and by the apparent nonchalance of the craftsman as he swings and shapes white-hot glass. The craftsman may use a contoured wooden mold or paddle and even a great wad of wet newspaper to force the glass into the shape he wants. He makes the form larger by taking additional gathers of glass from the furnace and by blowing to expand the air within the form. To lengthen a piece, he swings the blowpipe in great sweeping arcs, using centrifugal force to elongate the form.

Below: Laurie L. Thal *extends the colored bowl of each goblet into its clear stem. This is made possible by working with glass in a molten state and then letting it set as the glass cools. Tallest goblet 8" ht. Shortest goblet 6½" ht.*

patterns within the glass.

It is a mistake to approach the craftsman's glass with mass-produced precedents in mind. For example, removing bubbles from glass is a product of high technology and equipment. It became important only after mass production and mass marketing made necessary a predictable similarity in glass products.

The studio glass artist works with traditional methods of blowing, which are subject to the same eccentricities as glass blown centuries ago. Far from being upset by bubbles in a finished piece, the studio craftsman is more likely to feel that bubbles, air trapped within the hot glass, enhance the individuality of the piece.

Caring for Stemware

Unfortunately, the craftsman's work rarely can be replaced more than a year or two after its purchase because the craftsman has moved on to working in another style. That fact increases your sense of loss if one of your goblets should be broken, and it usually stimulates greater care in handling and washing.

Thicker, heavier stemware, both glass and clay, may be safely

Below Left: Latticinio, the process by which colored rods of glass are spiraled through the stems of these exquisite goblets, is a Renaissance technique recently revived by contemporary glass artists. Steven Maslach is the creator of these.

Bottom Left: John and Jan Gilmor use subtle translucent colors in their highly refined tumblers and stemware, available in five different shapes. Photo by Joseph Kugielsky.

Below Right: Dramatically slim black glass stems support handblown bowls, each graced with an intricate monochromatic pattern. Randy Strong uses a mold to form the bowls of the goblets in order to create a uniform set. Each, 8¾" ht.

Below: *After throwing delicately thin chalices on the wheel, Sally Silberberg incises the porcelain. The thinness she achieves becomes evident after the final firing, when the copper red glaze applied to the interior of the bowl shows through the translucent porcelain, gently coloring the outside surface. Each, 7 × 4 × 3".*

cleaned in the dishwasher, but with more delicate styles, you risk breakage. If undecided, you should ask the craftsman for assurance that his work is dishwasher-safe. Silver and pewter goblets should be handwashed, as commercial dishwasher detergent will quickly dull them. Even with handwashing, they will require periodic polishing to maintain their original gleam.

What About Price?

Refined porcelain goblets fall within the price range of $20 to $50 each, but casual stoneware goblets are generally lower priced —from $15 to $25.

Silver goblets, though expensive at $700 to $1000 each, are treasured pieces to be valued and used for many generations. You can enjoy the polished, luxurious look of silver at a lesser price with pewter goblets, typically priced between $45 and $75.

Striking overlays of 14 karat gold highlight the deeper flame colors of this copper vessel by Douglas Steakley. The simple shape of this piece allows you to focus on its surface and enjoy the subtle variations in color and texture. 4" diameter × 6". Photo by Lee Hocker.

Hollowware & Flatware

There are two broad categories of metalwork available for the home: hollowware and flatware. *Hollowware* is the term applied to container forms in metal, such as bowls, vases, boxes, decanters, and coffee pots. And *flatware* is the term aptly used for knives, forks, spoons, plates, and other metal forms that are more or less flat.

Top: Chunghi Choo's *silver decanter, an innovative shape that is fluid and asymmetrical, has been selected for the permanent collection of the Museum of Modern Art, New York City. 5½ × 7¾ × 4¼".*

Bottom: *These small forms, also by Chunghi Choo, are easy to grasp for use as sugar bowl and creamer or as individual decanters. Each is embel-* *lished with concentric circles that form a herringbone pattern where they overlap; the surface decoration re-iterates the form itself. These designs are also in the permanent collections of the Museum of Modern Art and the American Craft Museum, New York City. Each 5½ × 5 × 5".*

Right: *The spherical form of this teapot is repeated in the curve of the han-dle, creating a strong design state-ment in a functional object by Komelia Hongja Okim. Teapot, 7" diameter × 14"; sugar bowl, 3" diameter × 5"; creamer, 3" diameter × 6". Photo by Breton Littlehales.*

All current metalwork builds upon a rich tradition of silversmithing—when silversmiths were known as much for their designs as for their craftsmanship. With the industrial revolution, metalsmithing did not cease, but the independent metalsmith began to lend his skills and design talents to large scale manufacturers. Therefore, the present activity among metalworkers represents an exciting revival of original designs in silver, copper, pewter, and stainless steel after an over one hundred year hiatus.

Contemporary metalworkers still employ traditional hand-forging techniques, such as raising, stretching, and planishing, but they also utilize processes that were developed for industry, such as spinning, electroforming, and dieforming. While some of the new metalwork, like coffee services and candelabras, is clearly meant to be used, other pieces, such as vase forms and jewel-like boxes, are not meant to hold things but simply to enhance your home. On the following pages, you will see examples of the best functional and decorative work available in hollowware and flatware.

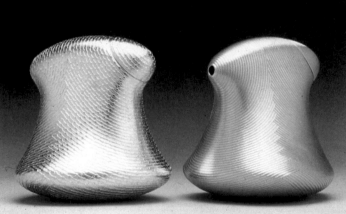

Hollowware

Over the past twenty years hollowware craftsmen have followed the lead of those working in glass and ceramics to create more sculptural designs with a presence beyond function. Yet many of those producing hollowware today have a serious concern for function more often associated with the industrial designer.

Unique historical influences have combined in the tradition of hollowware craftsmanship to create an unusual emphasis on form with surface decoration. Eighteenth- and early nineteenth-

century silversmiths used decoration lavishly in fanciful baroque pieces that were lost to us once the independent silversmith began producing under the manufacturer during the industrial revolution. In the twentieth century, metalsmithing, like the other decorative arts and architecture, turned to the unadorned form. Primarily through the influence of Scandinavian design, traditional techniques of metalworking such as chasing and repoussé to create decorative relief, were abandoned in the search for perfect form. Recently there has been a return to experimentation with surface texture and even color in metal, but not at the sacrifice of good functional form.

Now we can enjoy remarkably fine designs in functional metals that combine simpler and more straightforward forms with integral decoration.

The concentric circles on Chunghi Choo's pair of small decanters, on page 66, are a fine example of beautiful surface decoration that accentuates the form. Douglas Steakley turned from working predominantly in silver to copper in order to take advantage of the lustrous color variations possible with copper. As you can see in the pieces pictured on

Below: "Fine silver" designates silver that is 99 percent pure, as compared with "sterling silver," which may be as low as 95 percent silver. Richard Mafong has used both in this detailed box. The design also features shibuishi, a Japanese technique combining fine silver and copper to achieve subtle gray colors, such as that of the central crosshatched area. 2½ × 2½ × 3½".

Right: In this decanter, Helen Shirk has created an interesting form by using different sized elements. The large flowing body is topped by smaller geometric shapes. Smaller still are the brass and copper inlays on the top. Delicate protruding seams draw attention to the contour of the piece. 10" ht.

page 71, he further enriches the surface with subtle hammer marks and punched patterns and sometimes even with a pattern of 14 karat gold overlay.

There is a rhythm to making hollowware that, while not apparent in the finished piece, is essential to traditional hand-forging techniques. First, there is the rhythm of the hammer striking metal in even, controlled blows of equal force, altering the shape with each blow. Then, there is a rhythm set up by a continuous cycle of forging (hammering), bouging (using a leather or wooden mallet to true the shape), and annealing (heating the piece to soften the metal to a workable state before the cycle begins again). Each complete cycle of forging, bouging, and annealing is called a course. Even a fairly simple bowl may take ten or more courses to raise a flat sheet of metal into a hollow container form. A large and intricate piece, such as Harold Rogovin's teapot on page 69, required as many as forty courses to shape the body alone.

Forging is a general term applied to the shaping of any metal with hammers and a metal stake or anvil. The metalsmith may use one of several more specific terms to describe his forming method: raising, stretching, or constructing. If a hollowware form is shaped by hammering on the outside of the form, the process is known as raising. Douglas Steakley's vase forms, on page 71, and Hans Christensen's candelabrum , on page 70, are examples of forms raised from a flat sheet of metal. If, however, the form takes shape by hammering on the inside surface, it is referred to as *stretching.* It happens that none of the pieces pictured here were stretched, which is more commonly used to make larger bowls. The advantage of either raising or stretching a form is that it eliminates seams in the finished piece (spinning and electroforming also make it possible to form a piece without seams, but they are not considered hand-forging techniques). Pieces that are seamed or soldered to create hollow vessel forms or those which have a spout or handle attached are said to be constructed. Of the constructed pieces shown, Helen Shirk incorporates the seam as a

Left: *According to Harold Rogovin, this teapot is the most complex piece he has ever made. The body of the teapot required forty courses to raise a flat sheet of sterling into this graceful spherical form. 12¼ × 9½ × 6". Photo by Joseph Kugielsky.*

Below: *This elegant coffee and tea service, architectural in feeling, was constructed by Richard Mafong of sterling silver with rosewood handles.*

Bottom: *In his sterling silver teapot, Curtis LaFollette has achieved a dynamic balance between the mass of the body of the teapot and the linear shapes of the handle and spout. The handle is weighted visually by the use of mokumé, a Japanese process in which a variety of metals are aligned in layers and fused together to create a wood grain pattern. The term refers both to the process and to the fused metals. 6½" diameter × 7". Photo by Joseph Kugielsky.*

design element in her decanter, see page 68, while Richard Mafong conceals all the seams in his coffee and tea service, shown on this page.

When you see hand-hammered marks in a piece of hollowware, these are not the marks that remain from shaping the form, but rather are the marks from a planishing hammer used to finish the surface. Once a piece reaches its final form, it must be planished with a smaller hammer to eliminate the heavier, uneven marks made in raising or stretching. Planishing may, again, require five or more courses, each one with progressively lighter blows. Although some metalsmiths follow planishing with filing, sanding, and polishing to create an unblemished reflection, such as in Hans Christensen's brass candelabrum, others may leave the planishing marks as part of the surface decoration. This is the case with Douglas Steakley's vase forms pictured on page 71.

Below: Sensuous curves distinguish this three-arm candelabrum by Hans Christensen. A protégé of Georg Jensen, Christensen, who began teaching at the Rochester Institute of Technology in the 1950s, was one of the first to teach metalsmithing in an American university. 12 × 8″ ht. Photo courtesy of American Craft Council, by Mitch Bader.

Right: Douglas Steakley works almost exclusively in copper, exploiting the metal's rich color variations. These two vessel forms were each raised from a flat sheet of copper, using traditional hand-forging techniques. Steakley has embellished the surfaces of his simple forms with subtle hammer and punch marks. Left, 3″ diameter × 8″; right, 7″ diameter × 5″. Photo by Lee Hocker.

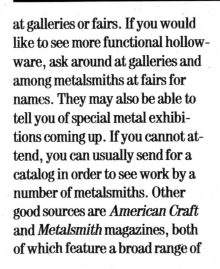

Below: Copper takes on unexpected color and pattern in the hands of David Paul Bacharach. *This raised form, though contemporary in spirit and decoration, appears at the same time to be ancient.*

Hollowware requires patience and painstaking labor at each step —forging, planishing, finishing. Although malleable, silver, copper, and pewter must be raised or stretched very slowly and evenly. The metalsmith may spend hours on a single course, which is just one of fifteen or twenty courses required to shape and planish the piece. In handcrafted hollowware, the time and réputation of the artist are often just as much a factor in pricing as is the cost of the materials. The recent popularity of copper among metalsmiths has made remarkable designs available at prices ranging from $600 to $1000, compared to silver hollowware which usually requires an investment of several thousand dollars. Even so, a growing number of collectors are avidly supporting the exceptional work of these independent metalsmiths in return for the great pleasure and pride of owning and using handcrafted silver.

Functional hollowware still represents a small proportion of the work available from metalsmiths, who generally do more nonfunctional metalwork or jewelry. That fact, plus the cost of silver, means that you won't see a lot of functional silver on display at galleries or fairs. If you would like to see more functional hollowware, ask around at galleries and among metalsmiths at fairs for names. They may also be able to tell you of special metal exhibitions coming up. If you cannot attend, you can usually send for a catalog in order to see work by a number of metalsmiths. Other good sources are *American Craft* and *Metalsmith* magazines, both of which feature a broad range of metalwork by craftsmen from all over the country. If someone's work strikes you, the metalsmith or his gallery will be happy to send you slides so that you can review more of his work. Don't assume that a metalsmith who exhibits only nonfunctional work will not accept a commission for a functional piece. To the contrary, most will, and you will benefit when they apply their sculptural sensibilities to functional work.

Below: *The curve of a shell inspired Susan Noland's silver berry spoon. The contour of the handle follows that of the shell, and the spoon curves sensuously up and away from the table, defying the traditional idea of "flatware." The well-intentioned curve also prevents the hand from slipping while serving. 9" length. Photo by Leslie Becker.*

Right Top and Bottom: *Through the seventeenth century, eating utensils were considered as personal as toothbrushes are today, so people carried their own flatware with them in uniquely designed, interlocking sets. These historic traveling sets, as well as contemporary camping gear, inspired Anne Krohn Graham's version. The spoon and fork fit within the knife handle, which forms a case. Photo by Tony Gaye.*

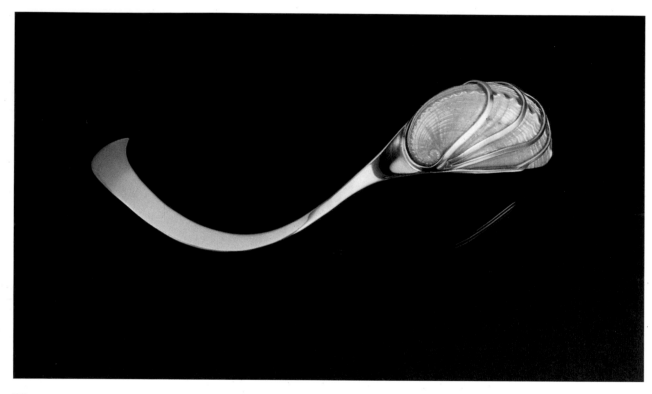

spoon, Graham pays close attention to the negative spaces created between the three pieces in a place setting. While the artistic concept of designing with negative spaces is as old as the Greek temples, its application to the design of flatware is entirely new. In her shell spoon on this page, Susan Noland dramatizes the special relationship created between the piece and the flat plane of the tabletop by curving the spoon gracefully up and away from the table. Thus, she achieves a dimensional quality in the spoon that is not common to flatware, as the name implies.

What to Look for When Buying Flatware

The real test of any flatware is how it feels in your hand and how it will feel in your mouth. Try out a cutting motion. Can you keep a firm grip while applying pressure in cutting? How does the handle feel in use? Are the fork and spoon well balanced? Run your finger along the edges. Are there rough edges on the bowl of the spoon, the tines of the fork, or in between the tines? It is possible for both manufacturers and craftsmen to get carried away with the decora-

Flatware

Flatware serves a dual purpose on the table: It is used to spear, cut, and scoop food, while it is also used to adorn a table setting. Today, metalsmiths are exploring both these aspects of flatware in their innovative designs. And whether you have a traditional or contemporary placesetting, there is work available to complement your current style.

Pewter, though still produced in styles that accurately capture the spirit of the eighteenth century, is not limited to traditional styles. Walter White's delightful asparagus spears pattern, on page 73, would handsomely underscore a floral or vegetable pattern typical of traditional place settings, or it would provide a lively contrast to an unembellished plate of modern design.

The pewter look of Brian Cumming's flatware is actually stainless steel with a dishwasher-safe finish. His designs, are in part inspired by the no-nonsense functionalism of Shaker designs. And like Shaker designs, his flatware is equally appropriate to a traditional or contemporary interior.

A few metalsmiths have introduced a new, sculptural approach to the forms of the knife, fork, and spoon—forms that we have taken for granted for so long. Anne Krohn Graham, for instance, whose work is shown on page 73, is concerned not only with the functional purposes of flatware, but also with the sculptural design of the forms. In planning the overall shape of a knife, fork, and

Below: Walter White's asparagus-spear tableware is available in pewter or silver. The sterling silver pattern is shaped by lost-wax casting, with fork tines and spoon bowls hand-hammered and polished afterwards. Each cast is slightly different, making the asparagus tips as varied as those in a garden. Photo by Jim Cummins.

Bottom: Because we have become accustomed to the cold look of commercially manufactured stainless steel, it is surprising to see the warmth that craftsmen glean from this metal. Brian Cummings contrasts the polished blade, tines, and bowl of his flatware set by burning a smoky, dark finish onto the handles. The finish is durable and dishwasher safe.

tion or design of the form at the expense of the more practical, functional aspects. Be sure the craftsman has taken pains to excel in all these areas, and you'll have a rewarding design that is both enjoyable and practical.

Metalsmiths making flatware generally show one or more prototype settings, which you can order in any quantity needed. As with commercial flatware, costs are based on time and materials. Naturally, the craftsman's prices must reflect the often considerable time involved in perfecting a design as well as the meticulous handwork required to fashion each piece. Although handmade silver flatware can be costly, as much as $600 to $800 for a three-piece place setting, it is, like any commercially produced silver setting, a treasure for generations to enjoy. Those craftsmen who work in pewter or stainless steel can offer their designs at lower prices, from $100 to $300 for a three-piece place setting, mainly because of the lower cost of the materials. Though distinguished in other ways, the unique designs from independent metalsmiths still require polishing just as often as commercial silver patterns.

Executed in pristine porcelain, this nonfunctional teapot by Marek Cecula is sliced by planes and cylinders, forming handle, spout, base, and lid.

Teapots

One stroll through a juried craft exhibition quickly reveals the wide range of teapots—both for use and for display—being fashioned by ceramic artists today. Even if you are not a tea drinker, it's hard to pass up the chance to own one of these marvelous teapots. There are stout little teapots and light, graceful ones, to be sure. But there are also Mad Hatter teapots, where everything seems delightfully out of kilter, and others where animal and human forms emerge organically from the handle, spout, or foot. At times whimsical, at times surreal, these teapots instantly capture the imagination.

Below: *This unusually thin-walled stoneware teapot functions beautifully. Its classic form features a shapely handle well-placed for balance in pouring. Ragnar Dixon Naess glazes just the lip of the spout, creating a sharp edge to break the flow of the water properly. Although his own high-fired stoneware pot can be used over the oil burner he produces, he warns that few ceramic teapots are safe from breakage over a direct flame. Teapot, 11½ × 7½ × 7½". Photo by Joseph Kugielsky.*

Bottom: *David Nelson uses a resist technique to obtain a strong pattern within the matte black glaze of his faceted teapot. Many potters believe that a horizontal lip, such as Nelson has made, is the closest to a no-fail spout design. Photo courtesy of American Craft Council, by Mitch Bader.*

Some teapots echo the serene, self-contained shapes, glazes, and carving of oriental teapots, while others mirror the forms and styles of twentieth-century painting and sculpture. On the following pages, you'll find a fine selection of all these types. If your new teapot is actually to be used to serve tea, you should examine the pot carefully with an eye to its design and construction.

What to Look for When Buying a Teapot

Unless you serve tea to a sizable party, you will probably be more satisfied with a smaller pot—one that serves two to four cups at a time and is lighter and easier to handle. With any teapot, however, remember to consider its weight when the pot is filled.

A large teapot can be comfortable for serving, but it must be well designed. Balanced weight while pouring is essential. This is determined primarily by the design of the handle. Lift and tilt the pot as though you were pouring tea into a cup. If the mass of the pot rests directly below your hand, or nearly so, it is much easier to stabilize the weight and

Below: Mary Anne Roehm's *porcelain work is wood-fired for ten to fourteen hours, during which time she must continuously stoke the kiln with split wood. This, the oldest of all firing methods, produces beautiful natural ash glazes created by the spewing and popping wood fire.*

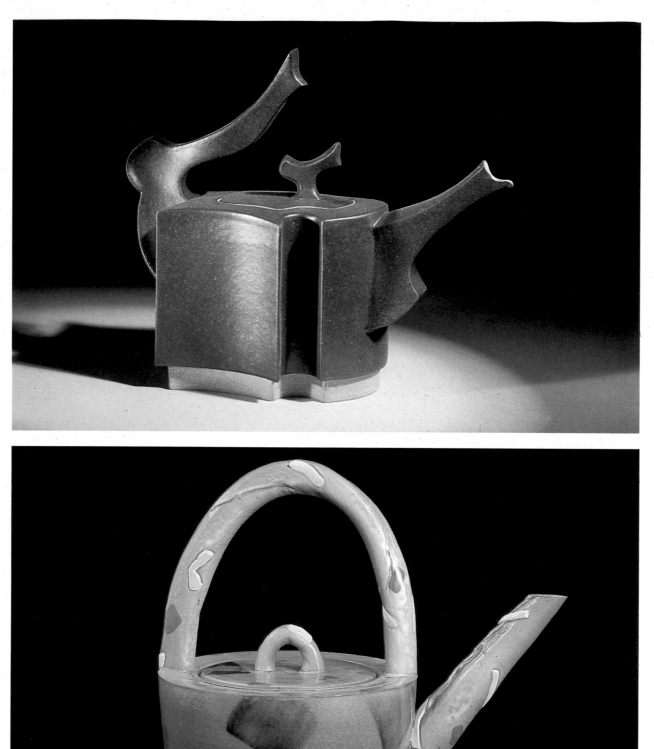

Left: Jean-Pierre Hsu's slab-constructed stoneware teapot successfully takes liberties with a conventional teapot form. Especially effective is his angular handle, which keeps the weight of the pot directly beneath your hand for comfortable pouring. In addition, it's easy to fill the pot with boiling water because of the design of the handle.

Bottom: Stanley Mace Andersen builds up color on his earthenware teapot, first by brushing on large and small patches of glaze color, and then by pressing small strips of brightly colored clay into the body of the teapot.

Right: This teapot was inspired by the variegated patterns of tropical fish and winged insects. Kaete Brittin Shaw creates this pattern by mixing pigment into porcelain before forming, as an alternative to surface glazing. Photo by Bob Hanson.

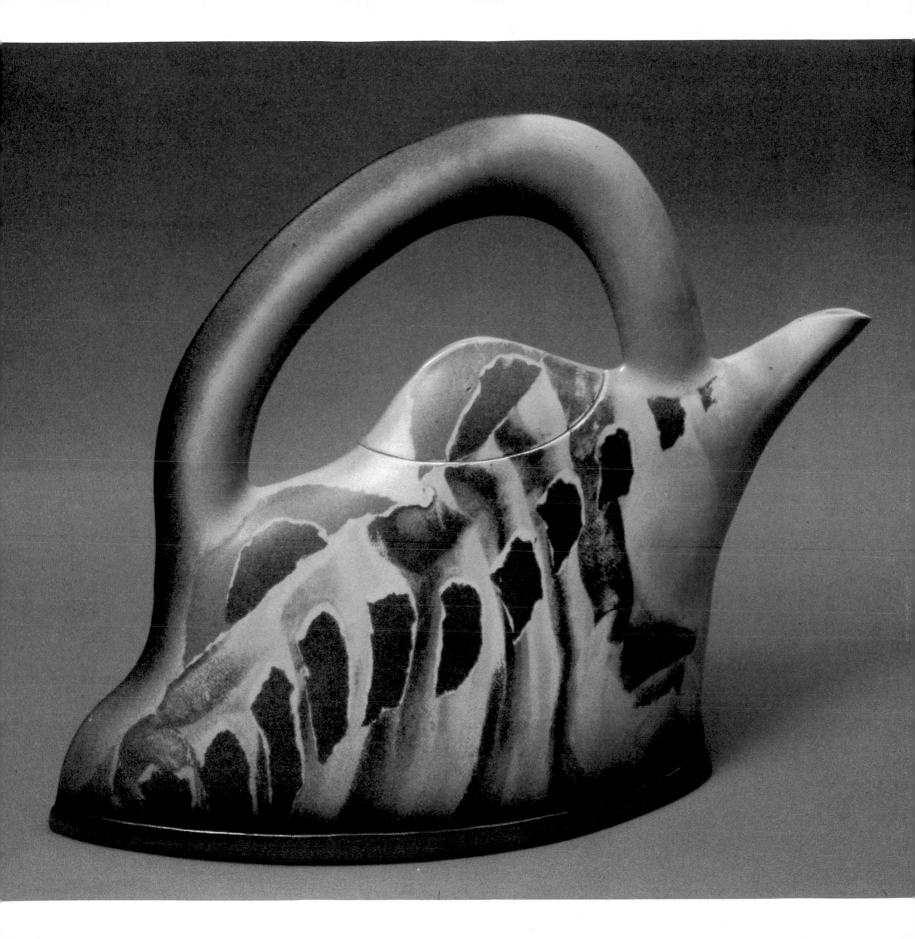

control the flow of liquid. If the pot is in front of your hand when you pour, it will require a strong wrist or a second hand to support the teapot.

Many American potters imitate the Japanese teapot by attaching a standing handle on the top of the pot to make pouring easier. A top-mounted handle may be bamboo or cane-wrapped wire, which drops to one side when not in use, or it may be a stationary handle made of clay. Another alternative is a clay handle mounted on the side of the pot, in a manner similar to an antique British or Chinese teapot. In all cases, however, remember that the mass of the teapot should rest almost directly below your hand when pouring.

There are at least as many variations on the spout as there are teas to brew within the pot. Here, you should evaluate the shape of the spout in relation to the pot itself and the mouth of the spout. Obviously, the spout should be compatible with the overall form of the teapot. The point where the spout joins the pot affects the overall form, so it's best if the spout appears to be a natural extension of the body of the pot, rather than an appendage. A good sharp edge on the spout helps to

Left: *The shape and color of this lovely teapot by Elaine Coleman are derived from traditional Chinese porcelains. The intricately incised pattern is made more prominent by the pale green celadon glaze that settles into the grooves and becomes darker in the deeper areas. 10 × 8½".*

Bottom: *Tom Coleman's porcelain teapot and cups are wheel-thrown and then altered by hand to create soft swells and ridges. His cups without handles imitate Japanese teacups and should be filled only halfway, so the top of the cup remains cool enough for the tea drinker to grasp. Teapot, 8" diameter × 10".*

Right: *The mottled glaze on Anne Shattuck's substantial teapot reinforces its irregular and elemental form. 8½" ht. Photo by Bob Barrett.*

Below: This whimsical porcelain tea set fashioned by Mara Superior seems to be inspired by a gentler time, when afternoon tea was an unhurried social occasion.

Below: Using real fruits, vegetables, and bamboo, Lynn Turner creates molds for her slip-cast porcelain forms. The inside of each piece is fully glazed in a traditional manner, but the exterior surfaces are airbrushed with thin glazes, recreating the subtle color variations of nature. Flask, 7" ht.

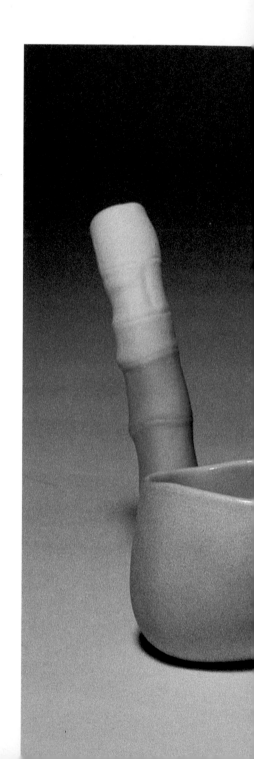

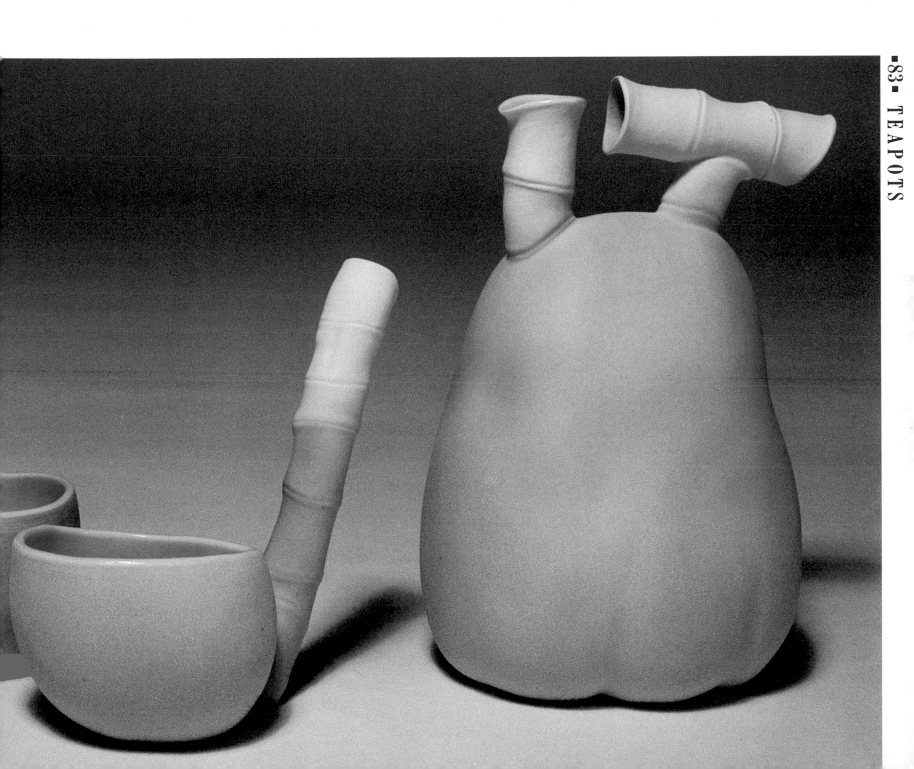

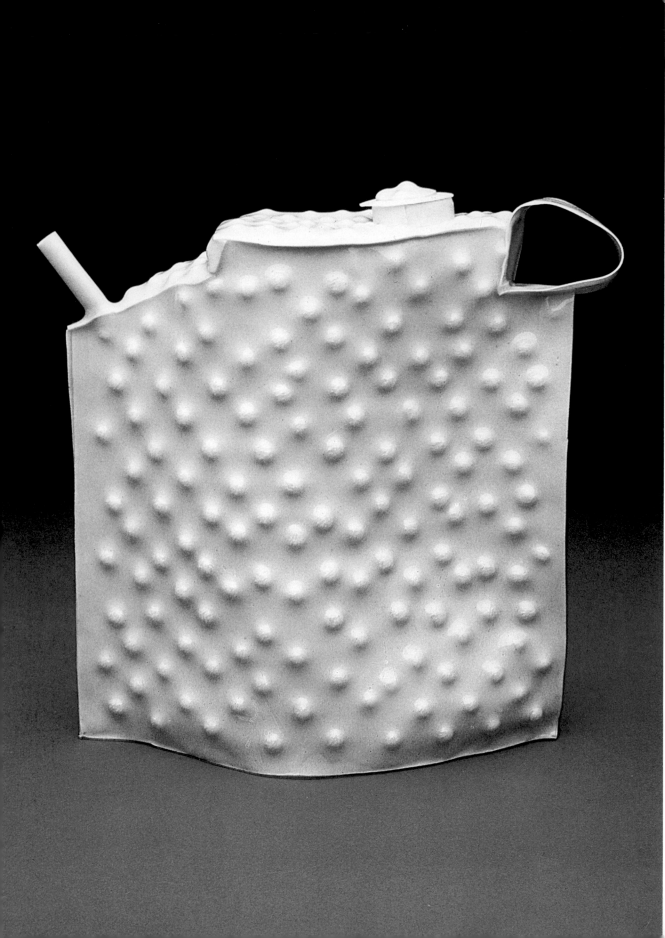

Left: *This wonderfully textured non-functional teapot by Philip Cornelius is disconcertingly lightweight, due to its hand-built, paper-thin porcelain construction. 9 × 7 × 3". Photo courtesy of Hadler-Rodriguez Gallery.*

break the flow of tea, forcing it to roll back into the teapot instead of down the side. The shape and mouth of the spout determine how the tea flows from the pot—in a predictable arc, dropping like a waterfall, or dribbling down the side of the teapot onto a saucer or the tablecloth. If you prefer a gentle stream of tea that falls straight from the spout, look for a wide mouth on the spout, like a pitcher that has a steady, slow pouring spout. The smaller the mouth of the spout, the faster the stream of tea, and the greater its tendency to flow in a graceful arc, like water in a fountain. One experienced potter compared the effect of a small mouth to water in a slow-moving river, which speeds up into rapids as it narrows in a gorge. Many devotees relish this arc as part of the ritual. By using a teapot often, you'll get to know the consistent leap of the stream and be able to get the tea into a cup and not onto the tablecloth.

A strainer to catch tea leaves may be incorporated within the spout, or it may not, requiring you to strain the tea before serving. An integral strainer is usually at the point where the spout and the body of the teapot are joined and usually consists simply of a

Right: *Enigmatic imagery and suggested movement result in a beguiling work, handbuilt of porcelain by Beth Fein. 12½ × 12 × 8".*

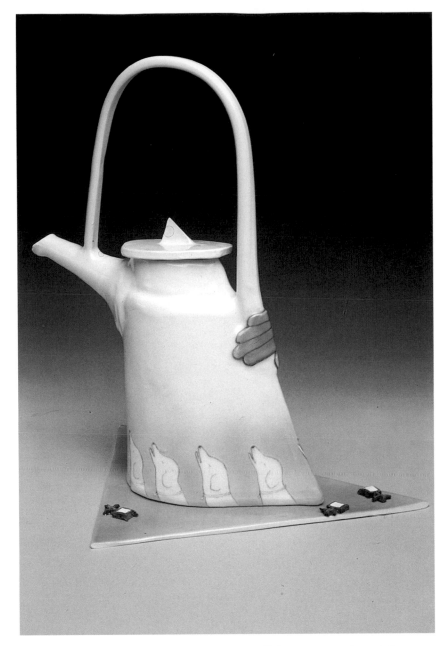

and in imitating these tea sets, often produce cups without handles. These cups are intended to be filled no more than half way with hot tea. Completely filled, the cup itself becomes so hot that it's impossible to hold. Half-filled, you can grip it easily near the top and comfortably sip without burning your fingertips.

How to Care for a Teapot

A teapot should not be confused with a tea kettle. The clay teapot brews tea after water is heated in a separate tea kettle. A clay teapot will shatter if placed directly on a range surface to heat water. Some craftsmen concede that you can keep tea warm in porcelain and stoneware teapots over an asbestos pad and a low gas flame on the range, but it's best to ask the maker. Serious tea drinkers will discourage you for another reason: The perfect brew is destroyed by continuous heat.

What about washing the teapot? Serious tea drinkers recommend that you never wash with soap or detergent, but simply rinse the teapot after each use. Why? These tea enthusiasts believe that with continuous use, there is a subsequent buildup of tannic acid

number of small holes punched through the clay.

Craftsmen have become very conscious of flanges and tabs to secure the lid while pouring. No lid can defy the laws of gravity, however, and if a teapot is tipped at an extreme angle, the lid may well fall off. If a well-designed teapot is of adequate capacity for the number of people you're serving, there's no reason to tilt the

pot all the way over to get the very last drop. If you're forced to hold the lid in place with one hand while you pour with the other, the problem may be solved by choosing a larger pot.

Often teapots are sold in sets with matching cups, as are many shown in this book. Many young American potters have been influenced by the design of antique Japanese and Chinese porcelains,

Below: *This brightly colored sculpture is a fantasy teapot by Peter Shire. He has abstracted the parts of a real teapot into bold geometric shapes. Photo courtesy of Janus Gallery.*

Right: *The twentieth century art movement known as Constructivism influenced Marek Cecula's design of this nonfunctional teapot.*

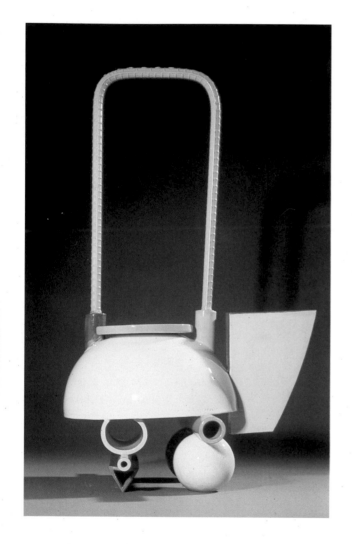

inside the pot which actually improves the pouring. Other serious tea drinkers take exception with this view. You'll have to discover for yourself which approach suits your taste buds!

What About Price?

A teapot is a difficult form to make. The body of the pot is usually thrown on a wheel, much as a vase or bowl would be. But then the potter must add a spout, a well-balanced handle with a comfortable grip in just the right place, and a snug-fitting lid. Because of the complexity of attaching all of these parts and the skill required to make them, the lower end of the price range for teapots typically begins at $75 to $100. Many well-established craftsmen, with museum exhibitions to their credit, continue to make teapots for the sheer joy of exploring the form. These teapots may sell for as much as $400 or more. Still another group of major clay artists fashion the classic teapot shape into sculptural forms that resemble teapots but don't hold water. These nonfunctional teapots are priced as sculpture and are meant to be displayed as such.

Handmade Furniture

You can purchase almost any piece of furniture you need for your home from a craftsman: coffee and end tables, console and dining tables, armoires, chests, wall cabinets, desks, secretaries, beds, chairs, and plant stands. Not only is there a great range of functional and decorative pieces, but a great diversity of styles, finishes, and woods. Contemporary woodworkers create furniture in traditional, modern, and innovative styles. Some of the more provocative pieces are designed to challenge the concept of what furniture is.

Detail of Rory McCarthy's gray lacquered coffee table (full view on pages 106-107). The richly colored and patterned interior surfaces that unfold from this table are an excellent example of the innovative use of decorative finishes in contemporary furniture. Photo by Balfour Walker.

Below and Right: An example of classically simple but beautifully executed work by Tage Frid, this table has a top that opens to double its surface area. In this closeup, notice that the beaded detailing is not applied, but rather is carved from the solid wood. Photographed at Pritam & Eames Gallery, by Joseph Kugielsky.

Whether your home is filled with formal antiques, country antiques, or mass-produced pieces of modern or traditional styling, the character of a handmade piece can greatly enhance the individuality of your home.

Contemporary woodworkers who are traditionalists at heart seek to enhance the natural beauty of the wood and take great pride in their mastery of fine woodworking techniques. Their's is a very philosophical approach to design, based upon an inherent respect for the wood itself. Typically, they favor native hardwoods, such as oak, birch, walnut, and cherry, but they may also incorporate exotic woods, such as ebony, padauk, and purpleheart, for the strong colors and striking contrasts these woods provide.

Their aim is to produce the finest piece of furniture possible a task that begins with the selection of the wood. To get the best pick, a craftsman often recruits the help of area lumberjacks to search for and save unusual and especially fine logs. At a lumbermill, the craftsman may pass over hundreds of logs or milled lumber before finding the five or six pieces of suitable quality for his work.

Left: Neil Barkon gives depth to this unusual wall-hung storage piece by contrasting straight and curved planes, which emphasize the active grain pattern of the wood. The piece is paired with a glass bowl by Stephen Dale Edwards and a quilt by Nancy Crow. Photographed at Pritam & Eames Gallery, by Joseph Kugielsky.

Below Left: John Dunnigan sets off the red padauk top of this exquisite little table with a painted rim and painted feet. The beveled top and skirt are also evidence of Dunnigan's meticulous craftsmanship. Photographed at Pritam & Eames Gallery, by Joseph Kugielsky.

Below Right: John Dunnigan's classic half-moon mirror echoes the shape of the table beneath in this distinctive pair. Photographed at the Pritam & Eames Gallery, by Joseph Kugielsky.

Long experience in working with wood makes the craftsman sensitive to subtle variations in the grain and color of raw lumber and uncut logs, characteristics that are hard to discern in the unrefined state but that are critical to the beauty of the finished furniture. Nothing but the finest wood will do. The craftsman simply will not invest his time in wood that is mediocre, so you can be sure you are not investing your money in anything but the best.

Sound construction techniques also distinguish the work of the individual craftsman from those of the mass-produced kind, ensuring that their handcrafted furniture will last for hundreds of years. For instance, traditional joinery, such as mortise and tenon, dovetail joints, and peg construction, allow for the natural expansion and contraction of the wood with changes in temperature and humidity. By contrast, mass-manufacturers use nails and glue to secure joints, a technique that does not allow for the natural and potentially damaging movement of the wood.

While a furniture manufacturer may attempt to conserve wood, the craftsman prizes the full depth of a piece of solid wood. Consider Tage Frid's table, on pages 90—

Left: *This wall-hung cabinet by Joyce and Edgar Anderson features expertly crafted traditional joinery. The walnut bust in the background is a jewelry case, also by the Andersons. The pottery that complements the warm wood tones is by (from left to right):* Karen Karnes, *the late* William Wyman, Bennett Bean, Karnes, *and* Toshiko Takaezu. *Photographed in the home of Louis and Sandra Grotta, by Tom Grotta.*

Below: Sam Maloof's *black walnut rocking chair is a design he has refined and perfected over the course of his thirty-year career as a fine woodworker. Its subtle curves conform gracefully to the body. His work is in the President's Oval Office as well as in the permanent collections of the American Craft Museum and the Boston Museum of Fine Arts. Photo by Jonathan Pollock.*

91, and the detailing on the shoulder—the horizontal support just beneath the tabletop. This very simple form is enriched by a beaded edge and a deeply cut channel. While a manufacturer creates this form by gluing pieces together and saving costly wood, Frid has meticulously carved the beading and the channel out of one solid piece of wood. This is but one step in the construction of the table that Frid values, even though it costs him more both in time and materials.

There are craftsmen today who have revived these traditional woodworking skills in the exact reproduction of antique furniture styles. But the contemporary woodworkers featured in this book, while drawing inspiration from traditional furniture, represent a group creating wholly original forms. Their work may capture the proportions, a distinctive line or silhouette, or a popular furniture form from the past, but always in a new and individual way. Variations on the ever popular rocking chair and the rolltop desk are examples of how contemporary craftsmen are refining and individualizing conventional furniture forms.

With a discipline rare in our

Below: Bob Trotman's *pair of occasional tables are aptly named Dancing Tables. Despite their fanciful form, these fine pieces were made with traditional inlay and lacquering techniques. 26½" ht.*

Right: Trent Whitington designed his eccentric "bedroom" chairs not for extended sittings, but rather for tying one's shoes. They are also intended to double as a clothes rack, since bedroom chairs usually end up being used that way anyway. The chairs are embellished with luxurious colors and mother-of-pearl inlay. Each, 30 × 26 × 20".

Below: Richard Scott Newman's *undulating blanket chest* makes the most of the natural grain of the Honduras mahogany. Even the integral handles at each end appear to be natural swells in the growth of the wood. Corner detailing on this cedar-lined chest dramatizes the traditional dovetail joint. 20 × 42 × 20". Photo by Northlight Studios.

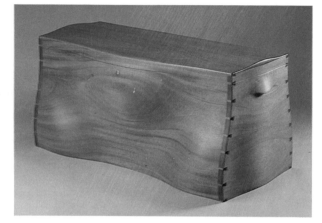

Left: *When faced with the challenge of creating a lingerie chest, David Ebner came up with a unique solution in this sculpted chest of Honduras mahogany. The handcarved slot that bisects the front of the chest serves as the handle or pull for the six drawers.* 55 × 30 × 16". *Photo by William Apton.*

Bottom Left: *The sloping sides of this richly grained chest of drawers by Michael Hurwitz distort its true height, creating an impression of monumentality.* 66½" ht. *Photo by Joseph Kugielsky.*

Bottom Right: *In an Art Deco-inspired vanity and bench, Marty and Fredi Shapiro juxtapose three different woods to accentuate the color variations in them—walnut (the darkest), mahogany (the lightest), and padauk (the red tones).* 60 × 40 × 20".

Below: Sara Jaffe's *armchair of Honduras mahogany, rosewood, and anodized black aluminum complements the bold geometrics of the painting. Photographed in the Showcase of Sherley Koteen Associates, by Breton Littlehales.*

fast-paced world, Sam Maloof, for instance, has been making rocking chairs for thirty years. And, he has refined the forms with each new rocker. Today, his rockers, like the one on page 95, reside in such prestigious places as the Oval Office of the White House and in the Boston Museum of Fine Arts. His work and his philosophy toward furniture have influenced younger American woodworkers to strive toward continually improving their furniture forms and construction techniques.

Some of the most adventurous furniture being designed today comes from innovative woodworkers who explore the basic principles of both representational and abstract art in their work. The most prominent among them is Wendell Castle. Almost two decades ago, he introduced a sculptural attitude toward the making of wood furniture that was to have a wide-ranging influence. He developed a technique for laminating many smaller pieces of wood into one large block and then carving it directly, similar to the way in which a sculptor might chip away at a block of wood or stone. Rather than assembling parts to create the whole, Wendell Castle reversed the traditional method of furniture-making by carving away to create the form.

More recently, Castle has turned to tour de force *trompe l'oeil* carvings on what appear to be conventional pieces of furniture. These laminated wood carvings, for example, of a pair of gloves dropped on a foyer table, or a tablecloth pulled awry (see page 105), suggest an unseen human presence. These arresting and innovative works have also understandably left their mark on many woodworkers.

John McNaughton's coffee table on page 105, a handsaw bent into a U-shape from which a hammer drips slowly to the floor, is another example of *trompe l'oeil* furniture as sculpture that invites an amusing double take. But not all sculptural furniture today is representational.

A growing number of young woodworkers are creating functional furniture that also looks like abstract sculpture. By manipulating conventional, functional forms to create new relationships of planes and angles, these craftsmen encourage us to see their pieces in altogether new ways.

Wendy Maruyama's desk, on page 108, stretches form and the viewer's mind by departing from

Right: Garry Knox Bennett *has created a marvelous contemporary version of the eighteenth-century piecrust table. It is seen here at the center of an effective display of contemporary American ceramics, and native Indian designs. Photographed in the home of Pat and Judy Coady, by David Arky.*

our conventional notion of what a desk should look like. Rather than creating a compact, symmetrical form, she uses sweeping lines and planes that extend beyond the body of the desk to create a marvelous sense of movement within a stationary piece of furniture.

Rory McCarthy's lacquered coffee table, on pages 106–107, is also a piece of sculpture that invites the owner's participation. Functional drawers that radiate from the mass of the piece can be arranged and rearranged at whim. To dramatize the effects of this changing form, McCarthy has highlighted the interiors of the drawers with gold leaf.

Other craftsmen make highly personal statements in their wood furniture. Edward Zucca's work is designed to make a pointed statement on contemporary values. His *Shaker TV* on page 109, for example, satirizes the anachronism of the family TV, symbol of modern electronics, in an Early American-style cabinet. This amusing piece features horizontally grained zebrawood for the screen and traditional handwoven Shaker webbing for the sound box.

Many furniture makers, like craftsmen working in other media, are returning to a more decorative

style, enriching their work with ornamental handcarving, inlay techniques, and colorfully painted finishes.

Although current carving styles may include classical and floral motifs, they are not limited to these. Most importantly, the carvings are designed to enhance the forms of the furniture and are carefully considered as integral to the total design aesthetic.

For many centuries, contrasting woods, ivory, and precious metals have been embedded in fine woods to create intricate inlays. Today's designers still use fine woods for their furniture; however, some, like Wendy Maruyama, may choose to spoof the venerable inlay technique by substituting textured sheet steel and colored epoxy resins.

Where once a clear, hand-rubbed finish to enhance the wood was *de rigueur,* painted finishes are now used very successfully to enhance the form of a piece. The chalky white paint on Judy McKie's console table, *Pete and Re-pete,* page 103, dramatizes the formal symmetry of the design. Tommy Simpson has drawn inspiration from the colors of Early American milk-paint finishes (see page 111) to underscore his origi-

Right: Judy Kensley McKie says that she turned to curves and animal imagery to make her furniture come to life. Sherley Koteen displays the softly waving lines of McKie's wood carving against the undulating colors of Cornelia K. Breitenbach's hanging. Photo by Breton Littlehales.

Right: Stylized and mystical creatures elegantly support a floating glass plane in this hall table by Judy Kensley McKie, delightfully titled Pete and Re-Pete. In the showcase of Sherley Koteen Associates, the glass top holds an oxblood-glazed vase by Catharine Hiersoux. Photo by Breton Littlehales.

nal interpretation of an American country rocker. Simpson's armoire, also page 111, takes on an anthropomorphic form through the use of light carving and heavily textured paints.

What to Look for When Buying Handmade Furniture

Because of, or perhaps in spite of, the special role handmade furniture will play in your life, comfort and function are still primary considerations. Apply the same tests you would when purchasing furniture in a store. Pull up to a table or desk. Sit in a chair. Is the surface of the table or desk the right height for you? If there are drawers, are they the right size and positioned where you need them? Are joints smooth and secure? Do the drawers move easily?

A chair should be comfortable not only to sit in, but to get out of as well. Unobstructed space beneath the seat makes it easier to stand, because you can put your feet directly beneath your body for greater stability.

Both the height and the angle of the seat also affect a chair's comfort. Recent ergonomic studies of how seating affects your spine, and thus your comfort, have shown that some of the conventional seating we accept through habit could be vastly improved.

Explore the options offered by individual craftsmen. A familiar form is not necessarily the most comfortable. What at first may seem odd in its departure from the norm may in fact be one of the most comfortable chairs you've ever experienced! Try out each piece with an open mind.

Caring for Handmade Furniture

A piece of handmade furniture should be cared for as if it were a fine antique. Protect wood against water marks, scorching from hot serving platters, and, whenever possible, from nicks and scratches. The furniture maker will usually recommend a particular polish by brand name. Use this periodically to protect your furniture and to prevent the wood from drying out.

Chances are you will not notice the drying right away, because it happens very slowly. As a result, many people neglect the periodic polishing or waxing that fine wood requires. If you have shopped for antiques, you have undoubtedly seen the damage that results from years of not replenishing the natural oils in wood. So it is extremely important that you take the time required for this minimal care. You will certainly be rewarded by the generations of use you can expect from handmade furniture.

What About Price?

Handmade furniture is not inexpensive. The kind of serious concern for quality that distinguishes work by contemporary craftsmen was reviewed earlier in this section. The craftsman's insistence on the best materials, the use of more difficult and more involved procedures, and on original, one-of-a-kind design, must of course influence the price just as it influences the quality of the piece you purchase. But if you compare its quality with the finest of commercial lines or with fine antiques, you'll begin to see the craftsman's price as the bargain it is.

Even on a budget, you still can

Below: *This contemporary interpretation of the classic rolltop desk is lightened by graceful legs and soft curves. Robert March chose padauk wood for these pieces, which gives them a warm, reddish glow. Desk, 60 × 46 × 33". Chair, 58 × 30 × 26".*

Below: *These graceful armchairs by Timothy S. Philbrick, with their fluid hand-carved arms and legs, seem to invite quiet conversation. Photo by Joseph Kugielsky.*

Right: John McNaughton's occasional table formed from plywood and mahogany is both a functional object and a playful sculpture. The bent saw supported by a melting hammer creates a witty juxtaposition of familiar objects in a surreal way.

Below: A square table seems to stand beneath a wooden cloth in this trompe l'oeil table laminated and carved by master woodworker Wendell Castle. Photographed in the home of Mr. and Mrs. Daniel Fendrick, by Breton Littlehales.

incorporate a handcrafted piece into a room if you buy wisely. Look to the mass manufacturers for neutral background pieces and upholstery, and put your money in a single spectacular piece from a craftsman. The very special quality of the handmade makes it possible to achieve impact out of proportion to the size of the piece. For instance, even a small occasional table or marvelous plant stand of original design can add a special touch to a room.

Mixing Handmade with Existing Furniture

In most homes, a mix of periods and styles of furniture is the norm rather than the exception, so the idea of combining styles is not new. Likewise, incorporating the handmade is mostly a matter of common sense.

Mixing furniture styles is very much like planning a guest list for a dinner party. For the most part, you choose people with common interests. You will avoid too many strong personalities and conflicting philosophies and will take care to seat two dominant characters away from each other. On the other hand, if the guest list looks a bit bland, a smart host or hostess often includes one lively figure who is sure to introduce provocative conversation.

When it comes to furniture selection, some common elements also are necessary for a congenial blend. And while too many strong personalities just won't mix, a little lively contrast is a good thing.

Furniture mixes should be compatible in their degree of refinement and formality, in scale, line, and decoration.

All furniture in one room should, as a rule, share a common level of refinement and a common degree of formality. A casual piece of furniture is out of place in a formal setting, and finely crafted furniture will show up the unfortunate qualities of cheap pieces.

Refinement and formality are defined by a number of things: materials, craftsmanship, and finishing details. While most formal pieces are crafted of dark woods, we associate lighter woods like birch and oak with informality. Heavier, chunkier forms are perceived as more casual than

Left: This monolithic coffee table by Rory McCarthy is made up of beautifully crafted segments that open, slide, and pivot from the table's mass to create ever-changing sculptural compositions at the whim of owner or guest. The interior of the drawers and compartments is painted and gilded in dramatic contrast to the smoked lacquer surface. 18 × 66 × 36". Photo courtesy American Craft Council, by George Erml.

Below: Defying conventional ideas about furniture, Wendy Maruyama applies sculptural principles to her bold desk design. Using a vibrant purple drawer lining (detail), Maruyama introduces lively color, while inlaid blocks of colored epoxy resins accentuate the position of the solid wood supports beneath. An endearing element is the playful crayon scrawl across the tabletop. Photographed in the home of Don Thomas and Jorge Cao, owners of Convergence Gallery. Photo by David Arky.

Opposite Left: A simple table at first glance, this piece by Wendy Maruyama is enlivened by textured black steel and brightly painted red borders that sit on top of the table and extend beyond its corners. It is handsomely placed beneath a pair of earthenware plates by Patrick Loughran. Table, 34 × 24 × 24". Photo by David Arky.

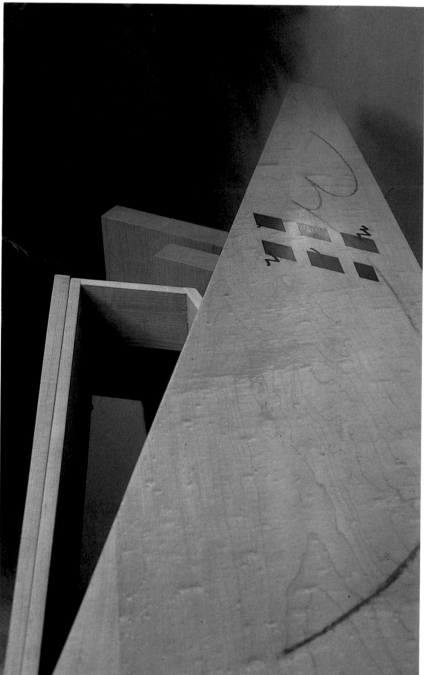

light, graceful lines.

Compatible scale is critical to a good blend. A graceful, light table with high, slim legs would work beautifully with the relative lightness of a Chippendale or Federal sofa, but would be overwhelmed by the popular new overstuffed sofa shapes. A massive rolled-arm sofa or expansive sectional sofa requires substantial companions, such as a stout, natural wood table or a lacquered cube form. When wooden chairs are paired with massive upholstered seating, a delicate chair may look as if it is about to float away. Guests may avoid it because discrepancies in scale are disconcerting, even when unconsciously perceived.

Just as the controversial guest adds life to a dinner party, however, a single contrasting piece of furniture brings out the best in both styles. An elaborately decorated desk is enhanced by the simple lines of a contemporary chair. A room of period furniture may be relaxed by the introduction of a simple coffee table of polished dark wood from a craftsman. Turning the formula around, a subdued neutral room of modern furnishings and art is warmed by a handmade addition with handsome carving or inlay work.

Handmade furniture, an individual expression of the craftsman,

Right: Edward Zucca has created a Shaker TV in satire of both our modern dependence on television and on its unlikely housing in an Early American-style cabinet. 36 × 24 × 18". Photographed in the showcase of Sherley Koteen Associates, by Breton Littlehales.

Below: Edward Zucca's *Middleboy is a
Post-modern interpretation of the
popular eighteenth-century highboy.*
52 × 60 × 19". Photo by David Arky.

often has a strong personality. The very distinctiveness that makes it a valuable anchor in the room can also make it difficult to mix with other eccentric furniture styles. One character per evening and one character per room is a good rule of thumb.

With these ideas in mind, you should be able to select handmade furniture for your home with some confidence. New handcrafted furniture blends exceptionally well with better antiques and good quality contemporary furnishings. Fine quality tends to make furniture compatible regardless of period or style.

Left: Tommy Simpson has decorated the surface of this armoire with an extravagant pattern. The piece, which houses a television and stereo, was originally created as a playhouse for his daughter, complete with hanging chandelier, tables and chairs. Photo by Joseph Kugielsky.

Below: In an homage to Early American folk art, Tommy Simpson captures the essence of a period in this wholly original rocker.

Working with glass in a molten state, Harvey Littleton encases several gathers of colored glass within clear glass. When the glass is cold, Littleton slices and polishes each piece. The slices reveal the interior structure of the piece, a visible history of the process. Photo by John Littleton.

Glass Art

Although glass has an ancient tradition that can be traced back to the Egyptians, in modern times it has been strictly a product of the factory; that is, until about 20 years ago. In 1962 a small group of determined craftsmen under the farsighted direction of Harvey Littleton (at the time a professor of art at the University of Wisconsin) developed a low-melting-temperature glass formula and a furnace small enough for an individual craftsman to blow glass in his own studio.

Below: *Though Michael Glancy's glass work is opaque, it retains glasslike qualities. Using deeply cut facets and electroplated copper, Glancy suggests the preciousness of cut stone. Photo courtesy of Heller Gallery, by Gene Dwiggins.*

Right: *William Morris evokes Stonehenge monumentality in his unusually large, three-foot-high glass forms. Partly freeblown, the pieces are finished in complicated molds to achieve the desired contours. In this demanding process, each mold may be used only twice. And even after hours of demanding work, three out of four blown forms will fail or crack. Photo by Lee Hocker.*

At that time, glass ceased to be merely a product created for a market. Instead, it became the artist's medium for making a personal, often dramatic, and highly individualized statement.

Unlike functional glassware, which is still strongly influenced by the decorative arts, this new direction in glass is essentially a sculptural movement. One sign of the acceptance of glass as a major art medium of the twentieth century is its inclusion in the permanent collections of the Metropolitan Museum of Art and the Museum of Modern Art, in New York City, as well as in other prestigious museums here and abroad. Forceful glass sculptures by Harvey Littleton, Dale Chihuly, Jon Kuhn, and Michael Glancy, for example, are among those on display at the Metropolitan Museum of Art.

The individual directions pursued by these new glass artists are extremely varied. If any single element links the diverse styles, it is that the final forms express the unique properties of hot glass. In blowing glass as a sculptural medium, the glass artist confronts an entirely different set of constraints and reference points than does a

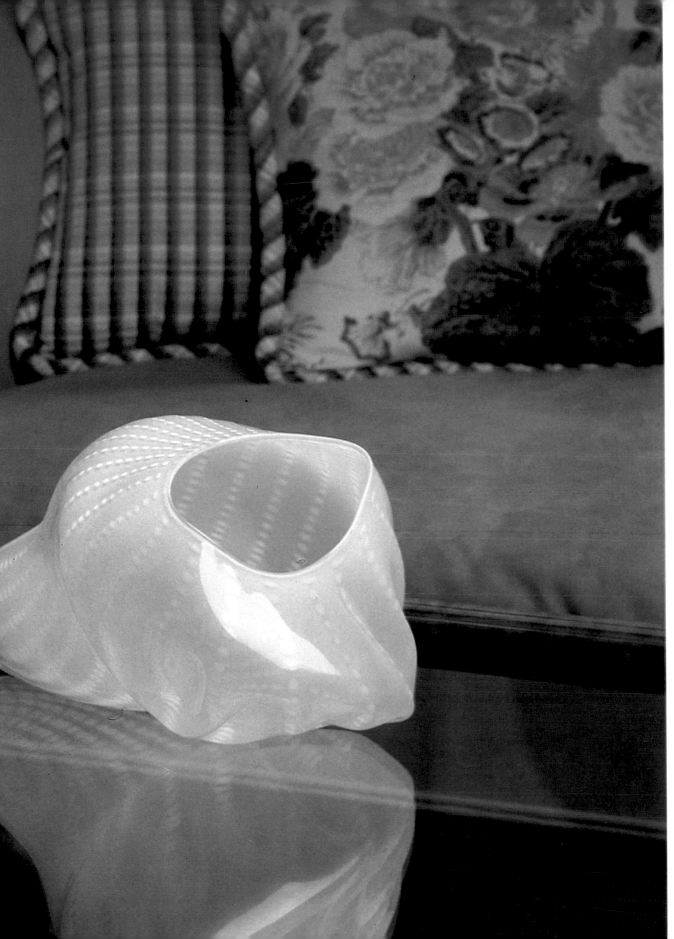

Left: Dale Chihuly's work is renowned not only for its beauty but also for its technical excellence. He is able to create both very large and extremely thin forms—a feat requiring great proficiency. Julia Walker displays his work by placing one piece inside another, creating multiple reflections on a glass tabletop. Photo by David Arky.

sculptor working in another material. Universally, sculpture has played off of the horizontal plane of the earth or floor. The glass sculptor has no such reference point, but creates his form in mid-air, attached only to the end of a four-foot blowpipe.

It is the immediacy of glass sculpture that these artists mention most often as what attracted them to glass over other materials. The form takes shape at once, directly in response to the artist's motions. A mistake cannot be amended; thus, the artist must be quick-witted and able to respond to the moment. Compared with a cast bronze or carved marble sculpture, which may follow a study or maquette, glass sculpture is a spontaneous interaction between the artist and the material, encompassing the unpredictable reactions of the flowing, molten glass and the artist's immediate responses to the forces of gravity that shape the glass at the end of the blowpipe. This immediacy and very personal spontaneity is unique among sculptural media.

The quality of light as it passes through glass has an ancient and universal fascination, but modern artists demand more from

Below: Carl Andree Davidt *combines glass and metal to create remarkable sculptures that are also tables. This single energetic piece would add a dramatic note to a sleek, contemporary interior. 4' diameter x 15". Photo courtesy of Heller Gallery.*

Below: Carl Andree Davidt *combines glass and metal to create remarkable sculptures that are also tables. This single energetic piece would add a dramatic note to a sleek, contemporary interior. 4' diameter x 15". Photo courtesy of Heller Gallery.*

themselves and from the medium than to rely on the beauty of the glass alone. Some have, in fact, purposefully reacted against the beauty of the glass, creating strong, almost aggressive forms, which contradict its inherent beauty. In all cases, they create forms that would stand alone as sculpture no matter what the material, and they use light as a tool to enhance their forms.

Fairly recently, major artists, such as Harvey Littleton whose work is on pages 112–113, have used cutting and polishing techniques to create many new light spectrums within a single form. Closely related is the layering of color to effect remarkable depth and perspective within the sculptural form—one more quality unique to glass. The work of Mark Peiser, for instance, is philosophically akin to the representative painter who explores perspective. The translucency and color possibilities of glass make it particularly suited to perspective studies. Other glass artists use layering of color and cutting to create amazing depth in abstracted compositions as well. The fragility of glass is another inherent quality of the material which artists push to its limit. Dale Chihuly, for instance, aims for extremely thin, delicate forms with an apparent undulating softness that contradicts the brittle, shattering potential of the material.

The work of Michael Glancy and that of collaborative artists. Margie Jervis and Susie Krasnican (shown , respectively, on page 114 and the back cover of this book) represents a departure from the exploitations of the translucency of glass. Michael Glancy varies his surface by electroplating copper and other metals on deeply cut facets of his vase forms. And glass enamels fired onto the surface of the Jervis/Krasnican slumped, polychrome bowl are responsible for its delicate, lustrous opacity.

Rarely is a single process used alone, but blowing, cutting and polishing, casting, and layering

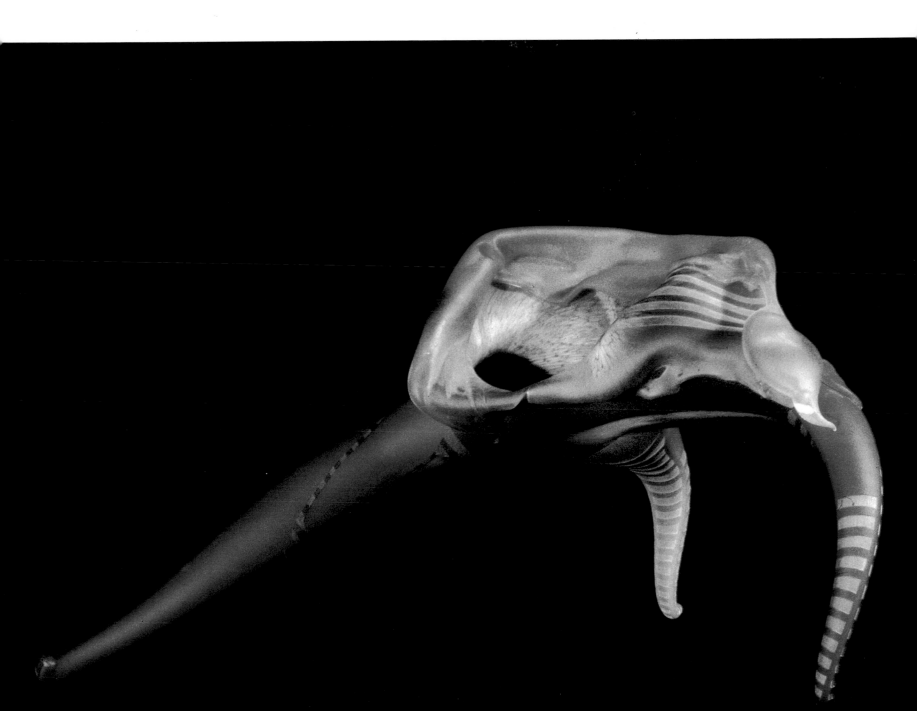

Below: *Using luminous colors, Stephen Dee Edwards evokes life and movement in his Sea Form series. 10 × 9 × 2". Photo by John Littleton.*

Below: Both the bowl by Gary Beecham *(left)* and the collaborative work of John Littleton and Katherine Vogel *(right)* feature layers of color encased within clear glass. Sherley Koteen displays the pieces on pedestals in front of large glass windows so that the changing daylight alters the color patterns within the glass. Photo by Breton Littlehales.

Left: *In a unique and demanding process, Rick Bernstein integrates images from contemporary life within his cone-shaped vessels. 7" diameter × 13". Photo courtesy of Heller Gallery. Photo by Susie Kuschner.*

Below: *Creating representational images in glass is admittedly quite difficult. A piece such as this one by Joey Kirkpatrick and Flora Mace is best understood by imagining a drawing on a deflated balloon that is then expanded by inflating the balloon. Photo courtesy of Heller Gallery.*

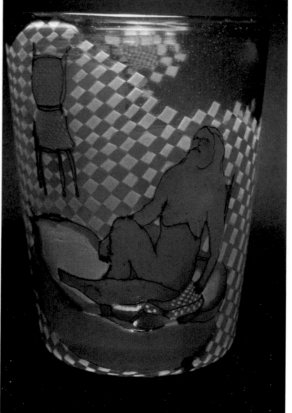

Left: *In his work, Jon Kuhn reminds us of the humble materials from which beautiful glass is made. The outer surface looks like the opaque sand (silica) from which glass is made, while a dramatic slice reveals the gemlike color possible in glass. Photo by Doug Long.*

Below: *In a substantial vase form, Fritz Dreisbach encases rods of colored glass within the blown form to achieve lively movement and energy. Photo by John Littleton.*

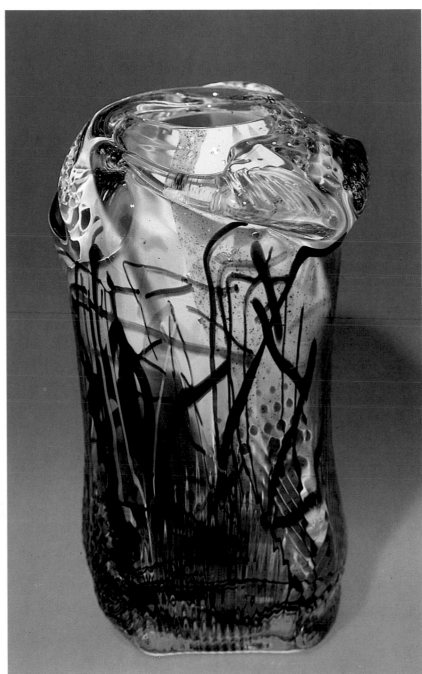

Below: Mark Peiser *may spend as many as fourteen hours without interruption on a single piece, creating detailed imagery within the multiple layers of glass. The scenes are so realistic, it almost feels as if you could walk into them. Photo by Ann Hawthorne.*

Right: Joel Philip Myers *first blows a simple vase form in black glass and then fuses to it fragments of colored glass salvaged from other pieces. By sandblasting, he gives the surface a subtle matte black finish. Photo courtesy of American Craft magazine, by David Riley.*

combine to create limitless possibilities for sculptural styles. Still part of a very young art movement, the glass artists continue to stretch the technical possibilities of their medium.

Price Ranges

The glass featured on these pages is essentially sculpture, and it is available at a price level you would expect to pay for sculpture. Regardless, with its inclusion in museum collections—a status favorably affecting its investment value—the best glass art is still priced at an acceptable level for the collector. If you are more interested in glass for personal rewards than for investment value, you can find glass vase forms for as low as $100 to $500 and an intermediate range of nonfunctional glass from $2000 to $5000.

Displaying

Proper display is essential to appreciate glass art. Both where the glass is placed and how it is lighted will affect a viewer's response to the work. Unlike the sculptor in marble or wood who works on a table or the floor, the sculptor who blows glass works without a frame

of reference, developing his form open-endedly. His creation, therefore, is best viewed from all sides, both during its creation as well as later, as a finished work. If shelf display is your only alternative, consider mirroring the wall behind. Pieces should not be crowded, so they can be viewed in the mirror.

Light is especially critical to glass art, and displaying glass objects on a tabletop or pedestal will give you an opportunity for dramatic lighting. Though some pieces are involved with form and are not so dependent on the influence of light, almost without exception, glass is enhanced by light. At first it is very helpful to move a piece several times and observe the effects of various lighting situations. Care should be taken to place objects so that there is no glare. An ideal situation for the placement of glass art is in front of a natural light source where the fullest spectrum of light can interact with the glass.

Purity of line and color are characteristic of Elsa Rady's porcelain bowls.
Finlike projections and a sweeping
horizontal silhouette give this bowl an
appearance of being in motion.

Ceramic Art

The history of the ceramic arts in America closely parallels the history of contemporary crafts here. About the time of the post–World War II revival of interest in crafts, young American potters came under the influence of Zen philosophy, the tea ceremony, and a long history of oriental ceramics. Then, in the late 1950s, a sculptural approach to clay gained momentum, opening up a new period of experimentation in ceramics. That vital energy has continued through today with new interest in color and surface decoration.

Below: *In this handsome display, Ken Deavers features the work of only one ceramist—Adrian Saxe. Though glaze colors and decoration differ from piece to piece, his distinctive style unifies five pieces on low tables. A single small piece gains special prominence on the mantle. The only exception to Saxe's work on display is Harriet Bellow's low-fired, boldly striped form to the right of the fireplace. Photo by Breton Littlehales.*

Top Right: *The translucency of porcelain is most apparent when it is worked thin. Here, Molly Cowgill exploits the inherent characteristics of this clay in a delicate bowl. She lets the bowl dry until it is leather-hard and then carves and incises it before glazing and firing. Photo by Jonathan Wallen.*

W ith the number of ceramic artists working today rapidly increasing, diverse styles proliferate. You can choose from classical oriental vessel forms, nonfunctional clay sculptures, and simple forms that are embellished either subtly or boldly with color and pattern.

One fact that distinguishes ceramic art from work in other media is the unpredictable nature of the clay, the glaze, and the firing. An oil painter can readily observe the colors he mixes and their effect on his canvas; the ceramic artist, in contrast, does not know until he opens the kiln what the outcome of his work will be. Even when the craftsman has years of experience, the unexpected can happen—sometimes a wonderful surprise and sometimes a disaster. Many ceramists romanticize this ultimate power of the clay and the kiln, and as you become more attracted to ceramic art and talk with the craftsmen who work in this medium, you will begin to sense their attraction to this intangible quality in the making of each piece.

Every step in the making of a ceramic vessel influences the final aesthetic. The choice of clay itself

Bottom Right: *This unusual "barnacle glaze," as Sally Bowen Prange calls this textured effect, is obtained by adding silicon carbide to the porcelain clay body. In high-temperature firing, the carbide becomes gaseous and bubbles through the glaze, cratering it throughout. 8 × 8½ × 11". Photo courtesy of American Craft Council Library.*

Left: Ralph Bacerra's *luxuriant decoration* is a modern interpretation of the rich patterning and colors of ancient Imari porcelain. Photo by Breton Littlehales.

Below: Adrian Saxe produces more monumental works than these, but few are more popular than his diminutive porcelain oil lamps. The tallest, only 6 inches high, is glazed with ox-blood and paired with an incised lamp glazed a pale celadon green. Photographed in the home of Ken Deavers, owner of American Hand, by Breton Littlehales.

is an essential part of the artist's statement. Only with porcelain, for instance, could Elsa Rady, whose work is on pages 124-125, achieve the thin, firm edges critical to her expression. Karen Karnes's ample forms, like the one on page 131, just as clearly express the natural qualities of stoneware, and Betty Woodman works in white earthenware (see page 133) in order to realize the bright, true glaze colors that the higher firing of porcelain or stoneware would wash out.

The ceramist similarly chooses a forming method that will best realize the shape he or she desires, and the method used is evidenced in the piece. Work such as that by Susan Loftin and Nancy Selvin (see page 132) is built up of flat slabs of clay. The mark of the potter's fingers as she pulls the clay up into the vessel form is still visible in the work of Toshiko Takaezu, on page 131. These marks are a sign of wheel-thrown work.

These technical considerations are much less likely to influence your response to a piece than is the strength of the work itself. Even a cursory knowledge, however, can increase your appreciation of the subtleties and often the difficulties of ceramic art.

Below: Thomas Hoadley uses an ancient Japanese technique known as nerikomi, in which colored clays are layered in a loaf shape and then stretched and folded to distort the layers. When a thin slice is cut from the loaf, it reveals a marbelized, striated pattern. Hoadley then presses these slices into vessel molds. Jar, 6½" diameter × 7¾".

Below: Although the larger vessel is clay and the other paper, each was formed by similar means: wet porcelain and wet paper pulp were pressed into a cast or mold. Reversing convention, Ruth Duckworth embellishes the interior of her large ceramic vessel with colored clays and contrasts it with an undecorated exterior. Sylvia Seventy's cast paper vessel has a black interior, also in contrast with its twine-bound exterior. Photographed in the home of Jack Lenor Larsen, by David Arky.

Right: Richard DeVore *handbuilds his stoneware vessels with unusually thin walls. These three pieces from the collection of Jack Lenor Larsen are typical of the fine crackle glazing and subtle glaze colors characteristic of DeVore's finest work. Photo by David Arky.*

As decoration has become more important in their art, ceramists have embraced techniques that allow them to embellish their forms with both color and texture. The renewed interest in color has resulted in greater use of earthenware. Because it is fired at relatively low temperatures, earthenware may be painted with brighter, stronger colors. These can be seen in the work of Curtis Hoard, where the colors are applied in a very painterly manner, making the style of painting as important as the form itself.

A fairly new way of introducing color in porcelain and stoneware is by using colored clay. In this technique, pigment is mixed into the clay before forming, resulting in an effect very different from that of surface glazing. Thomas Hoadley's vessel (page 129) illustrates the use of colored clays to achieve integral pattern. Hoadley presses the colored clays into a mold in order to retain clearly defined patterns, as is often done with inlaid color. In Ruth Duckworth's large bowl form, on page 129, the interior walls of the form were incised and colored clay pressed into the spaces.

Texture is another current concern in clay. It can be achieved by

Below: *The work of one accomplished potter, Toshiko Takaezu, is featured in this family room. Photographed in the home of Sandy and Fred Roth, by Tom Grotta.*

Bottom: *Karen Karnes has long been known for the strength and simplicity of the forms she creates in stoneware. In this robust piece, delicately glazed and with a subtly textured lid, she emphasizes the natural qualities of stoneware—stonelike, grainy, and muted. Typical of her work, the decoration remains subordinate to the form itself. Photo courtesy of Hadler-Rodriguez Gallery.*

Left: *This collector cleverly displays the vivid colors and architectural forms of Susan Loftin's works by juxtaposing them against a neutral contemporary interior. Photo by Jerry Burns.*

carving the surface, by adding chemicals to the clay body, and by applying particular glazes. Porcelain lends itself especially well to surface carving, and today's ceramists continue an ancient precedent well known in antique Chinese porcelains. The delicate ribbing of Adrian Saxe's oil lamp on page 128 as well as the more open, fluid pattern of Molly Cowgill's bowl on page 127, are created by incising the surface of the form when it has dried to a leather-hard stage between forming and firing. Leather-hard accurately describes the way a clay piece feels near the end of its drying stage before firing; the clay has dried to a point where it is firm enough to hold an incised design.

The fascinating, crater like surface of Sally Prange's porcelain vessel on page 127 is the result of adding silicon carbide to the clay

Near Left: *To build up lush surface colorations, Nancy Selvin is apt to apply as many as seven layers of glaze colors to a piece, always firing between applications. In this case, the result is an unusual glossy yellow glaze that drips and swells down the side of the otherwise simple, diminutive piece. 4 × 4 ×4". Photo by Charles Frizzell.*

Below Left: *Robert Forbes achieves great vitality in his low-fired terra cotta bowls by vigorously brushing on slip (liquid clay). Photographed in the home of Kay and George Eddy, by Joseph Kugielsky.*

Bottom Left: *Betty Woodman is considered one of the most influential artists working in low-fired earthenware. She is best known for the fluid application and the intensity of her glaze colors. Photo courtesy of Hadler-Rodriguez Gallery.*

Below: *Judith Salomon's hand-built white earthenware vessel looks architectural with its suggestions of windows and walls. The piece is painted with intense glaze colors that remain clear and bright throughout the low-firing temperatures. Photo by Breton Littlehales.*

Left: *In a delightfully unorthodox interpretation of traditional mantel arrangements, Judy Coady pairs two large vase forms by Andrea Gill. Even though their decoration and forms are somewhat different, these pieces are well balanced in scale and color. Within this strong framework, she has centered a brilliantly colored bowl by Phillip Maberry and surrounded it with his functional dinnerware. Photo by David Arky.*

Below Left: Some arrangements are the result of a preference for a particular style of ceramics. Here, Julia Walker has displayed Neil Tetkowski's shallow vessel on a transparent plate stand (left) behind Paul Soldner's raku-fired work. Donna Polseno's matte black, raku-fired vase form acts as a foil to these natural clay colors and the vivid orange wall covering. Photo by David Arky.

Below Right: Nancee Meeker has intentionally kept this bowl quite simple to dramatize the irregular crackle glaze that results from raku-firing. 9" ht.

Bottom Left: In raku firing, pottery is taken from a red-hot kiln and put immediately into a combustible material, such as straw, where the heat of the clay creates a great deal of smoke. The effects of raku firing can be seen on this urn by Cynthia Bringle. The unglazed lip and base are totally blackened, while the glazed body is darkened in the fine cracks that develop in the glaze. Photo by Ann Hawthorne.

Bottom Right: By placing together two different forms by the same ceramic artist, Sherley Koteen makes a more dramatic display. The lustrous, raku-fired platter and spherical vessel are by Harvey Sadow. An equally effective display is achieved by draping Nina Ackerson's wool and linen rug over a contemporary white sofa. Photo by Breton Littlehales.

Below: Paul Chaleff's striking stoneware jar is fired in a wood-burning kiln built into the side of a hill near his studio. The entire firing cycle may take as long as twenty days. Chaleff's work is represented in the permanent collection of the Museum of Modern Art, New York City. 13" diameter × 14". Photo by Jeff Fox.

Below: By adding wood ash to the glaze, Tom Coleman creates a running glaze that visually defines the form as it drips down the sides during firing. On this porcelain basket, Coleman has used a gnarled twig handle to symbolize the source of his marvelous glaze. 10½" diameter × 13". Photo by Rick Paulson.

Right: Tom Turner's variegated glaze, most visible on the shoulders of his generous urn shape, simulates the broken, runny appearance of an ash glaze.

body. As the glaze reaches a melting temperature at high firing, silicon carbide gas bubbles through the molten glaze, creating craters, or "barnacles" as Prange refers to them.

Wood ash added to the glaze changes it into a broken, runny glaze. This creates a warm, rich texture, as in the piece by Tom Coleman shown above. This very old glazing composition, which has been associated with traditional or folk pottery, is now being explored again with renewed interest in the surface variations. (While everyone else was cursing and cleaning away the fine volcanic ash from Mount St. Helen's, potters in the area were gathering it by the bucketful for ash glazes.)

Still other textural possibilities can be effected in the firing. Salt glaze, for instance, is the result of adding rock salt to the kiln during firing. The salt reacts with the glaze at the high temperatures of the kiln to create the distinctive orange-peel surface, such as you can see on Byron Temple's storage jars on page 21.

Raku is an ancient Japanese firing process that has recently been

revitalized and popularized by American potters. In this technique, a pot is pulled from the kiln while red-hot and put immediately into a combustible material—sawdust, leaves, straw, or shredded paper. This burning material creates smoke that blackens the surface of the pot and may leave a mottled texture or distinctive mark on the surface. The piece being fired may be glazed or unglazed for very different effects. Unglazed clay has a matte surface and can become very black (as with Donna Polseno's pot on page 135). If the pot is glazed, the glaze tends to crackle in raku firing. When first pulled from the hot kiln, the glaze cools slightly quicker than the clay body and develops hairline cracks without damaging the clay. Nancee Meeker exploits this property in her work on page 135 by contrasting the crackle in a white glaze. When her pots are removed from burning sawdust, they are black and sooty all over. When they are scrubbed down, only the cracks in the glaze, which have absorbed the smoke, remain dark, creating elegant contrast within the white glaze. The crackle is not always so noticeable, however, on darker glazes. To minimize the

Left: Often work by several different ceramic artists can be successfully grouped for display by seizing upon one element they all have in common. In this case, the scale of each piece is quite ample and becomes the unifying element. Left, Andrea Gill; top center, Ken Ferguson; bottom center, Jane Guston; right, John Gill. Photographed in the home of Helene Margolies, by David Arky.

Below Left and Right: Curtis C. Hoard literally paints with clay, brushing colored clay, in a liquid state known as slip, over red earthenware. His large pieces represent a stylistic trend among potters toward overscaled forms. Such imposing works are more suitably displayed on the wall or as floor sculptures than as tabletop decoration. Platter, 22" diameter. Covered vessel, 13" diameter × 56".

Below Left: *After an initial bisque firing to harden the clay, Rick Dillingham breaks the form. Decoration such as gold leaf and glaze are randomly applied to shards without forethought of how they will fit together in the end. Raku firing represents still another unpredictable element, which adds appealing fire marks. 14" ht.*

Below Right: *In a reversal of the usual steps in which firing is the last step in the process Bennett Bean does a great deal of work on a piece after it is fired. Blackened areas created in pit firing are contrasted with sumptuous painted decoration, applied after firing.*

Right: *Built-in shelving is an especially effective way to display a prized ceramics collection. Works by one artist or pieces in complementary styles may be grouped for greater impact. A deep charcoal wall color, in this case, dramatically sets off the individual works of art. Photographed in the home of Ken Deavers, by Breton Littlehales.*

crackle effect and to add color to raku-fired pieces, the potter may use a very thin glaze or colored slip that will provide color in the final piece without crackle or gloss.

More American craftsmen work in clay than in any other medium, and their spirit of experimentation has resulted in an enormous range of styles available to you. The collector's market for ceramics has matured tremendously over the past few decades, and a secondary market is just beginning to develop for the work of the most influential ceramic artists and a few renowned potters who are no longer living. The vessel forms illustrated here are, for the most part, within a price range of $750 to $1500, although a few pieces are considerably more. While a few of these potters still show their work at the more prestigious fairs, work of this quality is more likely to be found in better galleries.

Karen Hubert uses wild vines for the handles and skeletal ribs of her rustic baskets and then interweaves them with dyed splints. Right, approximately 18 × 16"; center and left, approximately 17 × 12". Photo by Jonathan Wallen.

Baskets

The techniques used today for making baskets—coiling and weaving—differ little from those used by the very earliest basketmakers. And in many cases, the materials are the same: natural vines, willow, tree bark, pine needles, oak and ash splints. The baskets available today come in a wide variety of styles, ranging from tightly woven containers and organically shaped vessels to nonfunctional, purely sculptural forms.

Below: *On a large trestle table, Kay Eddy arranges three pine-needle baskets by Fran Kraynek-Prince and Neil Prince with towering copper candlesticks by Thomas R. Markusen and a naive wood-carved figure by Louise Kruger. Individually, any one of these pieces would be underscaled for the large table and cathedral ceiling of the room, but together they create an arrangement suitable to the expansive table. Photo by Joseph Kugielsky.*

Historically, the materials available determined how baskets were made. And while today there is greater accessibility to a wider variety of materials, many contemporary basketmakers have returned to working with natural materials gathered near their home. The chosen material dictates whether the basketmaker coils or weaves. Long and sturdy materials, such as reed, splint, and wild vines, are generally woven, while shorter and more delicate materials, such as pine needles and grasses, must be coiled. By bundling these shorter materials together in a lengthening coil, these otherwise delicate materials gain structural strength and enable the basketmaker to create sturdy walls. A continuous coil is created by wrapping cotton cord or raffia around a bundle of pine needles, for example, that are about the thickness of a little finger. At the same time, wrapping stitches penetrate the coil beneath to firmly build the walls and secure the basket structure. The shape of the basket is determined by changing the alignment of the coils—sloping gently out, straight up, or inward.

Below: In a closer view of the baskets by Fran Kraynek-Prince and Neil Prince, you can see clearly how they have adapted the traditional coiling technique—carefully aligning the sheaths of Torrey pine needle clusters and using dye to accentuate the resulting spiral patterns. In another variation (right), they create rich texture by allowing the ends of the pine needles to remain loose. Photo by Joseph Kugielsky.

Below: *With meticulous care, Carol Hart weaves splint baskets in traditional forms. Miniature baskets, like the three in the right foreground, are an exacting test of her dexterity. Photo by Joseph Kugielsky.*

Right: *It requires great skill to split and weave extremely fine splints such as these made of black ash. Martha Wetherbee uses both old techniques and old shaker molds to shape her baskets. Photo by James Kittle.*

Fran Kraynek-Prince and Neil Prince, whose baskets are shown on page 145, have adapted ancient coiling techniques to their work, which incorporates unusual, found materials, such as palm fruiting blooms and sea grasses. They have also brought a distinctive new design element to the traditional pine needle basket. Instead of discarding the natural sheath that joins the bundles of needles to a branch, as was traditionally done in Indian pine needle baskets, they leave it attached. By carefully planned, regular alignment of these sheaths, they create a spiral pattern that dramatizes the spherical form of the basket,

clearly visible on the green basket shown on page 145. All three spectacular baskets pictured here are made of the exceptionally long needles of the Torrey pine, a rare tree that grows only in a very small area of southern California. In keeping with their personal respect for naturally regenerating materials, Kraynek-Prince and Prince gather only the fallen needles, leaving the pine cones to reseed and restore life for the endangered tree. With only the two of them working and a finite source of materials, gallery owners place orders for their work more than a year in advance. Certainly, they could hire additional

Top Left: *A trio of large baskets by Kari Lønning are fine examples of the finesse and surprising strength possible in baskets of reed, dyed and woven in an attractive contemporary style. Photo by Joseph Kugielsky.*

Bottom Left: *Reed may be used in a variety of ways to create different effects. Here, Joan Patton loosely weaves thick reeds to create a warm, rustic effect. Compare these baskets to the more tightly woven reed baskets by Karl Lønning.*

Right: *A basket woven by Carol Hart entirely of wild grapevine is a cozy napping spot for her cat. Photo by Joseph Kugielsky.*

help to work under their supervision and turn out the baskets more quickly to meet the already existing demand, but their attitude is exemplary of the contemporary craftsman's values. They will not exploit natural materials for profit nor will they allow someone else to produce under their name for profit. Their work, though not inexpensively priced, continues to be treasured for the unique philosophical and environmental values it incorporates.

In order to achieve a sturdy woven basket, the materials used must have inherent rigidity or strength (although they are made flexible by soaking), and they must be available in lengths long enough to weave in and out for several circumferences. Basketmakers loosely classify woven materials as round or flat. Reed, which is uniformly cut from the center of imported rattan, is the most popularly used round material. With it, the craftsman can achieve surprising strength and refinement. Kari Lønning's baskets, on page 148, are fine examples of the refined sturdiness possible with reed, in this case, dyed in luscious colors.

Other round materials for weaving include wild vines, such as honeysuckle, thicker irregular vines of wild grapevine, and slim branches of willow and dogwood. The use of irregular vines, such as grapevine and wisteria, has grown in recent years. Often, they are combined with uniformly cut reeds or roughly cut splints. Because grapevine has only limited plasticity, the natural curve of the grapevine affects the final shape of the basket and makes each one unique.

Flat splints shaved from the heart of a tree are also woven into baskets, and, like round materials, the refinement of the completed basket depends on the width of the splint and on how smoothly it is cut. The woven splint baskets of mountain origin are being made today by younger craftspeople who are impressed by the skill and folk tradition behind these sturdy baskets. Just as mountain families did a century ago, these young basketmakers learn to recognize the best trees for pliable splints. Making a splint is no small task in itself. The trick is to pull splints as long and as thin as possible, but of uniform thickness. Martha Wetherbee's traditional Shaker forms, on pages 146-147, highlight her skill in making black ash splints. Because she is able to

achieve the thinnest of splints, her baskets are exceptionally refined.

Others, such as John McQueen and Douglas Fuchs, have created purely sculptural forms using traditional techniques. John McQueen, an architect by training, was among the first of the new generation of basketmakers to insist upon using only natural, found materials. He creates a wealth of surprising textures and, in his piece at right, seems still to be exploring form and structure as he might in architecture. Fuchs harks back to the primitive beginnings of basketry in his ritualistic, columnar basket forms, on page 151, in which he incorporates feathers, sticks, and metal or stone.

The appeal of natural materials and the familiarity of woven basketry is universal, whether in functional or sculptural forms. Thus, for many people basketry is one of the most accessible types of sculpture for their homes.

Pricing and Care

Within the broad category of basketry, there is an enormous price range—from $45 for a small willow basket to several thousand dollars for some of the most noted sculptural works. You will not find new work priced as low as Philippine imports, but neither the construction nor the bland, anonymous look of these imports has the lasting quality of the work from today's conscientious craftsmen.

Treated with respect, you can expect generations of use and pleasure from contemporary basketry. Since all natural materials are damaged by prolonged exposure to dampness and direct sunlight, your baskets should be protected from these elements. Baskets, though, can be surprisingly sturdy, especially if they are meant to be serviceable. Others, intended for more decorative purposes, should be handled with care. Many of the decorative baskets do not have handles. These should be picked up with two hands at the base, just as you would pick up a delicate porcelain vase. Many other baskets contain fragile, natural elements that extend beyond the body of the basket itself, such as vine tendrils, brittle pine needles, twigs, and loose bark. While these materials give a piece its very special character, it also means these baskets require more careful handling. In fact, the less frequently they are handled, the better!

Top Left: *Formerly an architect, John McQueen now studies structure and form through his basket constructions. This four-part basket of basswood is rich in surface texture. Photo courtesy of Hadler-Rodriguez Gallery.*

Bottom Left: *Susan Lyman's nonfunctional pieces may be termed "baskets" only in that they are container forms and are composed of materials common to many baskets. She is one of a growing number of American craftsmen exploring paper pulp as an artistic medium. Here, she constructs a skeleton of reed and then stretches a skin of subtly colored paper over the ribs, creating a lovely, fragile container.*

Right: *Douglas Eric Fuchs first became fascinated with basketry when he learned that it was most likely the first craft. His current work calls to mind the baskets of primitive cultures in which baskets were used for both storage and rituals. Tallest 6' ht. Photo by Doug Long.*

Solid buildings float through a darkening sky creating a sense of displacement, typical of the woven compositions of Sheila O'Hara. This is a detail from Taos Pueblo in Search of the Balloon Fiesta. O'Hara created an unusual triple warp technique to intensify the shifts of color on the surface of this piece. Full dimensions, 48 × 96"

Wall Hangings

A wall hanging can be ideal for a large space in your home—over a mantel or a sofa, for example, or in a large entryway. Like a large painting, fiber hanging in such a space serves as a distinctive focal point. A hanging, however, adds more warmth and texture to your home than does paint on canvas. Especially striking in a home of contemporary design, a fiber piece provides a pleasant contrast to the slick, polished surfaces of modern furniture.

R

egardless of your decor, the inherent warmth of fiber can make an appealing contribution to any interior. And the styles available are as diverse as the craftsmen drawn to the potential of this medium.

Styles Available

In the 1960s, in a break with the past that generated much excitement among weavers, fiber hangings came off the walls and began to appear in more organic forms as freestanding columnar shapes. With this new direction, fiber artists entered a whole new era, marked by their efforts to extend the possibilities of their craft. Today that same spirit of freedom and experimentation exists; however, it is being expressed in new styles.

Overall, there has been a return to an interest in creating a more refined surface. In recent years, a group of weavers have revived detail and imagery in their work, drawing inspiration from the legacy of the great pictorial tapestries of the past.

Tapestry is a flat weave that makes it possible for the weaver to depict recognizable things in meticulous detail. Technically, tapestry describes a weaving in which

Left: Tapestries, developed in the fourteenth century, were used to transform cold stone walls into warm, decorative ones. Pam Patrie's contemporary tapestry, which was woven on a European loom built in the Middle Ages, serves in much the same way to warm the dining room in this home. Photo by Franklin Engel.

Below Left: Many craftsmen draw inspiration from the cultural history of their area, and so has Janusz Kozikowski. In one of a series of Ghost Rugs, he has simulated an eighteenth-century Navajo Indian chief's blanket. Worn spots, faded dyes, irregular edges are superimposed on a New Mexico landscape. He incorporates both Navajo and Spanish motifs in his work, which is executed in wools and natural dyes from the southwest.

Below Right: Shadows give depth to this flat tapestry woven by Judith Poxson Fawkes. In a layering of images, we see both the shadow of the window pane and the shadowed silhouette of her loom. Studio, 1980, JPF is woven into the top of the piece, repeating the tradition of such identification being woven within early American coverlets. 78 × 42". Photo courtesy of the Elements Gallery.

Top Left: Cynthia Schira "paints" impressionistic brush strokes with ribbon overlays that are firmly secured to the tightly woven background. 51 × 64". Photo courtesy of Hadler-Rodriguez Gallery.

Bottom Left: Sherry Schreiber uses both hand-dyed and metallic yarns to achieve luminous color effects in her tapestries. Seen here is Desert at Night. 6 × 8'.

the weft yarns completely conceal the warp, so the design is created solely within the weft yarns. The various artists drawn to the tapestry tradition work in diverse styles. The works of fiber artists Pam Patrie, on page 154, and Sherry Schreiber, at left, for example, may be characterized as painterly. Were the texture removed, one would immediately see the strong compositional elements at work in the design—a concern for perspective, shadow, and detail. In this respect, their weavings can be viewed as monumental paintings in fiber.

The highly refined weavings of Judith Poxson Fawkes feature representational images. Her tapestry, on page 155, gives you a glimpse of her loom as seen through a window into the artist's studio. Sheila O'Hara's weaving, on pages 152–153, reflects yet another influence—that of twentieth-century Surrealist painting. In her mysterious work, buildings float in a void defined only by subtle gradations of light in the background.

Some contemporary tapestry artists exhibit the influences of yet another great weaving tradition—the bold, exquisite designs of the various American Indian tribes. The best of these contemporary

Below and Right: John Eric Riis has collaborated with metalsmith Richard Mafong to create a dramatic contrast between the cool sheen of silver and the lush wool textures. Horizontal cords wrapped with wool and metallic yarns lie on the surface of a firmly woven background. 6' × 4' × 3". Photo by Rob Wheless.

Below and Right: Jim Bassler *tightly wrapped old clothes discarded by his friends to form the diagonal cords which overlay the surface of this hanging. His use of "rags" was inspired by the traditional rag rugs he saw during his two-year teaching stint at the Appalachian Center for Crafts in Smithville, Tennessee. The background, woven in strips, is typical of early weavings from Africa and South America. 42 × 42".*

Below: Loose hemp strings cascade from a finely detailed horizontal band at the top of this restrained hanging by Lewis Knauss. Painting the ends of each string in pale blues and pinks helps to dramatize the natural color and texture of the hemp. 34 × 27".

Below: Diane Itter, a leader of a new group of fiber artists working on a miniature scale, effectively uses only one knot—the double half hitch—tied thousands of times in her work Summer Lattice. Knotted area 8 × 5". Photo by Aneta Sperber.

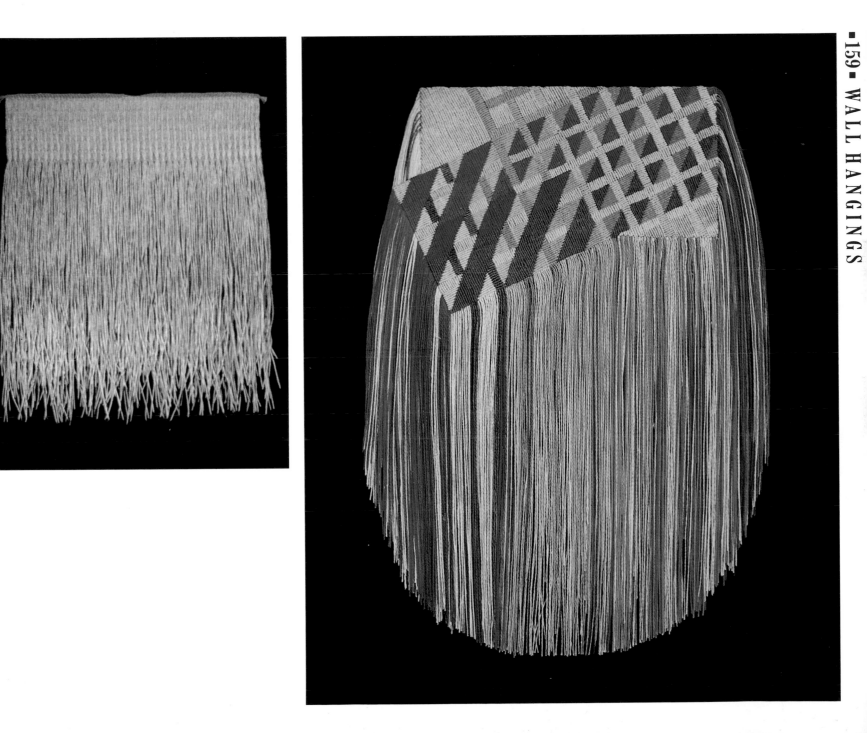

Left: *The color and pattern in this paper work is not applied surface decoration, but rather is integral to the paper fibers. In this respect handmade paper is similar to weaving and accounts for the increasing number of fiber artists drawn to it. This brilliantly colored piece by Nancy Albertson is one of five panels sandwiched between clear lucite to create a wall hanging or room divider. Single panel, 16 × 16".*

Below: *In a small apartment, Helene Margolies cleverly groups diminutive weavings by several artists (from left to right): Dawn MacNutt, Suzanne Swannie (above), a fragment by Warren Seelig (below), Ethel Stein, Diane Itter. Photo by David Arky.*

works draw upon elements indigenous to the Indian works but do not attempt to reproduce the traditional patterns exactly. Janusz Kozikowski's hanging on page 155 is a prime example of one such weaving, which sensitively reinterprets designs of the Navajo culture.

In contrast to the flat-weave, tapestry tradition, in which concrete imagery and detail are paramount, other weavings concentrate heavily on manipulating textural effects. Artists who concentrate on texture may introduce other materials, including some unexpected choices, into flat weavings of wool or linen. Jon Riis has incorporated silver discs into his weaving, on page 157, setting up an unusually striking contrast between the luster of the precious metal and the warmth and palpable surface of the fabric. Cynthia Schira often superimposes a ribbon overlay, such as that in *Prairie Grass* on page 156, to create an impressionistic play of light on the surface of her weavings. These artists, and others such as Lewis Knauss, whose work is on page 159, and Jim Bassler, see page 158, achieve extraordinarily rich surface effects.

Some weavers work on a vastly diminished scale, producing exquisite fiber miniatures. Diane Itter's knotted linen piece, on page 159, is an example of the very close, small-scale work being done. In the same way that larger wall hangings can be seen as paintings, these miniature fiber works, too, can be viewed as small paintings. On this page, you can see how one collector has grouped five fiber miniatures, most of them protected with plexiglass frames. For this particular collector, miniatures have made it possible for her to own and enjoy fiber works by major artists even though her small city apartment could not accommodate large-scale hangings.

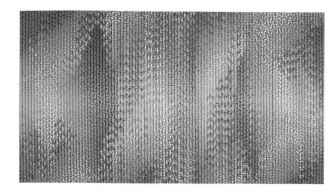

Left and Below: *Some contemporary artists working with fiber are not weaving it. Kris Dey, for example, airbrushes torn cotton strips and then wraps them onto lightweight plastic tubing. The tubes are strung together, forming rigid corrugated panels. Full size hanging, 6'4" × 8'.*

Right: *The remarkable play of light and color across Kris Dey's fabric surfaces is far from accidental. Carefully planned juxtapositions create a fascinating hanging that reminds one of the northern lights. 4 × 4'. Photo courtesy of Andrew Strauss Photography.*

Before You Buy a Wall Hanging

When you are considering buying fiber art for the wall, be sure it measures up to your expectations both from a distance and close up. Not only should its composition and coloration provide the appeal of a beautiful painting seen from across the room; the design and execution must also bear up under close scrutiny.

The Price of Wall Hangings

With the exception of miniatures, wall hangings are often priced by the square foot. The range starts at $75 per square foot and goes up to $500 a square foot for pieces by leading weavers who execute major commissions for public places. For example, a 4 x 6' hanging would cost from $1800 and up. If you are commissioning a hanging, price is quoted on a square foot basis. On a finished piece, the weaver usually translates the square-foot cost into a single amount. The time involved in creating the weaving and the reputation of the artist are the primary factors that influence the price range. This is especially true when it comes to pricing miniatures.

Quilts

Quilting is currently enjoying a revival throughout the United States—a revival, however, with a difference. Whereas quilters in the past were taught by their mothers and grandmothers to repeat favorite, traditional patterns, many of today's quilters are bringing a wholly new aesthetic to their craft. Trained in university art departments in painting, drawing, sculpture, and the principles of color, these new quilters are introducing highly original designs into their work.

Preceding Page and Below: An exciting detail from Michael James's quilt illustrates the painterly use of color and contrasting values utilized by contemporary quilt designers. Otherwise, James adheres to traditional piecing and quilting techniques. Like a painter working on a flat canvas, James creates remarkable depth and movement in his quilted wall hanging. 52 × 52".

Right: Nancy Crow has influenced many younger quilt artists, who have been inspired by her bold geometric patterns and pulsating colors. 60 × 60".

While they are still using the time-honored piecing and quilting techniques, contemporary quilters are striking out in imaginative and inventive ways.

Part of the magic of the new American quilt lies in its homage to traditional patterns and piecing techniques. The old log cabin pattern, for instance, has a light side and a dark side within each quilt block. Michael James, whose work appears on this page, has translated this traditional play of light and dark into an original contemporary pattern that contrasts black with soft, pastel tones. His work is a dramatic example of how a traditional pattern can inspire a modern treatment.

Quilt artist Nancy Crow, one of today's leading contemporary quilters, is best known for the arresting geometric patterns and color relationships of her designs. Viewing one of her quilts, like the one on page 167, is not unlike looking into a giant kaleidoscope.

Elizabeth Gurrier's white-on-white *May Day 1382*, page 170, is a fine example of the rich surface embellishment a quilter can achieve with traditional hand-quilting techniques. In this work, you can see the intricate,

closely worked quilting incorporated in her embossed, repeat
patterns.

At the same time that quilters
have eagerly assimilated traditional techniques, they have also
been quick to make use of new
techniques in their work, such as
photo-silkscreening on fabric.
Wenda von Weise, whose work is
pictured on page 169, often incorporates photo-silkscreened images
of elements that depict her concern for the natural environment
—clouds, beach grasses, and sediment layers. On special commission, von Weise will take your
family photographs and silkscreen these images into an original design to create the ultimate
personal quilt.

The influence of such schools of
painting as Op Art and the ever
popular paintings of Vasarely can
also be detected in contemporary
quilts. Jan Myers's quilt on page
169 of undulating blocks of color
draws inspiration from these
sources. She contrasts highly
modern, technical imagery with
soft colors dyed by hand.

With the artist-designed quilt
has come the quilt's presentation
as an art object, hung on the wall
for appreciation rather than
placed on the bed for use. In con-

Left: Pam Studstill's *dramatic quilt evokes images of an evening sky, when the stars pop out as the light fades. Her quilt as wall hanging is particularly well suited to the dining area of Helene Margolies's home, providing visual warmth as it offsets a glass table. Luster-glazed pottery on the table is by Beatrice Wood and the high stool in the background is by Tommy Simpson. Photo by David Arky.*

Below: *In a delightful parody of the famous American Gothic painting by Grant Wood, Wenda F. von Weise transfers photographic images to fabric by a process of photo-silkscreening for her Kneale Farm: Twilight. 80 × 68".*

Below: *By hand-dying her own fabrics, Jan Myers controls the subtle variations in color essential to her quilts. The illusion of depth is reinforced by the graduated sizes of the individual quilt pieces.*

trast to the traditional quilter, newer quilt artists compose their quilts in sizes to suit their designs, rather than adjust their compositions to suit standard bed sizes.

The quilts shown in this book are by some of the most respected quilt artists producing today. And the price range of the work illustrated is a broad $1000 minimum up to $9000 for large commissioned pieces. It is possible to find good work by younger artists ranging in price from $850 to $1500.

Chances are that no matter what price quilt you buy, you will be convinced of the advantages of hanging a quilt. In terms of its contribution to a room, it adds a great deal more if it is seen on the wall, simply because it is within easy view from any place in the room. And hanging a quilt is an easy way to add drama to an otherwise bland setting, particularly since most quilts are fairly large and many are brightly colored.

As with any large fiber hanging, it is necessary that the quilt's weight be evenly distributed to avoid damaging the fibers or stitching. Most quilt designers sew a fabric channel onto the back of the quilt, into which you can insert a wooden or brass rod as a safe and quick way to hang it. Lacking other means, you can resort to the popular method of hanging antique quilts. With firm stitches spaced closely together, attach fabric fastener tape the full length of the upper edge of the quilt, and then tack the companion fastener strip to the wall at the appropriate height.

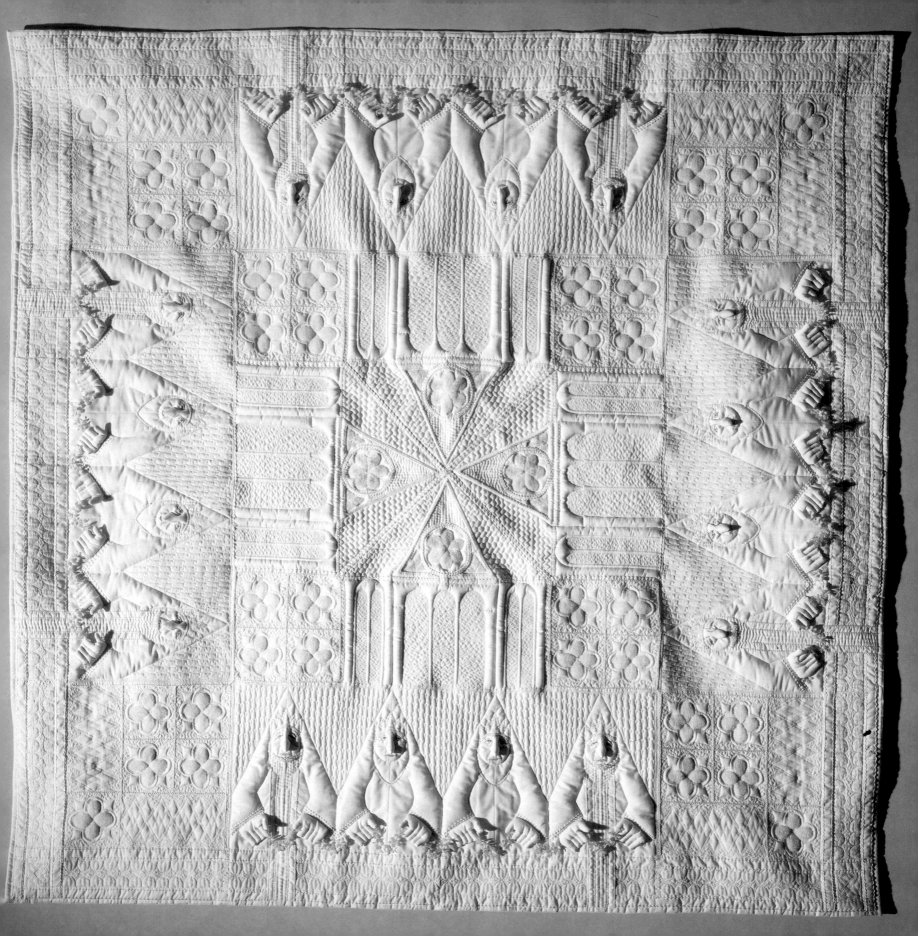

Left: Elizabeth Gurrier's design for "May Day 1382" is a tour de force of intricate quilting stitches—a display of technique more commonly associated with the fourteenth century than the twentieth. 63 × 63".

Right: A small hanging of quilted and pieced silk by Susan Webb Lee beautifully unifies a display of fine crafts in the home of Jack Lenor Larsen. The curvaceous silhouettes of Stephen Proctor's table and the late William Wyman's ceramic sphere contrast dramatically with the angular pattern of Lee's hanging. Photo by David Arky.

Using ribbed metal tools, James Johnston incises the surface of these shallow, slab-built stoneware vases and inlays them with colored clays for decorative effects. Approximately 12″ ht.

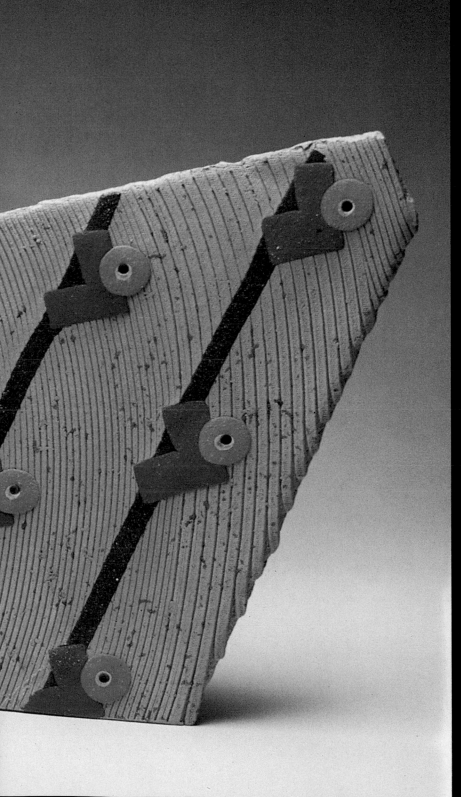

Gift Ideas

Deciding on the right gift is nearly always a quandary. Often, the more special the person or the event, the more difficult it is to choose. American craftsmen working in wood, glass, metal, fiber, and ceramics provide distinctive choices for gift giving. On the next few pages are just a sampling of gift ideas—for the person who has everything, or for the perfect gift to mark a special event, whether a wedding, anniversary, birthday, or graduation. These exceptional remembrances range from boudoir accessories to unparalleled gifts of museum quality.

Below: *This Magnifying Glass?* by Thomas McClelland *is a useful and unique desk accessory. 7 × 3". Photo by David Arky.*

Top Right: *Even the novice domino player will enjoy showing off the fine workmanship that went into this handsome set by Marty and Fredi Shapiro. Each playing tile is made of ebony with brass inlays, and the suede-lined case is of padauk, a wood notable for its rich red coloration.*

Middle Right: *In a parody of stately handmade timepieces, Garry Knox Bennett fashions a playful clock, that suggests quite accurately that "time flies." Photo by Nikolay Zurek.*

S ome, such as a silver letter opener or beautiful perfume bottle, have traditionally been popular for special occasions but become even more significant because of their singular designs. And in every craft fair or gallery show, there are surprises—like Linda MacNeil's small metal sculpture on page 182 that is actually a hand mirror, Seth Stem's wall-hung wooden and leather sculpture on page 184 that is a dramatic mirrored cabinet, and Garry Knox Bennett's fluid sculptural form on page 175 that is a clock that doesn't look like most clocks.

Here, too, are little indulgences for you–designs so unique that they spark a sense of discovery and an irrepressible urge to enjoy them at home. One-of-a-kind objects, these pieces grow out of the individual craftsman's experience, humor, and creativity. Always unique, sometimes eccentric, these special pieces should inspire you in your search for the perfect gift.

Desk Accessories

In furnishing the desk, you are often caught between very expensive, status leather or silver accessories and impersonal office supplies. The craftsman has responded to this gap by recreating standard desk accessories—pencil holders, blotters, clocks, in-and-out boxes, pen sets, and even briefcases—in rich wood tones. There are, of course, fine leather desk accessories, too, but they are, on the whole, much less remarkable than the hand-finished wood. The wooden accessories, while not innovative, do have a straightforward sincerity and warmth that make them a good substitute for the standard office fare. What really distinguishes the desk, either at home or in the corporate office, are special finds like Thomas McClelland's copper magnifying glass in the form of a question mark (shown above). The craftsman's novel designs may become both toys and conversation pieces, such as Trent Whitington's handsome gum-ball machine on page 175. For the fast-track executive, pen and pencil sets are passé, but an elegant domino set like the one on page 175, handcarved in ebony by Marty and Fredi Shapiro and encased in deep red padauk, symbolizes superior gamesmanship.

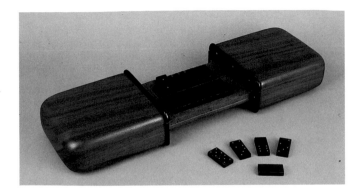

Bottom Left: Ron Pearson's sterling silver letter opener is a simple and beautiful gift sure to please anyone who might receive it. Susan Lange's handmade stationery, bound in a portfolio of her own design, adds still further to the art of letter writing. Photographed in the showcase of Sherley Koteen Associates by Breton Littlehales.

Above: Warren Durbin's elegant oak and teak candlestand echoes the simplicity and restraint of fine Japanese design, and, like it, is equally at home in traditional or contemporary settings.

Left: This beautifully crafted working gum-ball machine would surely delight any member of the family. Trent Whitington describes his work this way: "I take some chuckles and neat doodads and put them together using traditional woodworking techniques."

Far Left: *This candelabrum by Gregory Litsios is forged on a grand scale. Standing at 5'10" high, it would handsomely grace a large dining room, a massive stone fireplace, or an outdoor terrace.*

Top Left: *In this set of fireplace tools and stand, blacksmith C. Leigh Morrell forges steel in a graceful and light manner, defying the inherent characteristics of the dark, heavy metal. 36" ht. Photo by Jonathan Wallen.*

Bottom Left: *This appealing copper bin by Carolyn Dian Morris is a luxurious example of hand-forging and fabricating techniques. It can hold magazines, kindling, or dried grasses—or stand handsomely on its own. Photo by David Arky.*

Right: Marc Goldring has developed an unusual technique for shaping these leather vase forms: First, he immerses the stitched leather form in boiling water, where it bends, puckers, curls, and contracts. Then, when it dries, he sands and burnishes it to a lustrous finish. Photo by James Kittle.

Right: In a delightful departure from conventional fireplace tool sets, David Paul Bacharach creates a wall-mounted sculptural set. 48 × 42".

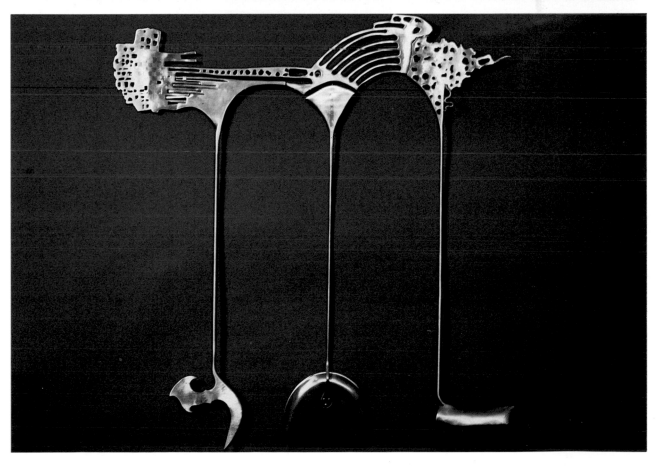

Left: June Schwarcz, a leading enamelist, electroplates copper foil to create this richly textured, basketlike surface, and then contrasts it with a glossy enameled interior. 5¼" diameter × 5". Photo by M. Lee Fatherree.

Left: David Paul Bacharach *shaped this vase form using thin copper strips and traditional basket-weaving techniques. Heat, chemical baths, and coatings of oxide were then applied to enhance the natural luster and color of the copper.*

Dressing Table Romance

The glamorous dressing table is again in fashion, and craftsmen are creating luxurious and beautifully handmade accessories for it. Make-up brushes with decorated silver and brass handles, like those of Carolyn Dian Morris on page 181, once again bring sophisticated elegance to a woman's dressing table. An occasional rethinking of the traditional form of hand mirrors, such as Linda MacNeil's glass and metal pieces adds a modern sculptural quality that appeals to today's self-confident woman. Beth Fein's lovely porcelain box, on page 179, is decorated with inlaid patterns of color, and gloves and a paper fan in *trompe l'oeil* relief.

Perfume bottles—jewel-like creations in glass, both clear, faceted shapes, and swirling layers of color within glass—are enjoying a great renaissance. Pretty floral designs can be found along with an abundance of lustrous, Art Nouveau-inspired bottles and dramatic geometrical pieces, created by slicing away part of the rounded bottle form. The sheer number and diversity of perfume bottles indicate that they are collected, or lovingly given, for the romance of

Below: *The designs on these Art Deco-inspired perfume bottles by Laura Wilensky are painted on porcelain. Photo by Ralph Gabriner.*

Bottom: *Playful, feminine imagery decorates this ceramic box by Beth Fein, a romantic addition to a vanity or boudoir. 6 × 16 × 10". Photo by Gary Sinick.*

Below: *This plush fantasy chair and ottoman were created by Norma Minkowitz, using traditional knitting and crocheting techniques. Furniture is a departure from her better-known wearable designs, which have been collected by the Costume Institute in the Metropolitan Museum of Art, New York.*

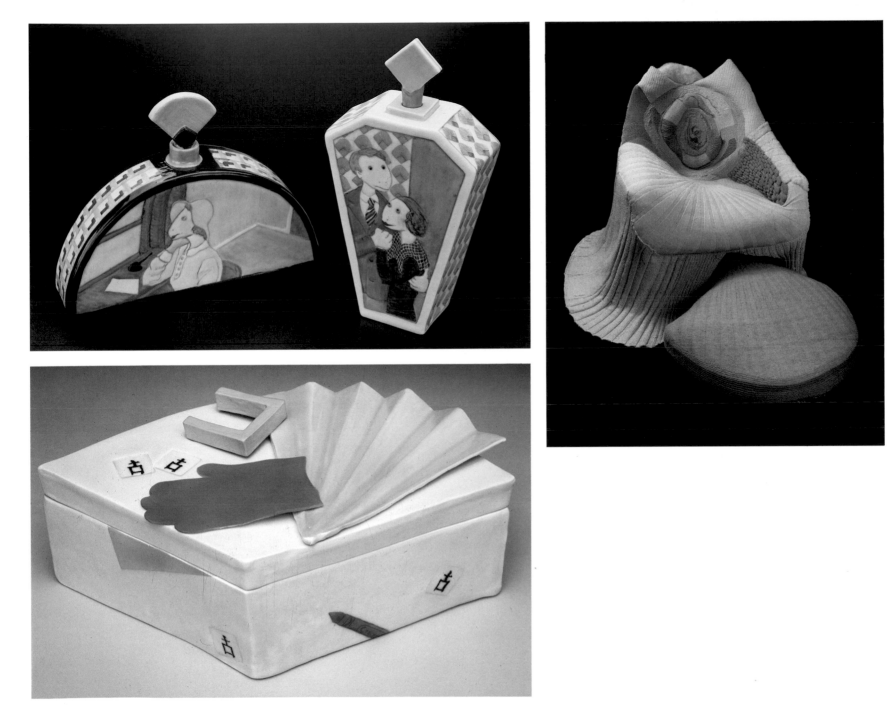

Below: These slip-cast vases in angular shapes by James Johnston are well-suited to dramatic groupings. From 4 to 14" ht.

Right: For the woman with style, sable make-up brushes by Carolyn Dian Morris combine bronze, nickel, and gold in a distinctive design. Photo by David Arky.

Below: After blowing colored glass into plump perfume bottle shapes, Janet Kelman sandblasts the glass to create intriguing surface patterns. Areas that are masked remain slick and reflective, while the unmasked areas become matte and slightly rough. She recommends occasional polishing with household vegetable oil to enrich the contrast of the sandblasted patterns. Photo by Joseph Kugielsky.

Bottom Right: A small gather of colored glass is encased within clear glass, then dramatically sliced and polished in these exquisite bottles by K. William LeQuier. Practically, the colored glass holds perfume; artistically, it represents the glassblower's first breath. Each 4 × 2 × 2"

Bottom Left: In the work of Andrew Magdanz and Susan Shapiro, soft, contemporary colors are handblown in simple shapes, then embellished with inlaid glass canes. Photo by Ken Riemer.

Below Left: Rich Landergren dramatizes the unusual graining of exotic woods in his handsome brush and comb sets. As with his mirrors, the shape follows the wood grain, creating distinctive differences in each one.

Bottom Left: Linda MacNeil is intrigued with the fact that "people have always collected (functional) objects which become so precious that they aren't put to their intended use," but become known as "art." Now she makes hand mirrors that are unmistakably sculptural and intended to be used. 12 × 6 × 4".

Bottom Right: David R. Rogers's brass and nickel straight razor would be a prize gift for any hirsute male.

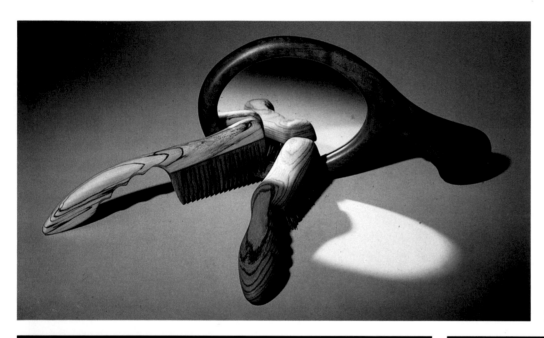

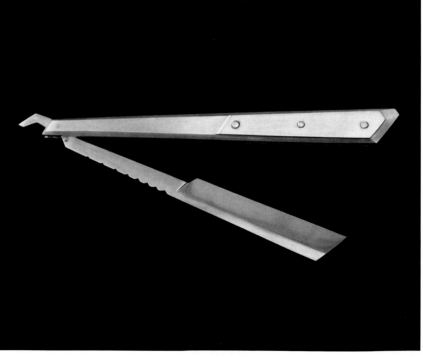

Left: Michael Graham's sensuous tabletop sculpture in wood conceals small compartments for loose change or fine jewelry. His remarkable design not only surpasses the conventional men's valet, but could work to fool the potential thief. Photo courtesy of American Craft Council, by Bror Karlsson.

Below Left: Both the luscious red coloration of natural padauk wood and the traditional tambour top contribute to the distinctive warmth of this small box for keys, change, and jewelry, by Bruce Erdman. 2½ × 4¾ × 7". Photo by Jonathan Wallen.

Below Right: Steve Madsen's work is deceptive. This superbly crafted piece, which has the monumentality of a chest of drawers or even a city building, is less than twelve inches high. Photo courtesy of American Craft Council, by Bror Karlsson.

Bottom Left: Steve Elling purposefully creates an understated box design to highlight its intarsia center. Intarsia is a technique for decorating a surface by inlaying one material into another; in this case, metal into wood.

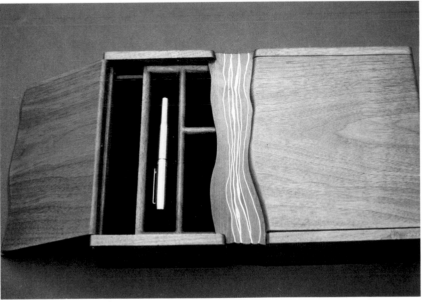

the work rather than as working perfume containers. For whatever reason, they are a fine example of the glamour and beautiful objects available.

Wooden Valet Boxes

Woodworkers produce handsome valet and jewelry boxes for loose change, keys, watches, and other paraphernalia likely to be emptied from pockets. Styles range from the rugged, simple box that dramatizes the natural color and form of the wood, through traditionally inspired tambour or roll-top valets, to sophisticated inlays of contrasting wood colors and

metals. Sculptural pieces, such as those of John Cederquist on page 184 and Michael Graham on page 182, may be hard to identify as storage boxes, thus serving a dual purpose as wooden sculpture and functional storage. For the man who is difficult to select a gift for, these special little boxes represent not only a serviceable gift but one that will enhance his appreciation for woodworking.

Below and Right: Seth Stem cares as much about how this sweeping sculptural wall cabinet looks as how well it functions. He has outfitted it for maximum use with shelves, drawers, a tray, and a mirror.

Below: John Cederquist's *unique, masculine wall sculpture in leather and wood has seven drawers for storage—ideal for the bedroom, study, or living area. Photo by Ron Leighton.*

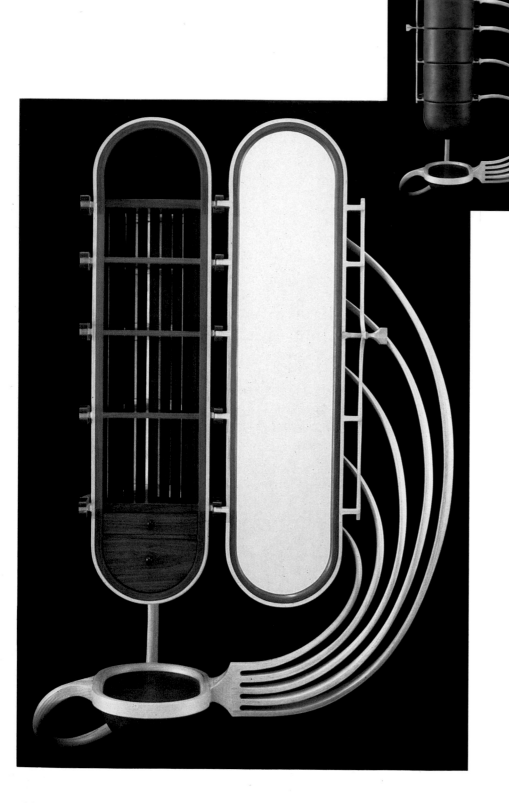

Turned Wooden Bowls

Classic vessel forms in wood are usually shaped on a power lathe. First the craftsman roughs out a wooden bowl or vase form and then he anchors it to a lathe. As the wood rotates at high speeds, the craftsman holds a cutting tool against the wood in a fixed position, thereby shaving away wood to create the container shape. The velocity of the lathe and the weight of the wood combine to create a powerful momentum that requires both great strength and skill to master.

For turned wooden bowls, craftsmen tend to favor woods with unusual colors and grain patterns. Many of the distinctive patterns you see in these forms are found in decaying trees and in the abnormal growths on trees. Melvin Lindquist's vase, on this page, is fashioned from spalted or decayed wood. It is the spalting which gives the wood its special figuring and character. David

Left: A sculptor of spalted or decayed wood, Melvin Lindquist has, with his son Mark, experimented extensively with translating traditional clay vessel forms into wood. This fine example of his pioneering work is made of manzanita burl. 7" ht. Photo by Robert Aude.

Below: Ed Moulthrop's voluptuous vessels are noted for their impressive size (as much as 36 inches in diameter) as well as for the artist's use of "exotic" native woods. One of the most unusual is turned from figured tulipwood, which is recognized by its distinctive red flashing within the grain pattern. Photo courtesy of the Elements Gallery.

Bottom: These beautifully turned and finished wooden bowls by Bob Stocksdale speak eloquently of his command of the medium. The bowls feature thin walls and perfectly formed shapes. Stocksdale's work appears in the permanent collections of the Oakland Museum, the Boston Museum of Fine Arts, and the Philadelphia Museum of Art. Photo by David Arky.

Below: Alan Stirt *first turns his bowl
forms on a wood lathe and then hand-
carves delicate fluting on the exterior.
This one is yellow wood from the
Osage orange tree. Photo by Jonathan
Wallen.*

Ellsworth's pieces, on this page,
derive their special qualities from
the burled wood he uses—the burl
being the knobby, abnormal
growth on a tree.

The outstanding work of Ed
Moulthrop, Mark Lindquist, and
Melvin Lindquist has been recognized nationwide by leading galleries, critics, and museums. All
three, in fact, have their work
represented in the collection
of The Metropolitan Museum of
Art in New York City. Thus, a gift
of a turned wooden bowl by any
one of these artists carries with it
the prestige of his impressive
credentials.

Top Left: *Irregular burls create natural craters in these otherwise smoothly polished, classical vessel forms by David Ellsworth. The forms in the background are turned from red maple and the low piece in the foreground from box elder burl. 2½ to 11" ht.*

Bottom Left: *The apparently unstudied form of this bowl by Mark Lindquist is deceiving, for Lindquist carefully examines the wood while drying it for several years before he ever begins cutting. His object in cutting is to get the most figure and character possible from the wood. 30" wide. Photo by Robert Aude.*

Below: *Hap Sakwa collects burl woods from trees in his native California. He explains that the exterior of the burl is deceptive, being gray with age and covered with dirt. Thus, much of his shaping and polishing on a wood lathe is directed toward revealing the rich colors hidden within the burl.*

Displaying Crafts

Once you've invested time and money in selecting handmade objects for your home, you will want to display them to their best advantage. Your handsome pottery bowl should not have to spend its life tucked into an already-overflowing bookshelf, where its pattern will go unnoticed in the visual din of its surroundings.

All of the baskets in this grouping have been plaited, an ancient technique in which three or more strands are braided. Two large, open basket forms by Lisa Martin (right) are combined with three smaller ones by Dorothy Gill Barnes (center), and an antique plaited sash. This effective display is enhanced by a porcelain puzzle by Brad Miller. Beautifully finished wooden boxes in graduated sizes by Michael Elkan provide a sense of scale to the arrangement. Photographed in the home of Jack Lenor Larsen, by David Arky.

Right: *The proper lighting makes an enormous difference in the presentation of crafts. Here, a skylight brightly illuminates a large area and calls attention to Bob Trotman's chair, Janet Bogush's hanging, Bennett Bean's ceramics (left of hanging) and Jan Yatsko's yarn basket form (right of hanging). Photographed in the showcase of Sherley Koteen Associates, by Breton Littlehales.*

Right: *In a room of pale neutrals, the turquoise finish on Jonathan Bonner's treated copper bowl adds a dramatic accent, while Dave Bigelow's large pit-fired urn echoes the color of the smoky brown carpet. Mark Forman's plates are especially well-suited to wall display. Photographed in the home of Don Thomas and Jorge Cao, owners of Convergence Gallery, by David Arky.*

When you visit craft galleries, notice the display techniques they use to highlight each piece of original work. You can recreate their thoughtful presentations in your home in a variety of ways: by raising the work on a base or pedestal, by applying sensitive lighting, and by grouping objects of similar materials or styles.

One of the simplest and least expensive ways to integrate new work into both traditional and contemporary interiors is to display a bowl or urn shape on a wooden or lucite base. Both the very plain platform and the more ornate oriental bases of carved rosewood are available in graduated sizes from about two to twelve inches wide so that you can match the base to the proportions of the bowl or vase form. The oriental bases are particularly effective in blending new porcelain pieces with antique porcelains or other traditional accessories, because they enhance the classical oriental character of some new pieces. A lucite base creates a more contemporary feeling, with the object appearing to float in space. These clear, slick bases are generally more suitable for displaying highly textured work,

such as basketry, wood, or paper.

Larger pieces of all media may be placed on simple pedestals, such as those used in galleries and museums. Even functional pieces, such as ceramic teapots or wooden bowls, take on a new presence when displayed on a pedestal. Of course, pedestals are only suited to fine work. Such display enhances a well-made piece, but it is likely to emphasize the faults of the inept craftsman. If you have several fine pieces to display, two or three simple pedestals in wood, lacquer, or laminate in heights from thirty to forty-two inches will give you great flexibility.

Whether a piece is shown to greatest advantage at table height or pedestal height is determined by the shape and decoration of the piece itself. For example, artists working in clay or wood often contrast a sweeping bowl form with an irregular edge distorted by cutting or tearing or by natural abnormalities in the growth of the wood. The edge is most noticeable when the piece is seen in silhouette, and so the piece is best displayed at eye level. Here a pedestal is particularly helpful in accenting the most dramatic element—the contrast of smooth

bowl with torn edge.

In deciding what height is best for display, ask yourself what the single most important element of each piece is—is it silhouette, texture, or surface decoration? In displaying a plate with bold surface embellishment, the goal is to present the full surface of the plate at one time. This can be accomplished by propping the plate up in a wooden plate stand, by hanging it on the wall, or by placing it on a low table so that the viewer looks down on it.

Potters often provide a decorative plate with holes, so that it can be displayed on the wall. You can also purchase inexpensive wire hangers that will hold even heavy platters securely on the wall. An increasingly popular alternative to flat art, ceramic plates may be hung singly or in groups of two or three.

Lighting can do a great deal to enhance the unique properties of a piece. Both the source of the light

(its position in relation to the object) and also the type of light influence the success of the display. Much can be accomplished with direct sources of light—built-in downlights or wall-washers, track lighting, or portable brass and chrome pharmacy lamps. Built-in lighting is usually effective only when it can be planned ahead of time to enhance a special commission, such as a major wall hanging, but track lighting and pharmacy lamps allow a good bit of flexibility in spotlighting your crafts.

Good lighting plays up the strongest, most distinctive quality of the craft object, be it texture, translucency, reflectiveness, high color, or some other characteristic. If you are lighting basketry or weavings, for example, your primary goal is to dramatize the rich textures in these pieces. Light from a source almost directly overhead will create shadows within the piece, highlighting even subtle textures. As the light source is placed farther away from a weaving, it tends to eliminate all shadows and visually flatten variations in texture.

A direct overhead source of light is also valuable in highlighting the translucency of glass and

thin porcelain vases and bowls. The unusual translucency of Molly Cowgill's porcelain bowl on page 127, for example, is made more apparent by the photographer's overhead lighting. With glass, a similar spotlight directed at the piece can make it appear as if the light comes from within the form. Natural lighting, achieved by placing a glass object near a window, is especially successful to enrich the colors and layers within glass art. A few special pieces, such as those of John Littleton and Katherine Vogel on page 120, seem to change colors as the angle and quality of light changes during the day.

Reflective surfaces, such as metal and glass, are trickier to light well, as you can produce a blinding glare if you overdo it. A diffuse source, such as a shaded lamp, seems to work better than an unshielded, direct source, and , of course, periodic polishing is essential.

At professional craft fairs, the exhibiting craftsmen are called upon to light their work well in less than ideal circumstances, and you can often get good ideas from observing their lighting techniques.

Much of the work of contem-

Left: *Jack Lenor Larsen conceals his collection of antique and contemporary crafts behind sliding fabric panels, highlighting one section at a time. By rotating pieces from storage, or from room to room, you are more likely to continue to notice and appreciate them. As your collection grows, consider Larsen's glass shelves and overhead lighting as an excellent means of displaying and protecting small and fragile works. A few major pieces, such as Ed Moulthrop's wooden sphere on the floor (left) and Dale Chihuly's glass (right) are most effectively displayed when seen alone. Photo by David Arky.*

Near Right: *Here's an excellent example of how you can group objects of different materials and techniques to achieve a harmonious and striking display. Kay Eddy, partner in The Elements Gallery, has successfully combined work by four craftsmen: (left to right) Paul Soldner's large raku vessel, John McQueen's basket, Bennett Bean's pit-fired vessel, and Dominic DiMare's paper and wood sculpture. Photo by Joseph Kugielsky.*

Far Right: *In a surprising and successful juxtaposition, Karen Karnes's salt-glazed pottery (left) and Ellen Schon's pit-fired stoneware (second from left) are seen on a formal eighteenth-century style chest. Carol Shaw-Sutton's woven wall piece is an exciting contemporary complement to the antique American Indian basket. Photographed in the home of Kay and George Eddy, by Joseph Kugielsky.*

Right: *Potters who make plates often provide a way for you to hang their work. Three plates by Richard and Sandra Farrell take on new aesthetic interest when hung together on a fabric-covered panel.*

Right: *You can create dramatic effects by deliberate understatement, such as is seen here with a single stoneware bowl by Richard DeVore. The refined form of the bowl is highlighted when seen in silhouette, and the serenity of the piece is underscored by the same quality in William Bailey's painted still life. Photographed in the home of Mr. and Mrs. Daniel Fendrick, by Breton Littlehales.*

porary craftsmen is so highly individual that it must stand alone. There are, however, occasions when grouping objects together gives them greater visual impact in your home. If you are collecting the work of one craftsman, for instance, several of his pieces displayed together will be more noticeable to a visitor than the same number of pieces scattered throughout the room or house.

In any grouping, there should be a unifying element—a consistent style, form, material, or technique. If you have a special interest in celadon glazed porcelain, for example, you may successfully combine celadon pieces by several different craftsmen. In Jack Lenor Larsen's table arrangement on pages 188–189, the unifying element is more subtle; plaiting, an ancient weaving or basketry technique, is common to all of the pieces here, which include both new work and an antique sash.

Thoughtful selectivity is critical to effective display. One of the greatest mistakes made by serious collectors and by those just beginning to acquire is to put out everything they have purchased. The collection of Jack Lenor Larsen, president of the American Craft Council and a weaver himself, is a good example of selective presentation (see page 192). Sliding fabric panels in his home conceal his very fine collection while allowing him to feature a few distinguished pieces—making more of an impression on guests than if they were overwhelmed by his full collection at once. Even without his comprehensive collection, you can exercise the same principle by presenting a few key pieces and rotating all of your crafts from room to room.

Another excellent example, shown at right, is the beautiful still life created by Mrs. Daniel Fendrick with just a single bowl. Her restraint in displaying the very fine work of Richard DeVore produces a remarkable sense of discovery when one walks into the room.

The most effective display helps the viewer to appreciate the special characteristics that make a piece unique. That will change with each piece, each material, and each artist. A little thought can add enormously to the impact of a fine piece of work.

Detail of Stephen Bondi's hardware.
(see page 202 for full view).

Commissioning Crafts

What can you commission from craftsmen? Most craftsmen would answer spontaneously, "Anything!" In fact, commissions may range from designs for a canopy bed to a weaving that helps dramatize a two-story stairwell. You can commission a stained glass window to block an unfortunate view, or even a forged iron stair railing so that it is designed as an outstanding architectural feature of your home.

C ommissions are possible in wood, fiber, forged iron, precious metals, stained glass, and even ceramics. And there are certainly times when a commission will make a great deal more sense than trying to find just the right piece to suit your particular requirements. Architectural or structural installations and large furniture pieces and fiber works, for instance, are usually available only through a commission.

Wood

In wood, there are a great many things you can commission. Major furniture pieces, of course, account for most commissions. You can commission such pieces as a bed, armoire, and a coordinated dining table and chairs in nearly any style you prefer, from traditional to contemporary. For smaller occasional tables, desks, and accent chairs, you're more likely to find just the special piece you want among the diverse styles of work already produced and being shown in fairs and galleries. It's just plain impractical, however, for a craftsman to have a complete array of styles, particularly larger pieces, for you to

Left: *This mantelpiece by Tommy Simpson was designed for easy removal from the wall; the owners considered this an important feature. Should they move some day, this prized commission could be installed in Mr. ane Mrs. Christoph Nostitz's next home. Other fine crafts featured include Rina Peleg's woven clay basket (on the floor to the left of the fireplace) and Barbara Tiso's porcelain bowl (second from left). Photo by David Arky.*

Below: *Judy and Pat Coady discovered their antique brass lever-operated wine opener on a trip to London. Since Judy Coady, director of Workbench Gallery in New York City, a non-profit furniture gallery, knew the possibilities and benefits of commissioning furniture, she asked Jere Osgood to design and build a cabinet that would feature their special find and provide storage for wine bottles, goblets, and linens. Photo by David Arky.*

foresight and planned the design of the mantelpiece so that it could be easily removed if the owner moved. This was a lifetime commission, which would go with them wherever they went.

Forged Iron

New technology, which makes it possible for the blacksmith to lift greater weight, has encouraged commissions on a grander scale - stair railings, freestanding staircases and fireplaces, supporting and decorative columns, security screens for windows and doors, and monumental exterior gates.

Albert Palcy, one of this country's foremost blacksmiths, creates magnificent pieces for private homes as well as public and commercial institutions. Paley has been particularly successful in achieving remarkable lightness and fluidity in iron on a monumental scale. One of his graceful bannisters, pictured on pages 200–201, might well be on a tour of historic homes a century from now.

Ivan Bailey draws the inspiration for his pieces from local or regional motifs (his home is in Georgia), incorporating palmettos, pine trees, and water birds of

choose from on hand. Imagine a craftsman investing the time and materials required to make a double bed only to have a prospective buyer announce, ''I want that bed exactly, only in a king size!'' Sometimes, the best way to get precisely what you want is by commissioning the work after

much discussion and a clear plan of action.

One especially noteworthy commission in wood was crafted by Tommy Simpson, who built and carved a magnificent mantelpiece to adorn a bedroom fireplace (page 198). Simpson worked closely with the owners, and they used

Below: *On an otherwise unadorned entrance, Ivan Bailey's highly stylized over-scaled door hinges become the dominant element setting this home apart from its neighbors. The door is studded with hand-wrought nails.*

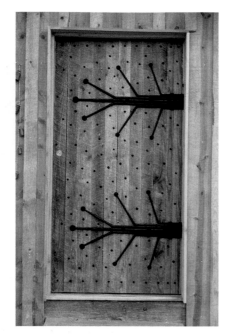

the lowland marshes. His stylized trees are featured as distinctive overscaled door hinges in one commission (pictured here). Stephen Bondi's ornamentation on the door seen on page 202 is another fine example of how superbly handmade hardware can be incorporated into an architectural design.

Silver

Silver has historically been associated with special events. For the young bride and groom, for the retirement or graduation gift, for the first grandchild, or to mark a silver anniversary, what better way to commemorate the occasion than with a precious silver object? You can commission a coffee service, a small bowl, or a baby's first set of silver. Admittedly, these are not inexpensive gifts, but when you are seeking a tangible way to celebrate the passage of one of life's most important moments, a handmade silver gift is surely a worthwhile choice.

Fiber

There are definite advantages to commissioning a work from a weaver or quilter. Although the fiber artist may offer you an impressive collection of already-completed pieces to choose from, a commission allows you to have a work tailor-made for your home. You can adjust dimensions of the piece to suit a particular room—a tapestry to dramatize cathedral ceilings, for example. Just as you can plan a particular piece to accentuate positive features in your home, so too can you plan a piece to help detract from any unattractive element—using a hanging quilt to visually balance an awkwardly placed door or window.

Much of the work of America's contemporary weavers deserves consideration as art, however, not just as decoration. To the artist, more is involved than how a piece fits in with your color scheme. Legitimate artists working in fiber are justly offended by the suggestion that they alter their personal expression to match fabric swatches. That's an old-fashioned notion that grew out of the relationship between the decorator and the skilled tradesman, and the results of such a partnership are likely to be old-fashioned, too. Realistically, you should choose a weaver who works in colors that you like rather than ask the weaver to change his or her aesthetics. Just as you wouldn't ask a

Left: Albert Paley is able to achieve remarkable fluidity and lightness in forged iron. Evident in this graceful stair railing commissioned for a new home, the vinelike tendrils appear to be blown by the wind. 20′ length. Photo courtesy of Fendrick Gallery.

painter whose oils you admire to work with a specific palette to suit your decor, it's also important to approach the fiber artist with the same good sense.

Craftsmen are very accommodating, however. Inherent in the creation of a piece is the necessity of its proper installation to maximize aesthetic appeal. A fabric artist, for instance, will be conscientious about assuring that his or her wall hanging is hung securely and lit properly. For example, it may be desirable to have a spotlight positioned at a certain angle to the hanging or track lights installed nearby, delineating shadows and maximizing textures. Indeed, it is advisable that a weaver see the location in which a piece is to be installed before beginning work on it. The amount of sunlight a tapestry will receive will have a bearing on the artist's choice of dyes; he will not want to risk using materials that will fade from too much exposure to the sun.

Stained Glass

Stained glass artists, like so many other craftsmen, are experimenting with great success in their chosen medium. No longer con-

Left: Stephen Bondi's *subtle hardware detailing echoes the wood grain of the door. Although it appears to be only decorative, the forged steel ornament incorporates working hardware.*

fined to religious subjects, nor to the dutiful imitation of Art Nouveau designs, these craftsmen are producing highly personal and innovative works. As a result, artists and homeowners are finding new applications for stained glass. In the house shown on page 203, Al Garber replaced the center panels of two wooden doors with companion stained glass designs, dividing the interior in a more practical and beautiful way. Heat and sound are better controlled in the dining room, and guests no longer feel cut off from the rest of the house.

Stained glass can also be used to block a bad view or to introduce light inside a house without jeopardizing privacy. A small stained glass panel displayed against a large expanse of window can also draw attention to a spectacular view. Large freestanding panels can create a foyer within a large open space or divide a room into smaller conversation areas—and always without sacrificing light.

But stained glass need not be used only to solve problems. In fact, much of the new work being created today rivals the beauty and quality of fine painting and can function in a room in much the same way.

Ceramics

Ceramics play a much smaller role in commissions today because such a broad choice of vessel forms already exists. There are, however, a few notable exceptions: bathroom and kitchen tiles, sinks, and ceramic murals. Just within the past few years, potters have begun to explore the design possibilities of handmade tiles, and as more ceramic artists have been attracted to this form of expression, the aesthetic styles available have begun to increase.

The tile designs you'll find differ from the country or provincial patterns common to imported Italian tiles. As with other forms of decoration in ceramics, the craftsman's tiles tend more toward abstract designs. Rather than use a repeat design, the craftsman paints an occasional tile which is installed in a random pattern, in keeping with a looser style of decoration.

For the natural or rustic bath, one can find stoneware sinks and tiles in soft glaze colors. More recently, potters have begun to imitate decorative commercial porcelain sinks, embellished with shells and made with tiles to match. In all cases the sinks are cast to fit standard plumbing sizes. The ceramist, in most cases, not only creates and executes the design, but also calculates the number of tiles required and participates in their installation.

In addition to their traditional use in the bath, cast tiles are now being used as hanging wall murals for any room in the house. These may range from a panel of four to six square feet, as with Kathi Yokum's pieces on page 207, to a permanent installation that covers an entire wall. Some take on the effect of a quilt-block repeat, while others present a painterly design. Tiles can be very effective in a room where the cool, smooth surface of the tile offsets a lot of wood or carpet.

What is a Special Order?

Commissions are not necessary when a special order can fulfill your requirements. To distinguish from commissions, special orders do not require interaction between the purchaser and the craftsman. You may see a prototype design exhibited—a potter's single place setting of ceramic dinnerware, for instance. If you like the work, you can then order as many place settings as you re-

Below: Al Garber replaced a central wooden panel in a dining room door with etched and stained glass. Julia and Carter Walker commissioned the panels to bring more light into the room and to create a greater sense of openness. Photo by David Arky.

quire. This is when you would request a special order. The same situation could apply to hand-blown goblets and silver or pewter flatware.

There are other situations in which a commission may not be appropriate. Suppose, for instance, you favor an older style of a craftsman's work, which he feels he has outgrown. He may not be willing to repeat the old work. In this case, a craftsman may decline to accept a commission for reasons both personal and practical.

At the opposite extreme, if your commission requires a technique or process that he is not comfortable with, he is likely to be candid and even suggest another craftsman. No one appreciates more than the craftsman the time required to master and refine a special technique, and rather than do poor work, he will probably say no.

Without thorough technical knowledge of the various craft processes, you may unwittingly ask a craftsman to create something that is simply not feasible for a single order. One potter was asked to develop a long tart tray using her current style of decoration. This was seemingly a simple request; however, it required a full year of experimentation to perfect a form that would not warp in kiln firing. As it happened, this commission was accepted by the potter because it was a very large wholesale order, but obviously such development and experimentation would have been too costly and time-consuming for a single order.

Although it's not a hard-and-fast rule, you'll probably be more satisfied with a commission after you've purchased several existing designs and become generally familiar with the potential in each craft medium.

How to Proceed

Perhaps the most important element in a successful commission is your own thoughtful analysis of your needs. Define first what a commission will provide that you have not been able to find in existing work and be prepared to communicate your thoughts and needs clearly to the craftsman.

The craftsman is often delighted to have the opportunity to create a new form for you, to solve a particular design problem and—within reason—to adapt colors and textures to your home. It is unfair and impractical, however, to ask a craftsman to change his aesthetic style for a single commission.

Although you should make clear your needs and hopes for the piece, the best work comes from giving the craftsman free rein. Thus, it's essential that you begin with someone whose style you truly like.

Narrow the field to a few craftsmen whose work you especially like, then look at a wide range of work by each of them. It is much wiser to assess the entire scope of an artist's work, rather than make a decision based on the appeal of a single piece. It's possible to be attracted to one piece and then feel differently when you see the rest of the craftsman's work. For one thing, by looking at numerous examples of one person's work, you are more likely to spot an immature designer—one whose work lacks consistency and clear direction.

A craftsman will always provide black-and-white photographs or color slides of past and current work. But it's also a good idea to see and examine several actual pieces of his work so that you can evaluate the quality of the craftsmanship. Then you can make a valid decision on the design from examining slides or photographs.

This portfolio will play an important role in your conversations with the craftsman. You will have examples of his work to refer to, and compare and contrast to the piece you want.

If feasible, ask the craftsman to visit your home to see for himself the scale, the natural light, and the other furnishings and art that you have. All of these factors may influence his proposed design. Particularly in new construction or remodeling, the earlier the craftsman is involved, the greater his contribution. That's true whether you are commissioning an installed architectural piece or a wall hanging. For example, the craftsman may suggest special lighting effects that can be easily and inexpensively installed during construction to greatly enhance the hanging.

What About Price?

You should bring up the subject of price range at the outset to make sure you're within your budget. Although an accurate estimate will be possible only after a decision has been made about both design and materials, a craftsman should be able to give you a ballpark estimate right away.

Once you've settled on a craftsman, discussed your preferences and, if possible, visited the site with him, the craftsman must then put considerable time into a design concept, materials, samples, and drawings or maquettes to present his proposed solution to you. The actual presentation may be very informal, but you should expect to pay a fee (generally, 10 percent of the total fee) for the initial concept. If, for some reason, you decide not to follow through on the commission, the craftsman is nevertheless entitled to compensation for his design. Should you agree to his concept and the commission proceeds, the initial fee paid to the craftsman is applied to the final charge. If you have chosen the artist carefully and are pleased with the initial design concept, the exciting step toward realization of your special piece begins. With a clear go-ahead, it's common practice to pay half of the total fee at this point, with the balance due upon installation.

Finding the Right Craftsman for You

Whether you're looking for a craftsman for a special commis-sion or for work to buy for your home, you'll find good work available all over the country. Apart from the centers of painting and sculpture in New York City and on the West Coast, craftsmen live and work in every state in the union. At a strictly local level, you may be disappointed in the quality or maturity of work available, but thanks to the phenomenal crafts revival over the past three decades, excellent work is never far away. State or regional craft member guilds, independent craft schools, and universities with strong craft programs ensure quality work in every area of the country. Here are eight good ways to find the right craftsman for your commission.

1. *Craft Galleries.* It's possible to work directly with a local craftsman on a special commission, but there are a number of advantages to working through a craft gallery. Not only will a gallery owner's experiences with previous commissions increase your chances for a smooth and satisfying relationship between you and the craftsman, but a gallery can save you a great deal of legwork in finding the right craftsman. Many craft galleries have extensive slide files on hand of a number of people whom they represent, and you can see a lot of work in one place. Even if you are working with a designer or architect, the gallery owner has the advantage of long exposure to a particular craftsman's work and his changing styles, and thus may be in the best position to direct you to someone suitable for your purposes.

The gallery's role is to facilitate the commission and installation of work by the craftsmen it represents. Many craftsmen, particularly more established artists, prefer to have the gallery owner or director take over the administrative details of a commission. A gallery's participation, however, does not eliminate your face-to-face contact with the craftsman. On the contrary, the gallery usually encourages a meeting, as that is part of both the success and the pleasure of a commission. In spite of popular belief, a gallery's involvement does not add to the price. The craftsman sets a fair price on his work based on materials and time involved. If a gallery administers a commission, the craftsman pays the gallery a percentage of his fee, much like an agent's commission on sales.

2. *Craft Guilds.* State or re-

gional guilds are generally noted for the quality of their members' work, because each member's work must pass the standards of the guild. By maintaining high standards, all members benefit from the guild's reputation. Two of the strongest member guilds in the country are the Piedmont Craftsmen, Inc. (based in Winston-Salem, North Carolina, with members from twelve Southeastern states) and the New Hampshire Guild of Craftsmen. These two guilds sponsor annual fairs, maintain slide registries, and operate retail shops that are open year-round. Programs available from other guilds vary, depending on the size and standards of the individual guilds. Although there are certainly exceptions, member guilds tend to attract craftsmen who are doing functional rather than sculptural work.

3. *Independent Craft Schools.* These private schools, some very old and well-known and some newcomers, offer courses and a limited exhibition schedule. Rapid growth in the number of these schools puts them within a day's trip from almost anywhere in the United States. For the beginning collector, they provide a chance to learn more. By refining your eye through courses in the crafts and attending occasional lectures and exhibitions, you will undoubtedly become more familiar with a variety of craftsmen's work and more discerning about the kind of work you prefer. If you want to know more about crafts, you should get acquainted at once with the school nearest you.

4. *Universities with Craft Curricula.* The enormous growth of the American crafts movement came about largely through our universities, when the art departments began after World War II to add courses in ceramics, fiber, metal, and later wood and glass to their core courses in painting and sculpture. The influence of these university programs is still strongly felt. In addition to the valuable sources for original work obtainable from highly respected instructors and promising students, these universities frequently attract a community of graduates who remain in the area to pursue their craft. As you become more knowledgeable in the craft world, you may be surprised to discover that an internationally respected metalsmith or ceramist lives and works in a university town near you.

5. *Publications.* With increasing sophistication and specialization in the craft world, publications have developed to document the best work in each medium. A selected list of these publications, along with subscription addresses, can be found at the back of the book. Many of these magazines, which concentrate on work in one medium, such as clay, wood, fiber, glass, or metal, are published independently by national organizations who represent the craftsmen. Should you be especially interested in buying in a certain medium, you can consult one of these magazines for more information. Generally, these publications are written with the practicing craftsman in mind. Therefore, they tend to feature stories with a great deal of technical information.

6. *Museums.* Increasingly, fine crafts are receiving recognition from such prestigious museums as the Metropolitan Museum and the Museum of Modern Art in New York City; the Smithsonian in Washington, D.C., in several of its specialized units; and the San Francisco Museum of Contemporary Art. In addition, three outstanding museums focus primarily on the work of contemporary craftsmen: the American Craft Museum in New York City, the Renwick Gallery, a part of the Smithsonian Institution, and the Museum of Craft and Folk Art in Los Angeles. Leaders in bringing the excellent work of craftsmen to the attention of the public, these museums have developed extensive traveling exhibitions that make museum-quality craft work accessible throughout the country. To develop a good eye, you should make every effort to see the work selected by the country's leading craft curators.

7. *Craft Fairs.* The quality of work in a fair, and thus your enjoyment of it, may vary widely. As mentioned earlier, guild-sponsored fairs are generally reliable because members' work has been prescreened. A juried fair is often an indication of better quality work, but to be sure, you must know who is on the jury or screening committee. Sometimes a private, commercial sponsor acts as his own jury or appoints a puppet jury so that "juried" may not be a guarantee of high standards, but rather a reflection of the organizer's interests.

American Craft Enterprises, the marketing arm of the American Craft Council, organizes

Right: Many ceramists are exploring the painterly possibilities of handmade tiles intended to be viewed as wall hangings, such as these two panels by Kathi Yokum. Displayed with her work is a painted wooden table by Edward Zucca. Photo by Joseph Kugielsky.

Left: *When Judy and Pat Coady purchased their grand old townhouse, the frosted glass of the existing parlor doors had been shattered. Stained glass artist Marni Bakst carefully salvaged the broken glass to reuse it in her design. The Post-modern column to the right of the doors is by furniture maker Trent Whitington. Photo by David Arky.*

five fairs annually. These fairs have become widely known for the consistently high quality work of the participating craftsmen and for being smoothly run and planned with the visitor in mind. These prestigious events are something of an exception in that they often include nonfunctional work as well as functional pieces. Scattered around the country at various times of the year, the fairs are planned to give maximum accessibility to everyone.

From one year to the next, specific dates for the fairs will vary within the months listed below. To find out the precise dates for each of the events, contact American Craft Enterprises, P.O. Box 10, New Paltz, NY 12561, or call (914) 255-0039: Baltimore, Maryland (February); Dallas, Texas (April); Rhinebeck, New York (June); Newport, Rhode Island (July); San Francisco, California (August).

8. *American Craft Council (ACC).* The services provided by the ACC are worth highlighting here. The Council is responsible for the publication of *American Craft* magazine, exhibitions at the American Craft Museum, which also travel, and the sponsorship of five regional fairs through American Craft Enterprises. Of

particular note is their extensive craft library, located in the American Craft Museum I in New York City. Nowhere in America is the work of so many craftsmen gathered together and catalogued. More than 2,000 craftsmen are represented through slides of their work, organized by media. In addition, all craft periodicals and catalogs of all major museum exhibitions are available at the library. As an example, the library is used often by gallery owners, invitational fair sponsors, museum curators, designers, and architects who want to see a lot of work quickly in order to locate appropriate craftsmen for exhibitions or commissions. You can also take advantage of this remarkable resource, but there are qualifications for its use. You must be a member of ACC and you must be in New York City on a Tuesday, Wednesday, or Friday afternoon when the library is open to members.

Besides access to their extensive library, membership in the American Craft Council includes a subscription to *American Craft* magazine, a bi-monthly publication covering the best work in all craft media, and free admission to the American Craft Museum in New York City. ACC's membership

is not limited to craftsmen alone, and the magazine would be valuable to anyone wanting to know more or to see more of fine crafts. The magazine covers major museum exhibitions and influential gallery exhibitions, profiles leading craftsmen, and highlights the work of emerging artists. Of particular help is their state-by-state calendar of craft events, fairs, workshops, school courses, as well as, museum and gallery exhibitions. For membership information, contact: Membership Department, American Craft Council, P.O. Box 561, Martinsville, NJ 08836.

DIRECTORY OF CRAFTSMEN

This appendix lists all of the craftsmen whose work appears in the book. For each, the entry includes: 1) the city and state where the craftsman lives at the time of publication; 2) a brief description of what the craftsman makes; 3) a selection of galleries where more of his work can be seen; 4) whether commissions are accepted, along with a rough estimate of the time necessary to fulfill an average commission; 5) an estimate of the retail price range of work. Please note that the information presented here does not represent a commitment as to prices or availability.

NINA ACKERSON
Baltimore, Maryland
Woven rugs
DISTRICT OF COLUMBIA: Sherley Koteen;
  MARYLAND: Baltimore, Off Broadway
Accepts commissions, allow 2-4 weeks
Approximately $300

NANCY ALBERTSON
Burnsville, North Carolina
Handmade paper and woven fiber wall hangings
GEORGIA: Atlanta, Eve Mannes; NORTH CAROLINA:
  Winston-Salem, Piedmont Craftsmen
Accepts commissions, allow 6-8 weeks
$150-9000

EDGAR & JOYCE ANDERSON
Morristown, New Jersey
Wood furniture
Contact the artists at: Tempe Wick Rd., Morristown,
  NJ 07960
Accept commissions, allow 1-3 years
$200-10,000

STANLEY MACE ANDERSEN
Penland, North Carolina
Earthenware for table use
DISTRICT OF COLUMBIA: American Hand;
  GEORGIA: Atlanta, Signature Shop; NEW YORK:
  New York City, The Elements; NORTH CAROLINA:
  Winston-Salem, Piedmont Craftsmen; PENN-
  SYLVANIA: Philadelphia, Sign of the Swan,
  The Works
Accepts commissions, allow 2-3 months
$7-150

GLENN APPLEMAN
New York, New York
Ceramic cookie jars
ILLINOIS: Chicago, A Show of Hands; NEW YORK:
  New York City, Incorporated, Surroundings
Does not accept commissions
$110-120

MITCHELL AZOFF
Port Washington, Wisconsin
Carved wood trays, vases, vessels, boxes, furniture
DISTRICT OF COLUMBIA: Appalachian Spring;
  ILLINOIS: Evanston, Mindscape; TEXAS:
  Houston, Hanson

Accepts commissions, allow 2-3 months
Production items, $10-90; commissions, $160 and up

JUDY AZULAY & JOE CHASNOFF
Lindside, West Virginia
Wood furniture and small gift items
DISTRICT OF COLUMBIA: Jackie Chalkley;
  MASSACHUSETTS: Boston, Signature; NORTH
  CAROLINA: Asheville, New Morning
Accept commissions, allow 6 months
$12-2200

RALPH BACERRA
Pasadena, California
Porcelain vessels
CALIFORNIA: Los Angeles, Garth Clark; DISTRICT
  OF COLUMBIA: American Hand; NEW YORK: New
  York City, Theo Portnoy
Does not accept commissions
$2000-3000

DAVID PAUL BACHARACH
Cockeysville, Maryland
Metal kitchen utensils, fireplace sets, and non-
  functional vessel forms
MAINE: Portland, Handcrafters; MASSACHUSETTS:
  Cambridge, Ten Arrow; OHIO: Cleveland, Sylvia
  Ullman
Accepts commissions, allow 6 months
$75-3500

IVAN BAILEY
Atlanta, Georgia
Metal, primarily iron, fireplace equipment, fountains,
  sundials, gates and railings
Contact the artist at: 1260 Foster St., Atlanta, GA
  30318
Accepts commissions, allow 1-3 months
$700-10,000

MARNI BAKST
New York, New York
Stained glass
NEW YORK: New York City, Heller
Accepts commissions, allow 1-6 months
$150-225 per square foot

NEIL BARKON
Melrose, Massachusetts
Wood furniture

MASSACHUSETTS: Boston, Society of Arts and
  Crafts; NEW YORK: East Hampton, Pritam & Eames
Accepts commissions, time varies
$300-4000

DOROTHY GILL BARNES
Worthington, Ohio
Baskets
Contact the artist at: 33 Wilson Dr., Worthington,
  OH 43085
Accepts commissions, allow 3 months to 1 year
$40-200

JIM BASSLER
San Pedro, California
Fiber wall hangings
DISTRICT OF COLUMBIA: Sherley Koteen;
  GEORGIA: Atlanta, Form and Function; NEW
  YORK: New York City, The Elements
Accepts commissions, allow about 3 months
$1500-3000

BENNETT BEAN
Blairstown, New Jersey
Non-functional white earthenware vessels
ARIZONA: Scottsdale, The Hand and the Spirit;
  CALIFORNIA: Los Angeles, Craft and Folk Art
  Museum; DISTRICT OF COLUMBIA: American
  Hand; GEORGIA: Atlanta, American Art; NEW
  YORK: New York City, Heller; PENNSYLVANIA:
  Philadelphia, The Works
Does not accept commissions
$200-1000

GARY BEECHAM
Spruce Pines, North Carolina
Glass vessels
CALIFORNIA: San Francisco, Contemporary Artisans;
  DISTRICT OF COLUMBIA: Sherley Koteen;
  MARYLAND: Baltimore, Barstons; NEW YORK:
  New York City, Heller; PENNSYLVANIA:
  Philadelphia, The Works
Accepts commissions, time varies
$700-1500

BRUCE BEEKEN
Shelburne, Vermont
Wood furniture
NEW YORK: East Hampton, Pritam & Eames;
  PENNSYLVANIA: Philadelphia, Richard Kagan

Accepts commissions, allow 6 weeks
$200-3500

HARRIET BELLOWS
Alfred Station, New York
Large porcelain vessels
DISTRICT OF COLUMBIA: American Hand; OHIO:
    Cincinnati, Private Collection; Cleveland, DBR
Does not accept commissions
$375-650

GARRY KNOX BENNETT
Oakland, California
Clocks and furniture of wood, metal and glass
ARIZONA: Scottsdale, The Hand and the Spirit;
    CALIFORNIA: Los Angeles, Craft and Folk Art
    Museum; ILLINOIS: Wilmette, Artisan Shop; NEW
    YORK: New York City, The Elements, Workbench;
    PENNSYLVANIA: Philadelphia, The Works
Does not accept commissions
$500-10,000

RICK BERNSTEIN
Watertown, Massachusetts
Glass vessel forms and architectural glass collages
FLORIDA: Palm Beach, Holsten; MARYLAND:
    Baltimore, Barstons; MASSACHUSETTS: Boston,
    Glass Veranda; MICHIGAN: Lathrup Village,
    Habatat; NEW YORK: New York City, Heller
Accepts commissions, allow 1-2 months
$100-500 for production work; $1000-5000 for
    commissioned work

DAVE BIGELOW
Santa Barbara, California
Raku-fired porcelain vessels
CALIFORNIA: San Francisco, Contemporary Artisans;
    DISTRICT OF COLUMBIA: American Hand;
    FLORIDA: Palm Beach, Holsten; NEW YORK: New
    York City, Convergence, The Elements
Accepts commissions, allow 6 weeks
$350-500

SARAH BODINE
New York, New York
Functional stoneware
NEW YORK: Albany, Forms and Foliage
Accepts commissions, allow 2 months
$5-75

JANET BOGUCH
Seattle, Washington
Non-woven wall hangings
CALIFORNIA: San Francisco, Meyer, Breier, Weiss;
    DISTRICT OF COLUMBIA: Sherley Koteen;
    WASHINGTON: Seattle, Traver Sutton

Accepts commissions, allow about 3 months
$300-1000

STEPHEN BONDI
Emeryville, California
Metal furniture, door hardware, fireplaces and fireplace
    tools, railings, lamps and architectural elements
Contact the artist at: 4300 E. Shore Highway, Emeryville,
    CA 94608
Accepts commissions, allow up to 1 year
$150-100,000 and up

JONATHAN GRAHAM BONNER
Providence, Rhode Island
Non-functional metalwork
ARIZONA: Scottsdale, The Hand and the Spirit;
    CALIFORNIA: San Francisco, Meyer, Breier, Weiss;
    NEW YORK: New York City, Convergence;
    RHODE ISLAND: Providence, Lily Iselin
Accepts commissions, allow up to 3 months
$200-1500

DAVID BOYE
Davenport, California
Knives
CALIFORNIA: Davenport, David Boye Knives; San
    Francisco, Meyer, Breier, Weiss; COLORADO: Vail, A
    Place on Earth; HAWAII: Honolulu, Following Sea;
    VIRGINIA: Charlottesville, Signet
Occasionally accepts commissions, allow 2 months to
    1 year
$65-400 and up

BRADFORD WOODWORKS
Worcester, Pennsylvania
Wood kitchenware
CALIFORNIA: Los Angeles, Craft and Folk Art
    Museum; PENNSYLVANIA: Philadelphia, Sign of
    the Swan
Do not accept commissions
$9-42

JOSEPH L. BRANDOM
Baton Rouge, Louisiana
Gold, silver, bronze, copper, and stainless steel vessels,
    utensils and door knockers
LOUISIANA: Baton Rouge, Crafts; MARYLAND:
    Annapolis, Pottery 'N Things; NEW YORK: Buffalo,
    Morgan; NORTH CAROLINA: Asheville, New Morn-
    ing; PENNSYLVANIA: Bryn Mawr, The Store;
    Verona, The Store
Accepts commissions, allow at least 1 month
$100 and up

CORNELIA K. BREITENBACH
Los Angeles, California

Painted and dyed fabric panels
CALIFORNIA: Los Angeles, Mandell Art Services; San
    Francisco, Allrich; DISTRICT OF COLUMBIA:
    Sherley Koteen; GEORGIA: Atlanta, Eve Mannes
Accepts commissions, allow 1-2 months
$2000-11,000 ($150-175 per square foot)

CYNTHIA BRINGLE
Penland, North Carolina
Raku-fired porcelain vessel forms
Contact the artist at: Penland School of Crafts,
    Penland, NC 28765
Accepts commissions, allow 3 months to 1 year
$50-500

WENDELL CASTLE
Scottsville, New York
Wood furniture and sculpture
DISTRICT OF COLUMBIA: Fendrick; NEW YORK: New
    York City, Milliken
Accepts commissions, allow 2 months to 1 year
$2000 and up

MAREK CECULA
New York, New York
Functional and non-functional vessels
NEW YORK: New York City, Contemporary Porcelain
Accepts commissions, allow 1-3 months
$22-1500

JOHN CEDERQUIST
Capistrano Beach, California
Wood and leather furniture
CALIFORNIA: La Jolla, Gallery Eight; Los Angeles,
    Craft and Folk Art Museum; PENNSYLVANIA:
    Verona, The Store
Does not accept commissions
$500-2000

PAUL CHALEFF
Pine Plains, New York
Wood-fired clay vessels and platters
NEBRASKA: Omaha, The Craftsmen's; NEW YORK:
    New York City, Aaron Faber
Does not accept commissions
$200-2000

BETH CHANGSTROM
Mill Valley, California
Stoneware and porcelain plates, bowls and tureens
CALIFORNIA: Mill Valley, Fireworks
Accepts commissions, allow 2-4 months
$7-125

JOE CHASNOFF & JUDY AZULAY
Lindside, West Virginia

Wood furniture and small gift items
DISTRICT OF COLUMBIA: Jackie Chalkley;
  MASSACHUSETTS: Boston, Signature; NORTH
  CAROLINA: Asheville, New Morning
Accept commissions, allow 6 months
$12-2200

DALE CHIHULY
Providence, Rhode Island
Non-functional glass
ARIZONA: Scottsdale, Kate Eliot; CALIFORNIA: San
  Francisco, Braunstein; ILLINOIS: Chicago, Betsy
  Rosenfield; MICHIGAN: Lathrup Village, Habatat;
  NEW YORK: New York City, Charles Cowles
Accepts commissions, allow up to 1 year
$900-10,000

CHUNGHI CHOO
Iowa City, Iowa
Metalwork
Contact the artist at: 2 Glenview Knoll, River Heights,
  Iowa City, IA 52240
Accepts commissions, allow 1 month to 1 year
$500-3000

HANS CHRISTENSEN
Rochester, New York
Silver hollowware
Contact the artist at: 119 Faircrest Rd., Rochester,
  NY 14623
Accepts commissions, allow 4-8 months
$200-9000

BRYANT CLARK
Clarksville, Delaware
Steel knives, choppers and cutting tools, with other
  metals and wood
DISTRICT OF COLUMBIA: Mimosa; NORTH
  CAROLINA: Kitty Hawk, Duck Blind, Ltd.
Accepts commissions, allow 3-6 months
$75-1100

HARRIET COHEN
Amherst, Massachusetts
Red earthenware vessels
DISTRICT OF COLUMBIA: American Hand; NEW
  YORK: Brooklyn, Clay Pot; PENNSYLVANIA:
  Philadelphia, The Works
Does not accept commissions
$200 and up

MICHAEL COHEN
Amherst, Massachusetts
Stoneware for table use
DISTRICT OF COLUMBIA: American Hand;
  MASSACHUSETTS: Brewster, Spectrum; Brookline,

Marion-Ruth
Accepts commissions, allow 3 months
$10-500

ELAINE COLEMAN
Canby, Oregon
Porcelain vessels
ARIZONA: Scottsdale, The Hand and the Spirit;
  DISTRICT OF COLUMBIA: American Hand;
  OREGON: Portland, Contemporary Crafts
Accepts commissions, allow 1-3 months
$20-2500

TOM COLEMAN
Canby, Oregon
Porcelain vessels
ARIZONA: Scottsdale, The Hand and the Spirit;
  DISTRICT OF COLUMBIA: American Hand;
  OREGON: Portland, Contemporary Crafts
Accepts commissions, allow 1-3 months
$20-2500

BOB COOGAN
Smithville, Tennessee
Knives
NEW YORK: East Hampton, Appalachian Art
Accepts commissions, allow about 3 months
$50 and up

PHILIP CORNELIUS
Pasadena, California
Non-functional porcelain
CALIFORNIA: Los Angeles, Garth Clark; NEW YORK:
  New York City, Hadler-Rodriguez; TEXAS: Houston,
  Hadler-Rodriguez
Does not accept commissions
$500-2500

MOLLY COWGILL
Richmond, Virginia
Porcelain vessels
ARIZONA: Scottsdale, The Hand and the Spirit;
  CALIFORNIA: Los Angeles, Craft and Folk Art
  Museum; DISTRICT OF COLUMBIA: Jackie Chalkley;
  PENNSYLVANIA: Philadelphia, The Works
Occasionally accepts commissions, allow 6 weeks to
  6 months
$50-1000

NANCY CROW
Baltimore, Ohio
Quilts
Contact the artist at: 10545 Snyder Church Rd.,
  Baltimore, OH 43105
Does not accept commissions
$1200-5000

BRIAN CUMMINGS
Rumney, New Hampshire
Forged iron flatware, cooking utensils, lighting,
  fireplace equipment and building hardware
CALIFORNIA: Los Angeles, Craft and Folk Art
  Museum; DISTRICT OF COLUMBIA: Appalachian
  Spring; NEW JERSEY: Tenafly, America House;
  NORTH CAROLINA: Asheville, New Morning
Occasionally accepts commissions, time varies
$8-500

KEN & KATHLEEN DALTON
Coker Creek, Tennessee
Split-oak baskets
CALIFORNIA: Berkeley, The Gift Horse; MAINE:
  Ogunquit, Maple Hill; MASSACHUSETTS: Orleans,
  Artful Hand; NEW YORK: New York City, Museum of
  American Folk Art; Scarsdale, The Craftsman's
Do not accept commissions
$25-2000

DALE DAPKINS
Delhi, New York
Ceramic wall plates and vessels
COLORADO: Denver, Panache; DISTRICT OF
  COLUMBIA: Smull's; NEW YORK: New York City,
  Convergence; NORTH CAROLINA: Chapel Hill,
  Cameron; PENNSYLVANIA: Philadelphia, Past
  Present Future
Accepts commissions, allow 6 months
$20-500

CARL ANDREE DAVIDT
Atlanta, Georgia
Metalwork
NEW YORK: New York City, Heller
Accepts commissions, allow 1-2 months
$2500 and up

RICHARD DEVORE
Fort Collins, Colorado
Porcelain vessel forms
DISTRICT OF COLUMBIA: Fendrick; ILLINOIS:
  Chicago, Exhibit A
Does not accept commissions
$4500 and up

KRIS DEY
Diamond Springs, California
Painted fabric wall constructions
CALIFORNIA: San Francisco, Allrich
Accepts commissions, allow at least 1 month
$1350 and up

RICK DILLINGHAM
Santa Fe, New Mexico

Non-functional ceramic vessels
DISTRICT OF COLUMBIA: American Hand; NEW
  MEXICO: Santa Fe, Eason; NEW YORK: Buffalo, Nina
  Freudenheim; New York City, Hadler-Rodriguez;
  TEXAS: Houston, Hadler-Rodriguez
Does not accept commissions
$400-4500

FRITZ DREISBACH
Penland, North Carolina
Glass stoneware and vessel forms
Contact the artist at: The Penland School of Crafts,
  Penland, North Carolina 28765
Does not accept commissions
Prices not available

RUTH DUCKWORTH
Ceramic sculpture, wall pieces and murals
ILLINOIS: Chicago, Exhibit A
Accepts commissions, time varies
$1000-30,000

JOHN DUNNIGAN
Saunderstown, Rhode Island
Wood furniture
NEW YORK: East Hampton, Pritam & Eames
Accepts commissions, allow 6-12 weeks
$500-5000 and up

WARREN DURBIN
Burlington, Vermont
Wood furniture, candlestands, trays
CALIFORNIA: Berkeley, Zosaku; MICHIGAN: Detroit,
  Gallery of Contemporary Crafts; PENNSYLVANIA:
  Philadelphia, The Works
Accepts commissions, allow 3-4 months
$50-1000

DAN DUSTIN
Contoocook, New Hampshire
Wood spoons
MASSACHUSETTS: Boston, Society of Arts and Crafts;
  NEW HAMPSHIRE: Concord, League of New
  Hampshire Craftsmen
Occasionally accepts commissions, allow 3-4 months
$15-400

CRAIG EASTER
Fresno, California
Stoneware lidded pots
MASSACHUSETTS: Brookline, Marion-Ruth; Lenox,
  Yamato; NEW YORK: New York City, Surroundings;
  Scarsdale, The Craftsman's; PENNSYLVANIA:
  Philadelphia, Sign of the Swan
Does not accept commissions
$15-200

DAVID N. EBNER
Brookhaven, New York
Wood furniture and functional sculpture
NEW YORK: Bridgehampton, Elaine Benson; East
  Hampton, Pritam & Eames; Fishers Island, Pandion
Accepts commissions, allow 6-18 months
$500-10,000

STEPHEN DALE EDWARDS
Kirkland, Washington
Sandblasted glass bowls
CALIFORNIA: San Francisco, Contemporary Artisans;
  DISTRICT OF COLUMBIA: Jackie Chalkley;
  MASSACHUSETTS: Boston, Glass Veranda; NEW
  YORK: East Hampton, Pritam & Eames; New York
  City, Heller; WASHINGTON: Seattle, Foster/White
Accepts commissions, allow up to 2 months
$400-1500

STEPHEN DEE EDWARDS
Penland, North Carolina
Glass sculpture
MICHIGAN: Lathrup Village, Habatat; NEW YORK:
  New York City, Heller
Accepts commissions, allow 2 months
$900-1500

BARBARA EIGEN
New York, New York
Earthenware serving vessels
PENNSYLVANIA: Philadelphia, Sign of the Swan
Occasionally accepts commissions, allow 4-8 weeks
$22-75

MICHAEL ELKAN
Silverton, Oregon
Wood boxes
FLORIDA: South Miami, Netsky; MASSACHUSETTS:
  Brewster, Spectrum; NEW YORK: Scarsdale, The
  Craftsman's; OREGON: Portland, Real Mother Goose;
  PENNSYLVANIA: Philadelphia, The Works
Accepts commissions, allow 3-6 months
$40-1000

STEVE ELLING
New York, New York
Metal inlaid in wood boxes and furniture
HAWAII: Honolulu, Rare Discoveries; NEW YORK:
  New York City, Gallery 10; Scarsdale, The
  Craftsman's
Accepts commissions, allow 1-10 weeks
Boxes, $15-500; furniture, $250 and up

DAVID ELLSWORTH
Quakertown, Pennsylvania
Turned wood vessels

CALIFORNIA: Los Angeles, Del Mano; Mendocino,
  Gallery Fair; PENNSYLVANIA: Philadelphia, Richard
  Kagan
Does not accept commissions
$100-3500

BRUCE A. ERDMAN
Mt. Horeb, Wisconsin
Wood tambour cabinets and containers, especially roll-
  top desks
CALIFORNIA: Santa Monica, A Singular Place;
  HAWAII: Honolulu, Following Sea;
  MASSACHUSETTS: Brewster, Spectrum
Accepts commissions, time varies
$38-1600

LYN EVANS
New York, New York
Porcelain dinnerware and serving pieces, and
  architectural elements and tiles
NEW YORK: New York City, Gordon Foster;
  Southampton, Works; TEXAS: Dallas, At Home
Accepts commissions for tiles and architectural
  elements, allow 3-4 months
$30 and up

RICHARD & SANDRA FARRELL
East Killingly, Connecticut
Handbuilt and wheelthrown porcelain dinnerware,
  serving pieces, sinks, tiles, murals and architectural
  elements
DISTRICT OF COLUMBIA: Jackie Chalkley;
  MASSACHUSETTS: Brookline, Marion-Ruth;
  PENNSYLVANIA: Philadelphia, Sign of the Swan
Accept commissions, allow about 1 year
$20 and up ($150 per place setting, average)

JUDITH POXSON FAWKES
Portland, Oregon
Woven tapestries and rugs
NEW YORK: New York City, The Elements; OREGON:
  Portland, Contemporary Crafts
Accepts commissions, allow 2-3 months
$75 per square foot

BETH FEIN
Oakland, California
Ceramic teapots, cups, saucers, plates and boxes
ARIZONA: Scottsdale, The Hand and the Spirit;
  HAWAII: Honolulu, Following Sea; NEW YORK: New
  York City, The Elements
Accepts commissions, allow 6 months to a year
$150-1000

KEN FERGUSON
Shawnee Mission, Kansas

Stoneware and porcelain pots
CALIFORNIA: Los Angeles, Garth Clark, KANSAS:
   Shawnee Mission, Morgan; MISSOURI: St. Louis,
   Ronnie Greenberg; NEW YORK: New York City,
   Hadler-Rodriguez; PENNSYLVANIA: Philadelphia,
   Helen Drutt
Does not accept commissions
$500-750

ROBERT FORBES
Philadelphia, Pennsylvania
Earthenware bowls, platters, jars and vases
DISTRICT OF COLUMBIA: American Hand;
   MICHIGAN: Detroit, Gallery of Contemporary Crafts;
   NEW YORK: New York City, The Elements;
   PENNSYLVANIA: Philadelphia, Helen Drutt
Rarely accepts commissions, allow 3 months
$50-450

MARK FORMAN
Cherry Hill, New Jersey
Large ceramic wall plates
NEW JERSEY: Haddonfield, By Hand; NEW YORK:
   New York City, Convergence; PENNSYLVANIA:
   Philadelphia, Webster/Wallnuts
Accepts commissions, allow 2 months
$100-3000

NANCY L. FREEMAN
Olivebridge, New York
Glass goblets, bowls, pitchers and vases
MARYLAND: Baltimore, Tomlinson Collection;
   MASSACHUSETTS: Cambridge, Ten Arrow;
   MICHIGAN: Ann Arbor, Selo/Shevel; Lathrup Village,
   Habatat; NEW YORK: New York City, Jorice
Rarely accepts commissions
$28-200

TAGE FRID
Foster, Rhode Island
Wood furniture
NEW YORK: East Hampton, Pritam & Eames
Accepts commissions, time varies
$500 and up

DOUGLAS ERIC FUCHS
New York, New York
Non-functional baskets
NEW YORK: New York City, The Elements
Accepts commissions, allow 1-4 months
$100-1000

AL GARBER
New Haven, Connecticut
Stained glass wall pieces and screens
FLORIDA: Palm Beach, Holsten; MASSACHUSETTS:

Stockbridge, Holsten; NEW YORK: New York City,
   The Elements
Accepts commissions, time varies
$1000 and up

NADINE GAY
San Francisco, California
Ovenproof ceramic vessels
CALIFORNIA: San Francisco, Contemporary Artisans;
   NEW YORK: Rochester, Rochester Museum;
   PENNSYLVANIA: Philadelphia, Sign of the Swan
Accepts commissions, allow 2 months
$20-300

ANDREA GILL
Kent, Ohio
Non-functional ceramics
ARIZONA: Scottsdale, The Hand and the Spirit; NEW
   YORK: New York City, The Elements
Does not accept commissions
$300-1000

JOHN GILL
Kent, Ohio
Non-functional ceramics
NEBRASKA: Omaha, Craftsman; OHIO: Cleveland,
   DBR; NEW YORK: New York City, Hadler-Rodriguez
Does not accept commissions
$500-1000

JOHN & JAN GILMOR
Pine Plains, New York
Glass perfume bottles, stemware, platters and vase
   forms
CALIFORNIA: San Francisco, Compositions; NEW
   YORK: New York City, The Glass Store
Occasionally accept commissions, allow 2 months
$18-2500

MICHAEL M. GLANCY
Rehobeth, Delaware
Glass vessel forms
CALIFORNIA: Los Angeles, Ivor Kurland; GEORGIA:
   Atlanta, Great American; MARYLAND: Bethesda,
   Glass; MICHIGAN: Lathrup Village, Habatat; NEW
   YORK: New York City, Heller
Does not accept commissions
$850-4500

JOHN GLICK
Farmington, Michigan
Stoneware and porcelain dinnerware
MICHIGAN: Birmingham, Yaw; Farmington Hills, Plum
   Tree Pottery; PENNSYLVANIA: Philadelphia, Helen
   Drutt
Rarely accepts commissions (no dinnerware

commissions), allow up to 1 year
$10-400, occasionally to $800

MARC GOLDRING
South Acworth, New Hampshire
Sculptural vases and bowls of leather
MASSACHUSETTS: Chestnut Hill, Quadrum; NEW
   YORK: New York City, Convergence; White Plains,
   Westlake
Accepts commissions, allow 2-6 weeks
$40-500

BARRY GORDON
Baldwinsville, New York
Domestic utensils of wood
CALIFORNIA: Berkeley, Zosaku; NEW YORK: East
   Hampton, Engel Pottery; Rochester, Shelter Goods
Accepts commissions, allow 4-8 weeks
$8-28, occasionally to $120

ANNE KROHN GRAHAM
Newark, Delaware
Jewelry, flatware, and sculpture of gold, silver and
   other metals
DELAWARE: Wilmington, Artisans III; Delaware Art
   Museum; NEW YORK: New York City, Aaron Faber
Accepts commissions, allow 1-4 weeks
$25-2000

MICHAEL GRAHAM
Los Osos, California
Functional and non-functional wood sculpture
CALIFORNIA: San Francisco, Compositions
Accepts commissions, allow about 1 year
$1500-8500

ELIZABETH S. GURRIER
Hollis, New Hampshire
Quilted wall hangings and pillows
MAINE: Boothbay Harbor, Abacus; MASSACHUSETTS:
   Nantucket, Cockeyed Dove; NEW YORK: New York
   City, Julie; PENNSYLVANIA: Philadelphia, The Works
Accepts commissions, allow up to a year
$100-2000

JANE GUSTON
Guilford, Connecticut
Terra cotta vessels and platters
CALIFORNIA: San Francisco, Meyer, Breier, Weiss;
   DISTRICT OF COLUMBIA: American Hand;
   GEORGIA: Atlanta, Signature; MICHIGAN:
   Birmingham, Carol Hooberman; MISSOURI: St. Louis,
   Crafts Alliance; NEW YORK: New York City, Hadler-
   Rodriguez; TEXAS: San Antonio, Objects
Accepts commissions, allow about 4 months
$150-350

DOROTHY HAFNER
New York, New York
Porcelain tableware
CALIFORNIA: Los Angeles, Garth Clark; FLORIDA:
Palm Beach, Carani; NEW YORK: New York City,
Incorporated, Tiffany; TEXAS: San Antonio, Objects
Accepts commissions, allow 2 months
Dinner plates $65-130

JERRY HARPSTER
Monroe, Oregon
Metal cooking vessels, flatware and containers
CALIFORNIA: San Francisco, Extravagance;
MASSACHUSETTS: Cambridge, Ten Arrow; NEW
YORK: Riverhead, Elegant Extras; OKLAHOMA:
Tulsa, Art Signatures; OREGON: Portland,
Contemporary Crafts
Accepts commissions, allow 2 months
$30-2000

CAROL GRANT HART
Salisbury, Connecticut
Functional and decorative baskets
NEW YORK: New York City, The Elements
Does not accept commissions
$45-600

PIA & TOM HART
Unionville, Connecticut
Glass stemware
ARIZONA: Scottsdale, The Hand and the Spirit;
CALIFORNIA: Los Angeles, Craft and Folk Art
Museum; ILLINOIS: Evanston, Mindscape;
MASSACHUSETTS: Boston, Glass Veranda; NEW
YORK: New York City, The Elements
Occasionally accept commissions, allow at least 3
months
$25-800

FRANCES LEE HEMINWAY
West Simsbury, Connecticut
Porcelain tableware, sculpture and tile
COLORADO: Denver, Panache; CONNECTICUT: New
Haven, Creative Arts Workshop; MICHIGAN: Detroit,
Gallery of Contemporary Crafts; NEW YORK:
Brooklyn, Meuniers
Accepts commissions, allow 6 months to a year
$6-300

CATHARINE HIERSOUX
Berkeley, California
Porcelain tableware, wall plates and vase forms
ARIZONA: Scottsdale, The Hand and the Spirit;
CALIFORNIA: Los Angeles, Craft and Folk Art
Museum; San Francisco, Contemporary Artisans;
DISTRICT OF COLUMBIA: Sherley Koteen; MAINE:

Portland, Handcrafters; MARYLAND: Kensington,
Plum
Accepts commissions, allow 2-3 months
$12-1200

THOMAS A. HOADLEY
Pittsfield, Massachusetts
Porcelain plates and vase forms
DISTRICT OF COLUMBIA: Jackie Chalkley; FLORIDA:
Palm Beach, Holsten; MASSACHUSETTS:
Stockbridge, Holsten
Accepts commissions, allow 2-3 months
$65-750

CURTIS C. HOARD
St. Paul, Minnesota
Painted ceramic vessels and platters
MINNESOTA: Minneapolis, Vermillion Editions; NEW
YORK: New York City, The Elements; Scarsdale, The
Craftsman's
Accepts commissions, allow 1-2 months
$100-4000

JEAN-PIERRE HSU
Berkeley Springs, West Virginia
Stoneware tea sets
DISTRICT OF COLUMBIA: American Hand; NEW
YORK: New York City, Convergence; VIRGINIA:
Richmond, Lewis/Schaal
Accepts commissions, allow 3-9 months
$18-245 and up

KAREN HUBERT
Bethesda, Maryland
Baskets
ARIZONA: Scottsdale, Mind's Eye; CALIFORNIA:
Berkeley, Gift Horse; DELAWARE: Rehobeth Beach,
Tide Line; MASSACHUSETTS: Orleans, Artful Hand;
OHIO: Cincinnati, Private Collection; VIRGINIA:
Virginia Beach, Decker Studio
Accepts commissions, allow 1-3 months
$38-300

JANET HULING & JONATHAN KAPLAN
Bowmansville, Pennsylvania
Stoneware kitchen vessels and dinnerware
NEW YORK: Ithaca, People's Pottery; TENNESSEE:
Nashville, American Artisan
Accept commissions for dinnerware only, allow
3-5 months
$7-80

MICHAEL HURWITZ
Cambridge, Massachusetts
Wood furniture
NEW YORK: East Hampton, Pritam & Eames;

PENNSYLVANIA: Philadelphia, Richard Kagan
Accepts commissions, allow 2 weeks to 4 months
$500 and up

STEPHEN HYER
Cambridge, Massachusetts
Metal tea kettles and silver objects
Contact the artist at: 107 Pinckney St., Boston, MA 02114
Accepts commissions, allow 1-3 months
Up to $1500

DIANE ITTER
Bloomington, Indiana
Fiber wall pieces and small-scale knotted works
ARIZONA: Scottsdale, The Hand and the Spirit;
CALIFORNIA: Los Angeles, Mandell Art Services;
NEW YORK: New York City, Heller; PENNSYLVANIA:
Philadelphia, Helen Drutt
Does not accept commissions
$700-900

SARA JAFFE
Berkeley, California
Wood furniture
CALIFORNIA: Berkeley, Zosaku; Palo Alto, Los Robles;
DISTRICT OF COLUMBIA: Sherley Koteen
Accepts commissions, allow 4-6 months
$350 and up

MICHAEL JAMES
Somerset Village, Massachusetts
Wall quilts
Contact the artist at: 258 Old Colony Avenue, Somerset
Village, MA 02726
Accepts unrestricted commissions only, allow 6 months
to a year
$1500-8500

MARGIE JERVIS & SUSIE KRASNICAN
Falls Church, Virginia
Non-functional cast glass
DISTRICT OF COLUMBIA: Sherley Koteen;
MICHIGAN: Lathrup Village, Habatat, NEW YORK:
New York City, Heller
Accept commissions, allow 4-6 months
$500-2100

JAMES JOHNSTON
New York, New York
Earthenware vases and wall plates
CALIFORNIA: Los Angeles, Craft and Folk Art
Museum; NEW YORK: New York City, Convergence;
PENNSYLVANIA: Philadelphia, The Works
Accepts commissions, allow 1-6 months
Production items, $25-60, commissioned murals,
$1000-15,000

KEN JUPITER
Ithaca, New York
Wood cutting boards, serving trays and boxes
NEW YORK: Ithaca, People's Pottery
Accepts commissions, allow 2 months
$14-5000

JONATHAN KAPLAN & JANET HULING
Bowmansville, Pennsylvania
Stoneware kitchen vessels and dinnerware
NEW YORK: Ithaca, People's Pottery; TENNESSEE:
  Nashville, American Artisan
Accept commissions for dinnerware only, allow 3-5
  months
$7-80

KAREN KARNES
West Danville, Vermont
Ceramic bowls, large covered jars and vases
NEW YORK: New York City, Hadler-Rodriguez
Accepts commissions, allow 3-6 months
$500-2000

TED KELLER
Union, Maine
Porcelain teapots and dinnerware
DISTRICT OF COLUMBIA: American Hand
Occasionally accepts commissions, allow 2-4 months
$5-250

JANET KELMAN
Royal Oak, Michigan
Blown and sandblasted glass bottles
CALIFORNIA: San Francisco, Light Opera; MICHIGAN:
  Lathrup Village, Habatat; NEW YORK: New York City,
  Heller
Accepts commissions, allow 1 month
Approximately $120

BILL KENDALL
Nashville, Tennessee
Wood cutting and serving boards and tables
CALIFORNIA: Berkeley, Zosaku; MASSACHUSETTS:
  Brookline, Marion-Ruth; NEW YORK: Rochester,
  Creator's Hands
Does not accept commissions
$15-250 for boards, $250-2500 for tables

JOEY KIRKPATRICK & FLORA MACE
Stanwood, Washington
Enamelled glass vessel forms
CALIFORNIA: Los Angeles, Ivor Kurland; San
  Francisco, Contemporary Artisans; MICHIGAN:
  Lathrup Village, Habatat; NEW YORK: New York City,
  Heller; WASHINGTON, Seattle, Foster/White

Accept commissions, time varies
$800-2000

LEWIS KNAUSS
Philadelphia, Pennsylvania
Fiber wall-hangings
PENNSYLVANIA: Philadelphia, Helen Drutt, TEXAS,
  San Antonio, Objects
Accepts commissions, allow 6 weeks to 6 months
$175 per square foot and up

KNOCK ON WOOD
Freeville, New York
Wood kitchen ware
CALIFORNIA: Santa Barbara, Ruth Walters; MAINE:
  Bar Harbor, Caleb's Sunrise; MARYLAND: Baltimore,
  Calico Cat; NEW YORK: East Hampton, Engel
  Pottery; VERMONT: Stowe, Stowe Pottery
Do not accept commissions
$3-300

JANUSZ KOZIKOWSKI
Nedanales, New Mexico
Woven tapestries
NEW MEXICO: Nedanales, Kozikowski Tapestry Studio;
  Santa Fe, Enthios
Accepts commissions, allow 6 weeks to 3 months
$300-1200 for works in editions; $2000-20,000 for
  unique works

SUSIE KRASNICAN & MARGIE JERVIS
Falls Church, Virginia
Non-functional glass
DISTRICT OF COLUMBIA: Sherley Koteen;
  MICHIGAN: Lathrup Village, Habatat, NEW YORK:
  New York City, Heller
Accept commissions, allow 4-6 months
$500-2100

FRAN KRAYNEK-PRINCE & NEIL PRINCE
Encinitas, California
Baskets
ARIZONA: Scottsdale, The Hand and the Spirit;
  CALIFORNIA: La Jolla, Gallery Eight; Santa Barbara,
  Elizabeth Fortner; HAWAII, Honolulu, Following Sea;
  NEW YORK: New York City, The Elements
Do not accept commissions
$60-1500

LOUISE KRUGER
New York, New York
Wood and bronze figures
NEW YORK: New York City, Condeso Lawler
Accepts commissions, allow 1-6 months
$1200-25,000

JON KUHN
Staunton, Virginia
Glass vessel forms
GEORGIA: Atlanta, Great American;
  MASSACHUSETTS: Boston, Signature; MICHIGAN:
  Lathrup Village, Habatat; NEW YORK: New York City,
  Heller; TEXAS: Dallas, Human Arts
Accepts commissions, allow 3 months
$600-6000

CURTIS K. LAFOLLETTE
Hudson, Massachusetts
Silver hollowware
MASSACHUSETTS: North Hatfield, Baracca
Accepts commissions, allow 3 months to a year
$500-12,000

RICH LANDERGREN
Bloomington, Indiana
Wood furniture and accessories
CALIFORNIA: Berkeley, Zosaku; ILLINOIS: Evanston,
  Mindscape; MASSACHUSETTS: Orleans, Artful
  Hand; NEW JERSEY: Haddonfield, By Hand; NEW
  YORK: Mamaroneck, Of Cabbages and Kings
Accepts commissions, allow 3 weeks to 6 months
$12-3000

SUSAN LANGE
East Stroudsburg, Pennsylvania
Handmade paper
DISTRICT OF COLUMBIA: Sherley Koteen;
  MICHIGAN: Birmingham, Carole Hooberman;
  PENNSYLVANIA: Philadelphia, The Works; TEXAS:
  Houston, Eve France
Accepts commissions, allow 2-6 months
$20-1000

TYRONE & JULIE LARSON
Bakersville, North Carolina
Ceramic ovenware, mixing bowls and canisters
DISTRICT OF COLUMBIA: American Hand;
  MICHIGAN: Detroit, Gallery of Contemporary Art;
  NEW YORK: New York City, Surroundings; NORTH
  CAROLINA: Bakersville, Larson Pottery Showroom
Do not accept commissions
$50-$450

SUSAN WEBB LEE
Oak Ridge, North Carolina
Quilts
NORTH CAROLINA: Greensboro, Green Hill
Accepts commissions, allow at least 6 weeks
$300-600

K. WILLIAM LEQUIER
Branford, Connecticut

Blown and sandblasted glass vessels
CALIFORNIA: Los Angeles, Del Mano; San Francisco,
 Compositions; FLORIDA: Palm Beach, Holsten;
 MASSACHUSETTS: Boston, Glass Veranda;
 MICHIGAN: Lathrup Village, Habatat;
 PENNSYLVANIA: Philadelphia, The Works
Does not accept commissions
$95-2000

MARK LINDQUIST
Henniken, New Hampshire
Turned wood vessel forms
ARIZONA: Scottsdale, The Hand and the Spirit;
 FLORIDA: Bay Harbor Island, Galerie 99; NEW
 YORK: New York City, The Elements;
 PENNSYLVANIA: Philadelphia, The Works;
 TEXAS: Dallas, Human Arts
Occasionally accepts commissions, allow at least 8
 months
$2000-8000

MELVIN LINDQUIST
Henniken, New Hampshire
Turned wood vessel forms
FLORIDA: Bay Harbor Island, Galerie 99; NEW YORK:
 New York City, The Elements; PENNSYLVANIA:
 Philadelphia, The Works; TEXAS: Dallas,
 Human Arts
Does not accept commissions
$150-4500

GREGORY LITSIOS
Pine Plains, New York
Iron tables, plant stands, chandeliers and candelabra
NEW YORK: Rochester, Contemporary Metalsmithing;
PENNSYLVANIA: Philadelphia, Sign of the Swan
Accepts commissions, time varies
$150-3000

HARVEY LITTLETON
Spruce Pines, North Carolina
Glass sculpture
CALIFORNIA: Los Angeles, Ivor Kurland; FLORIDA:
 Palm Beach, Holsten; MICHIGAN: Lathrup Village,
 Habatat; NEW YORK: New York City, Heller; TEXAS:
 Houston, Perception
Does not accept commissions
$1500-25,000

JOHN LITTLETON & KATHERINE VOGEL
Spruce Pines, North Carolina
Glass Sculpture
DISTRICT OF COLUMBIA: Sherley Koteen; NEW
 YORK: New York City, Heller; PENNSYLVANIA:
 Philadelphia, The Works; SOUTH CAROLINA: Hilton
 Head, Artistic Sass; WISCONSIN: Fish Creek,

Edgewood Orchard; Milwaukee, D. Erlien
Do not accept commissions
$550-1200

SUSAN LOFTIN
Atlanta, Georgia
Earthenware handbuilt and decorated vessels
DISTRICT OF COLUMBIA: American Hand; NEW
 YORK: New York City, The Elements; NORTH
 CAROLINA: Winston-Salem, Piedmont Craftsmen
Rarely accepts commissions
$200-1000

KARI LØNNING
Ridgefield, Connecticut
Reed baskets
CALIFORNIA: San Francisco, Cole-Wheatman
 Interiors; FLORIDA: Palm Beach, Holsten
Accepts commissions, allow 1-6 months
$168-700

PATRICK LOUGHRAN
New York, New York
Earthenware wall plates and dinnerware
NEW YORK: New York City, Convergence
Occasionally accepts commissions, allow 6-8 weeks
$35-600

SUSAN LYMAN
Provincetown, Massachusetts
Non-functional works in paper
MICHIGAN: Birmingham, Robert L. Kidd; NEW YORK:
 New York City, The Elements
Occasionally accepts commissions, allow 6 months to
 1 year
$500-2500

PHILLIP MABERRY
Garrison, New York
Porcelain plates, cups, bowls, picture frames and tiles
NEW YORK: New York City, Hadler-Rodriguez; TEXAS:
 Houston, Hadler-Rodriguez
Occasionally accepts commissions, allow 2 months
$175-1800

FLORA MACE & JOEY KIRKPATRICK
Stanwood, Washington
Enamelled glass vessel forms
CALIFORNIA: Los Angeles, Ivor Kurland; San
 Francisco, Contemporary Artisans; MICHIGAN:
 Lathrup Village, Habatat; NEW YORK: New York City,
 Heller; WASHINGTON: Seattle, Foster/White
Accept commissions, time varies
$800-2000

LINDA MACNEIL
Amesbury, Massachusetts
Metal and glass jewelry and hand mirrors
MICHIGAN: Lathrup Village, Habatat; NEW YORK:
 New York City, Heller
Accepts commissions, time varies
$500-2000

STEVE MADSEN
Albuquerque, New Mexico
Wood containers and furniture
CALIFORNIA: San Francisco, Compositions; NEW
 MEXICO: Albuquerque, Mariposa; PENNSYLVANIA:
 Philadelphia, Richard Kagan
Accepts commissions, allow 6 months to 1 year
$1000-10,000

RICHARD MAFONG
Dunwoody, Georgia
Metal, principally silver, containers and jewelry
NEW YORK: New York City, Fine Arts Acquisitions
Accepts commissions, allow 1 week to 1 month
$500-10,000

ANDREW MAGDANZ & SUSAN SHAPIRO
Rochester, New York   Cambridge, Massachusetts
Glass vase forms and perfume bottles
CALIFORNIA: San Francisco, Meyer, Breier, Weiss;
 MASSACHUSETTS: Boston, Glass Veranda;
 MICHIGAN: Lathrup Village, Habatat; NEW YORK:
 New York City, Heller; PENNSYLVANIA:
 Philadelphia, Helen Drutt
Accept commissions, allow 1-3 months
$70-4000

JAMES D. MAKINS
New York, New York
Porcelain dinnerware and vessel forms
DISTRICT OF COLUMBIA: American Hand; ILLINOIS:
 Chicago, Exhibit A; NEW YORK: New York City,
 Hadler-Rodriguez
Accepts commissions, allow about 5 months
$25-2500

SAM MALOOF
Alta Loma, California
Wood furniture
Contact the artist at: 9553 Highland Ave., Alta Loma,
 CA 91701
Accepts commissions, allow at least 1 year
$500 and up

ROBERT MARCH
Worcester, Massachusetts
Wood furniture
MASSACHUSETTS: Worcester, The Craft Center;

MICHIGAN: Detroit, Gallery of Contemporary Crafts;
NEW YORK: East Hampton, Pritam & Eames; New
York City, The Elements
Accepts commissions, allow 6 months
$500 and up

THOMAS R. MARKUSEN
Kendall, New York
Hollowware lamps and furniture of various metals and
wrought-iron work
CALIFORNIA: Ojai, Running Ridge; GEORGIA:
Atlanta, Signature Shop; ILLINOIS: Evanston,
Mindscape; MASSACHUSETTS: Cambridge, Ten
Arrow; NEW MEXICO: Santa Fe, Running Ridge;
NEW YORK: New York City, The Elements
Accepts commissions, allow 4-6 months
$50-12,000

LISA MARTIN
New York, New York
Baskets and wall pieces
CALIFORNIA: La Jolla, Gallery Eight; San Francisco,
Contemporary Artisans; MARYLAND: Baltimore,
Tomlinson Collection; MASSACHUSETTS: Newton,
Jubilation; PENNSYLVANIA: Philadelphia, Sign of
the Swan
Accepts commissions, allow 1 month
$10 and up for baskets; $200-500 for wall pieces

WENDY MARUYAMA
Smithville, Tennessee
Wood, glass and metal furniture, decorated with paint
and dye
GEORGIA: Atlanta, Form and Function; NEW YORK:
East Hampton, Pritam & Eames; New York City,
Convergence
Accepts commissions, allow 1-6 months
$300-3000

STEVEN MASLACH
Greenbrae, California
Glass stemware, bowls, lights and non-functional vessels
CALIFORNIA: La Jolla, Gallery Eight; San Francisco,
Contemporary Artisans; MICHIGAN: Lathrup Village,
Habatat; NEW YORK: New York City, Gallery 10,
Heller; PENNSYLVANIA: Philadelphia, The Works
Accepts commissions, allow 8-10 weeks
$10-750

RORY MCCARTHY
Tucson, Arizona
Wood furniture
Contact the artist at: 385 N. Meyer Ave., Tucson, AZ
85701
Accepts commissions, allow 6-12 months
$2000-25,000

THOMAS W. MCCLELLAND
Boston, Massachusetts
Functional and non-functional metalwork
Contact the artist at: 105 Pinckney St., Boston, MA
02114
Accepts commissions, allow 2-6 weeks
$400-3500

SCOTT MCDOWELL
New York, New York
Hand-painted porcelain dinnerware
CALIFORNIA: Los Angeles, Craft and Folk Art
Museum; NEW YORK: New York City, Convergence;
TEXAS: Dallas, Human Arts
Occasionally accepts commissions, allow 3-4 months
$25-150

JUDY KENSLEY MCKIE
Cambridge, Massachusetts
Wood furniture
DISTRICT OF COLUMBIA: Sherley Koteen;
MASSACHUSETTS: Cambridge, Van Buren-
Brazelton-Cutting; NEW YORK: New York City, The
Elements
Accepts commissions, allow at least 1 year
$1500-5000

JOHN W. MCNAUGHTON
Evansville, Indiana
Wood tables
INDIANA: Indianapolis, Editions, Ltd.; MICHIGAN:
Birmingham, Carole Hooberman; NEW YORK: New
York City, Workbench
Accepts commissions, allow 6-8 weeks
$1000-4000

JOHN MCQUEEN
Alfred, New York
Non-functional basketry
NEW YORK: New York City, Hadler-Rodriguez
Does not accept commissions
Prices not available

NANCEE MEEKER
Rhinecliff, New York
Raku and pit-fired ceramic vases and lamp bases
DISTRICT OF COLUMBIA: Jackie Chalkley;
MASSACHUSETTS: Brookline, Marion-Ruth;
PENNSYLVANIA: Philadelphia, The Works
Does not accept commissions
$20-450

BRAD MILLER
Snowmass Village, Colorado
Non-functional ceramics
CALIFORNIA: Los Angeles, Craft and Folk Art

Museum; Santa Barbara, Elizabeth Fortner;
COLORADO: Denver, Sebastian Moore; OREGON:
Portland, Contemporary Crafts
Accepts commissions, allow at least 6 weeks
$100-1500

NORMA MINKOWITZ
Westport, Connecticut
Crocheted and knitted wearable art and soft furniture
FLORIDA: South Miami, Ophelia; MASSACHUSETTS:
Cambridge, Mobilia; NEW YORK: New York City, Julie
Accepts commissions, allow 1-3 months
$200-4000

MINEO MIZUNO
Los Angeles, California
Porcelain dinnerware and non-functional objects
CALIFORNIA: Los Angeles, Janus; DISTRICT OF
COLUMBIA: American Hand
Accepts commissions, allow about 6 weeks
$100-1800

C. LEIGH MORRELL
Brattleboro, Vermont
Metal knives, fireplace sets and chandeliers, principally
of iron and steel
NEW HAMPSHIRE: Concord, League of New
Hampshire Craftsmen; VERMONT: Middlebury, Frog
Hollow
Accepts commissions, allow 6-8 weeks
$5-400

CAROLYN DIAN MORRIS
Newport, Rhode Island
Metal vessels and cosmetic brushes
DISTRICT OF COLUMBIA: Smull's; MARYLAND:
Baltimore, Tomlinson Collection; MICHIGAN:
Detroit, Gallery of Contemporary Crafts; NEBRASKA:
Omaha, Craftsmen's; NEW JERSEY: Layton, Peter's
Valley; NEW YORK: New York City, The Elements;
NORTH CAROLINA: Winston-Salem, SECCA;
TEXAS: Dallas, Human Arts
Accepts commissions, allow 4-6 months
$50-650

WILLIAM MORRIS
Carmel, California
Sculptural glass
CALIFORNIA: Los Angeles, Ivor Kurland; ILLINOIS:
Chicago, Betsy Rosenfield; MICHIGAN: Lathrup
Village, Habatat; NEW YORK: New York City, Heller;
WASHINGTON: Seattle, Foster/White
Accepts commissions, time varies
$1000-4000

ED MOULTHROP
Atlanta, Georgia
Turned wood vessel forms
ARIZONA: Scottsdale, The Hand and the Spirit;
 GEORGIA: Atlanta, Signature Shop; HAWAII:
 Honolulu, Following Sea; NEW YORK: New York City,
 The Elements
Does not accept commissions
$200-5000

GINA MOWRY
Binghamton, New York
Copper and silver objects, including omelet pans, ladles
 and letter openers
NEW YORK: Binghamton, The Goldsmith
Accepts commissions, allow 6-8 weeks
$150 and up

JAN MYERS
Minneapolis, Minnesota
Hand-dyed quilts
GEORGIA: Atlanta, Image South; ILLINOIS: Evanston,
 Mindscape; MINNESOTA: Minneapolis, Textile Arts
 Alliance; NEW YORK: Southampton, Gayle Willson;
 PENNSYLVANIA: Philadelphia, Sign of the Swan
Accepts commissions, allow 6-8 months
$500 and up

JOEL PHILIP MYERS
Normal, Illinois
Non-functional glass vessels
FLORIDA: Palm Beach, Holsten; ILLINOIS: Chicago,
 Betsy Rosenfield; MICHIGAN: Lathrup Village,
 Habatat; MISSOURI: St. Louis, B.Z. Wagman; NEW
 YORK: New York City, Heller
Does not accept commissions
$3000-5000

RAGNAR DIXON NAESS
Brooklyn, New York
Functional wheel-thrown stoneware vessels
MASSACHUSETTS: Cambridge, Ten Arrow; NEW
 YORK: Brooklyn, Clay Pot; New York City,
 Surroundings; VIRGINIA: Alexandria, Full Circle
Accepts commissions, allow 2-4 months
$10-450

CHARLES B. NALLE
Trenton, New Jersey
Ceramic tableware
ILLINOIS: Chicago, Randolph Street; MICHIGAN:
 Birmingham, Carole Hooberman; NEW YORK: New
 York City, The Elements
Does not accept commissions
$10-60

DAVID NELSON
Weaverville, North Carolina
Stoneware and porcelain teapots, platters and covered
 vessels
DISTRICT OF COLUMBIA: American Hand; NEW
 YORK: New York City, Surroundings; NORTH
 CAROLINA: Asheville, New Morning;
 PENNSYLVANIA: Philadelphia, The Works
Accepts commissions, allow 3 months
$30-450

RICHARD SCOTT NEWMAN
Rochester, New York
Wood furniture
NEW YORK: East Hampton, Pritam & Eames;
 PENNSYLVANIA: Philadelphia, Richard Kagan
Accepts commissions, time varies
$1000 and up

GARY NOFFKE
Farmington, Georgia
Metal cooking utensils
Contact the artist at: Route 1, Box 178, Farmington, GA
 30638
Accepts commissions, time varies
$100-70,000

SUSAN R. NOLAND
Des Moines, Iowa
Gold and silver fine utensils
Contact the artist at: 902 42nd St., Des Moines, IA
 50312
Accepts commissions, allow 2-3 months
$250-5000

SHEILA O'HARA
Oakland, California
Tapestries
NEW YORK: New York City, Modern Master Tapestries
Accepts commissions, allow at least 2 months
$5,000 and up ($150-$200 per square foot)

KOMELIA HONGJA OKIM
Rockville, Maryland
Metal, primarily silver, sculptural jewelry and
 hollowware
Contact the artist at: 722 Anderson Ave., Rockville, MD
 20850
Accepts commissions, allow 1-2 months
$150-3000

JERE OSGOOD
Wilton, New Hampshire
Wood furniture
NEW YORK: East Hampton, Pritam & Eames; New York
 City, Workbench; PENNSYLVANIA: Philadelphia,

Richard Kagan
Accepts commissions, allow 6 months to 1 year
$1000-7000

RUDE OSOLNIK
Berea, Kentucky
Turned wood lamps, candlesticks and vessels
KENTUCKY: Berea, Benchmark; NORTH CAROLINA:
 Asheville, Folk Art Center
Accepts commissions, allow 3-4 months
$10-1000

ALBERT PALEY
Rochester, New York
Forged iron tables, candelabra, gates and architectural
 work
DISTRICT OF COLUMBIA: Fendrick
Accepts commissions, allow several months to 1 year
$4500 and up

WILLIAM PATRICK
Arlington, Vermont
Wood rolling pins, plates, bowls, boards, wall pieces
HAWAII: Honolulu, Following Sea; NEW YORK: New
 York City, The Elements; Scarsdale, The Craftsman's
Accepts commissions, allow up to 2 months
$20-600

PAM PATRIE
Portland, Oregon
Tapestry
CALIFORNIA: San Francisco, Allrich; OREGON:
 Portland, Contemporary Crafts, Fountain, Patrie
 Tapestries; VIRGINIA: Arlington, Elizabeth Michael,
 consultant
Accepts commissions, allow at least 2 months
$100 per square foot

JOAN PATTON
New Lebanon, New York
Baskets
CONNECTICUT: New Milford, The Silo; NEW JERSEY:
 Montclair, Dexterity, Ltd. NEW YORK: Huntington,
 Basket; Woodstock, Gilded Carriage;
 PENNSYLVANIA: Spring House, Artisans Three
Accepts commissions, allow 6-8 weeks
$35-375

RONALD HAYS PEARSON
Deer Isle, Maine
Jewelry and home accessories in all metals
ARIZONA: Scottsdale, The Hand and the Spirit;
 DISTRICT OF COLUMBIA: Sherley Koteen;
 MASSACHUSETTS: Boston, Signature; MICHIGAN:
 Birmingham, Little; NEW YORK: New York City, The
 Elements; Rochester, Memorial Art Gallery;

PENNSYLVANIA: Philadelphia, Sign of the Swan
Accepts commissions, allow 1-6 months
$11-10,000

MARK PEISER
Penland, North Carolina
Glass sculpture
MICHIGAN: Lathrup Village, Habatat; NEW YORK:
New York City, Heller
Does not accept commissions
$1000-15,000

RINA PELEG
New York, New York
Non-functional ceramics
GEORGIA: Atlanta, Form and Function; NEW YORK:
Buffalo, Nina Freudenheim
Accepts commissions, allow 1-2 months
$600-5000

TIMOTHY S. PHILBRICK
Narragansett, Rhode Island
Wood furniture
NEW YORK: East Hampton, Pritam & Eames;
PENNSYLVANIA: Philadelphia, Richard Kagan
Accepts commissions, allow 2½ years
$1500 and up

TODD PIKER
Cornwall Bridge, Connecticut
Stoneware serving pieces, dinnerware, large urns
CONNECTICUT: Cornwall Bridge, Cornwall Bridge
Pottery; NEW YORK: New Paltz, Handmade
Accepts commissions, allow 6 weeks to 6 months
$5-1000

DONNA POLSENO
Floyd, Virginia
Stoneware vessels, containers and vase forms
DISTRICT OF COLUMBIA: American Hand;
MICHIGAN: Detroit, Gallery of Contemporary Crafts;
NEW YORK: New York City, The Elements
Does not accept commissions
$10-100

SALLY BOWEN PRANGE
Chapel Hill, North Carolina
Porcelain vessel forms
NEW YORK: New York City, The Elements; NORTH
CAROLINA: Winston-Salem, Piedmont Craftsmen
Accepts commissions, allow 3 months
$150-800

NEIL PRINCE & FRAN KRAYNEK-PRINCE
Encinitas, California
Baskets

ARIZONA: Scottsdale, The Hand and the Spirit;
CALIFORNIA: La Jolla, Gallery Eight; Santa Barbara,
Elizabeth Fortner; HAWAII: Honolulu, Following Sea;
NEW YORK: New York City, The Elements
Do not accept commissions
$60-1500

RON PROPST
Winston-Salem, North Carolina
Flameware skillets, butter warmers and casseroles
NORTH CAROLINA: Asheville, New Morning;
Winston-Salem, Piedmont Craftsmen; TENNESSEE:
Chattanooga, Plum Nelly; Nashville, American
Artisan
Accepts commissions, allow about 6 weeks
$15-70

ELSA RADY
Venice, California
Hand-thrown, hand-carved porcelain vessel forms
CALIFORNIA: Los Angeles, Janus; San Francisco,
Quay; MASSACHUSETTS: Boston, Impressions; NEW
YORK: New York City, Max Protech; TEXAS: Dallas,
Mattingly-Baker
Does not accept commissions
$900-1800

JON ERIC RIIS
Dunwoody, Georgia
Tapestry
Contact the artist at: 1309 Valley View Rd., Dunwoody,
GA 30338
Accepts commissions, allow at least 2 months
$50 per square foot and up

MARY ANNE ROEHM
Rochester, New York
Wheel-thrown and hand-built porcelain bowls
ARIZONA: Scottsdale, The Hand and the Spirit;
CONNECTICUT: Greenwich, The Elements;
DISTRICT OF COLUMBIA: Jackie Chalkley; HAWAII:
Honolulu, Following Sea; NEW YORK: New York City,
Convergence; PENNSYLVANIA: Philadelphia, The
Works
Accepts commissions, allow 6-10 weeks
$15-300

DAVID R. ROGERS
Coleman Falls, Virginia
Knives and wood furniture
Contact the artist at: Rt. 1, Box 432B, Coleman Falls,
VA 24536
Accepts commissions, time varies
$100-700 for knives; $250-6000 for furniture

HAROLD ROGOVIN
Califon, New Jersey
Metal, primarily silver, hollowware
Contact the artist at: P.O. Box 251, Califon, NJ 07830
Accepts commissions, allow 6-8 weeks
$350-25,000

HARVEY SADOW, JR.
Comus, Maryland
Wheel-thrown, raku-fired ceramic vessels
DISTRICT OF COLUMBIA: Sherley Koteen; FLORIDA:
Palm Beach, Holsten; MASSACHUSETTS:
Stockbridge, Holsten
Does not accept commissions
$500-3000

HAP SAKWA
Los Osos, California
Turned and carved wood vessels
CALIFORNIA: Los Angeles, Craft and Folk Art
Museum, Del Mano; NEW YORK: New York City,
Incorporated, Surroundings; PENNSYLVANIA:
Philadelphia, The Works
Accepts commissions, allow up to 9 months
$50-2000

JUDITH SALOMON
Cleveland Heights, Ohio
Functional hand-built whiteware pots
ARIZONA: Scottsdale, The Hand and the Spirit;
CALIFORNIA: Los Angeles, Garth Clark;
DISTRICT OF COLUMBIA: American Hand; OHIO:
Cleveland, DBR
Accepts commissions, allow several months
$50-1000

ADRIAN SAXE
Los Angeles, California
Porcelain vessels
CALIFORNIA: Los Angeles, Garth Clark; DISTRICT OF
COLUMBIA: American Hand
Does not accept commissions
$150-2000

CYNTHIA SCHIRA
Lawrence, Kansas
Woven wall hangings
NEW YORK: New York City, Hadler-Rodriguez;
PENNSYLVANIA: Philadelphia, Helen Drutt
Accepts commissions, time varies
$175 per square foot and up

ELLEN SCHON
Watertown, Massachusetts
Raku-fired stoneware vessel forms
DISTRICT OF COLUMBIA: Jackie Chalkley; Sherley

Koteen; MASSACHUSETTS: Chestnut Hill, Quadrum;
NEW YORK: Scarsdale, The Craftsman's;
PENNSYLVANIA: Philadelphia, Sign of the Swan
Accepts commissions, allow at least a month
$24-350

SHERRY SCHREIBER
New York, New York
Tapestry
NEW YORK: New York City, Incorporated, Modern
Master Tapestries, Pindar
Accepts commissions, allow at least 6 weeks
$1850 and up

JUNE SCHWARCZ
Sausalito, California
Enamelling on copper bowls and wall pieces
CALIFORNIA: San Francisco, Meyer, Breier, Weiss,
Contemporary Artisans; GEORGIA: Atlanta, Great
American
Occasionally accepts commissions, allow 6 weeks
$400-1200

WARREN SEELIG
Elkins Park, Pennsylvania
Fiber wall hangings
CALIFORNIA: San Francisco, Miller-Brown; NEW
YORK: New York City, Hadler-Rodriguez;
PENNSYLVANIA: Philadelphia, Helen Drutt
Accepts commissions, allow 6-8 months
$600-4000

NANCY SELVIN
Berkeley, California
Earthenware teabowls
ARIZONA: Scottsdale, The Hand and the Spirit;
CALIFORNIA: Los Angeles, Jacqueline Anhalt
Does not accept commissions
$250-800

SYLVIA SEVENTY
Healdsburg, California
Paper vessel forms
CALIFORNIA: San Francisco, Allrich; NEW YORK:
New York City, The Elements; WASHINGTON:
Seattle, Traver Sutton
Accepts commissions, allow at least 2 months
$100-550

MARTY & FREDI SHAPIRO
Saugerties, New York
Wood furniture and desk accessories
FLORIDA: Miami, Twenty-four Collection;
MARYLAND: Baltimore, Tomlinson Collection; NEW
JERSEY: Montclair, Dexterity, Ltd.; NEW YORK: New
York City, Gallery 10

Accept commissions, allow 1-3 months
$250-2500

ANNE SHATTUCK
Kingston, New York
Salt-glazed stoneware and porcelain functional vessels
CALIFORNIA: Santa Barbara, Elizabeth Fortner;
MASSACHUSETTS: Brookline, Marion-Ruth;
NEBRASKA: Omaha, Craftsmen's; NEW YORK:
Brooklyn, Clay Pot; Kingston, Shattuck Pottery; New
York City, Surroundings; PENNSYLVANIA:
Pittsburgh, Clay Place
Accepts commissions, allow up to 9 months
$10-500

KAETE BRITTIN SHAW
High Falls, New York
Porcelain teapots
NEW YORK: New York City, Convergence, Julie
Accepts commissions, allow 3 months
$175-500

CAROL SHAW-SUTTON
Fullerton, California
Painted willow constructions
CALIFORNIA: Los Angeles, Mandell; San Francisco,
Meyer, Breier, Weiss; NEW YORK: New York City,
The Elements
Accepts commissions, allow 1-2 months
$500-2500

PETER SHIRE
Los Angeles, California
Non-functional teapots
CALIFORNIA: Los Angeles, Janus
Does not accept commissions
$500-1800

HELEN SHIRK
San Diego, California
Silver, copper and brass jewelry and hollowware
CALIFORNIA: Los Angeles, Janus; PENNSYLVANIA:
Philadelphia, Helen Drutt
Accepts commissions, time varies
$400-3500

SALLY URBAN SILBERBERG
Plainfield, Massachusetts
Wheel-thrown porcelain vessels
FLORIDA: Palm Beach, Holsten; MARYLAND:
Baltimore, Craft Concepts; NEW YORK: Brooklyn,
Clay Pot
Accepts commissions, allow 2-3 months
$100-300

JOSH SIMPSON
Shelburne Falls, Massachusetts
Glass goblets, platters and vases
CALIFORNIA: Carmel, Walter White; HAWAII:
Honolulu, Following Sea; NEW YORK: Corning,
Museum of Glass; New York City, Jorice
Accepts commissions, allow 1 month to more than
1 year
$30-3000

TOMMY SIMPSON
Washington, Connecticut
Painted or naturally finished wood furniture
NEW YORK: Hartsdale, Alan Brown; New York City,
Theo Portnoy
Accepts commissions, allow 6 months to 1 year
$200-20,000

PAUL SOLDNER
Aspen, Colorado
Raku-fired porcelain
MASSACHUSETTS: Boston, Segal; NEW YORK: New
York City, The Elements
Does not accept commissions
$500-3000

DOUGLAS STEAKLEY
Carmel Valley, California
Metal, principally copper, hollowware and jewelry
CALIFORNIA: Carmel, Concepts
Accepts commissions, allow 2-3 months
$500-2000

ETHEL STEIN
Croton-on-Hudson, New York
Wall hangings
NEW YORK: New York City, Modern Masters Tapestries
Accepts commissions, time varies
$500-5000

SETH L. STEM
Marblehead, Massachusetts
Wood and leather furniture
MASSACHUSETTS: Boston, Society of Arts and Crafts
Accepts commissions, allow 6 months to 1 year
$500-5000

ALAN STIRT
Enosburg Falls, Vermont
Turned wood bowls and platters
ARIZONA: Scottsdale, The Hand and the Spirit;
MASSACHUSETTS: Cambridge, Ten Arrow; NEW
YORK: New York City, The Elements; VERMONT:
Middlebury, Frog Hollow
Accepts commissions, allow 2-3 months
$50-600

BOB STOCKSDALE
Berkeley, California
Wood bowls, plates and trays
Contact the artist at: 2145 Oregon St., Berkeley, CA 94705
Does not accept commissions
$25-1000

RANDY STRONG
Berkeley, California
Glass stemware
CALIFORNIA: San Francisco, De Young Museum Shop;
Santa Barbara, Elizabeth Fortner; NEW YORK:
Corning, Museum of Glass
Occasionally accepts commissions, allow 3 weeks
$58-1000

PAM STUDSTILL
San Antonio, Texas
Quilts
PENNSYLVANIA: Philadelphia, Helen Drutt
Accepts commissions, time varies
$1500-3000

MARA SUPERIOR
Northampton, Massachusetts
Porcelain dinnerware and tea sets
MASSACHUSETTS: Nantucket, Nantucket Loom;
Northampton, Pinch Pottery; Orleans, Artful Hand
Accepts commissions, time varies
$20-500

TOSHIKO TAKAEZU
Quakertown, New Jersey
Non-functional porcelain and stoneware
Contact the artist at: Quakertown, NJ 08868
Accepts commissions, allow up to 1 year
For price range, contact the artist

BYRON TEMPLE
Lambertville, New Jersey
Stoneware for table use, salt and sagger fired porcelain
lidded jars
MICHIGAN: Detroit, Gallery of Contemporary Craft;
PENNSYLVANIA: Philadelphia, Helen Drutt
Does not accept commissions
$10-350

NEIL TETKOWSKI
Granville, Ohio
Earthenware vessels
CALIFORNIA: Los Angeles, Garth Clark; San
Francisco, Meyer, Breier, Weiss; Santa Barbara,
Elizabeth Fortner; NEW YORK: New York City,
The Elements
Accepts commissions, time varies
$500-2000

LAURIE L. THAL
Jackson, Wyoming
Glass vases, bowls, perfume bottles, goblets, sculpture
and masks
CALIFORNIA: Los Angeles, Craft and Folk Art
Museum; DISTRICT OF COLUMBIA: Jackie Chalkley;
OHIO: Toledo, Museum of Art; TEXAS: Dallas,
Human Arts; WYOMING: Jackson, Artwest
Accepts commissions, allow at least 1-3 months
$75-600 for blown glass vessels; $600-1200 for cast glass
sculptural pieces

BARBARA TISO
New York, New York
Porcelain vessels, lamps and sculpture
MICHIGAN: Detroit, Gallery of Contemporary Crafts;
NEW JERSEY: Scotch Plains, Beautiful Things; NEW
YORK: New York City, Hadler-Rodriguez;
PENNSYLVANIA: Elkins Park, Gallery 500;
Philadelphia, Sign of the Swan
Accepts commissions, time varies
$50-300 for bowls; $200-500 for sculpture; $400-800 for
lamps

BOB TROTMAN
Casar, North Carolina
Wood furniture
DISTRICT OF COLUMBIA: Sherley Koteen; NORTH
CAROLINA: Winston-Salem, Piedmont Craftsmen
Occasionally accepts commissions, allow 1 year
$400-3000

LYNN TURNER
Berkeley, California
Porcelain tea sets, cruets, bud vases
ARIZONA: Scottsdale, The Hand and the Spirit;
DISTRICT OF COLUMBIA: American Hand; HAWAII:
Honolulu, Following Sea; NEW YORK: New York City,
The Elements
Does not accept commissions
$10-300

TOM TURNER
Medina, Ohio
Wheel-thrown porcelain jars and vases
ARIZONA: Scottsdale, The Hand and the Spirit;
CALIFORNIA: La Jolla, Gallery Eight; DISTRICT OF
COLUMBIA: American hand
Does not accept commissions
$30-400

KATHERINE VOGEL & JOHN LITTLETON
Spruce Pines, North Carolina
Glass Sculpture
DISTRICT OF COLUMBIA: Sherley Koteen; NEW
YORK: New York City, Heller; PENNSYLVANIA:

Philadelphia, Works; SOUTH CAROLINA: Hilton
Head, Artistic Sass; WISCONSIN: Fish Creek,
Edgewood Orchard; Milwaukee, D. Erlien
Do not accept commissions
$550-1200

WENDA F. VON WEISE
Cleveland Heights, Ohio
Photo-silkscreened quilts and quilted wall hangings
OHIO: Cleveland, Novart, New Gallery
Accepts commissions, allow 6 weeks
$1000 and up

TACHA VOSBURGH
South Portland, Maine
Stoneware serving pieces, dinnerware and lamps
MASSACHUSETTS: Brewster, The Spectrum
Does not accept commissions
$11-125

MARTHA WETHERBEE
Sanbornton, New Hampshire
Splint baskets
MASSACHUSETTS: Deerfield, Old Deerfield Museum
Shop; Pittsfield, Hancock Shaker Village; NEW
HAMPSHIRE: Concord, Concord Arts and Crafts
Accepts commissions, allow 2 months to 1 year
$45-500

WALTER WHITE
Seattle, Washington
Pewter and silver flatware and serving pieces, and
copper and brass weathervanes
DISTRICT OF COLUMBIA: Fendrick
Accepts commissions, time varies
$20-30,000

JOHN WHITEHEAD
Portland, Oregon
Wood bowls, dishes and utensils
GEORGIA: Atlanta, Great American; HAWAII:
Honolulu, Following Sea; OREGON: Portland,
Contemporary Crafts, Oregon School of Arts
and Crafts
Accepts commissions, allow 1-6 months
$100-500

TRENT WHITINGTON
Lafayette, California
Wood furniture
NEW YORK: New York City, Workbench
Accepts commissions, time varies
$450 and up

LAURA WILENSKY
Kingston, New York

Porcelain perfume bottles, containers and wall pieces
ARIZONA: Scottsdale, The Hand and the Spirit;
 CALIFORNIA: Santa Barbara, Elizabeth Fortner;
NEW YORK: New York City, The Elements;
Woodstock, Clouds
Accepts commissions, allow 2 months
$200-1800

DON WILLIAMS
Nottingham, New Hampshire
Porcelain and stoneware pitchers, casseroles and
 storage jars
MASSACHUSETTS: Wellfleet, Secrest; OHIO:
 Cincinnati, Vertu; PENNSYLVANIA: Philadelphia,
 Sign of the Swan
Accepts commissions, allow 8 weeks
$20-150

FRED WOELL
Deer Isle, Maine
Functional and non-functional metalwork
Contact the artist at: 156 Old Ferry Rd., Deer Isle,
 ME 04627

Accepts commissions, allow at least several months
$150-1000

BETTY WOODMAN
New York, New York
Ceramic vessels and architectural ceramics
CALIFORNIA: Los Angeles, Garth Clark; NEW YORK:
 New York City, Hadler-Rodriguez; PENNSYLVANIA:
 Philadelphia, Helen Drutt
Accepts commissions, time varies
$500-5000

JAN YATSKO
Lancaster, Pennsylvania
Coiled baskets
CALIFORNIA: San Francisco, Contemporary Artisans;
 DISTRICT OF COLUMBIA: Sherley Koteen; NEW
 YORK: White Plains, Westlake; PENNSYLVANIA:
 Philadelphia, The Works
Accepts commissions, allow 1-6 months
$250-550

KATHI YOKUM
Putnam, Connecticut

Ceramic tile murals
Contact the artist at: RR1, Park St., Putnam, CT 06260
Accepts commissions, allow 2 months to 1 year
$250-25,000

JAN ZANDHUIS
Galena, Maryland
Neon sculpture and glass stemware
GEORGIA: Atlanta, Signature; OHIO: Cleveland, Sylvia
 Ullman; MARYLAND: Baltimore, Tomlinson;
 MASSACHUSETTS: Cambridge, Ten Arrow; NEW
 YORK: New York City, The Elements
Accepts commissions, allow up to 6 months
$25-55 for goblets; $700-1800 for neon sculpture

EDWARD ZUCCA
Putnam, Connecticut
Wood furniture
NEW YORK: East Hampton, Pritam & Eames; New York
 City, Workbench; PENNSYLVANIA: Philadelphia,
 Richard Kagan
Accepts commissions, allow up to 8 months
$500 and up

GALLERIES

This appendix lists all of the galleries mentioned in the Directory of Craftsmen along with other important galleries worth visiting: alphabetically, by *state, city, and gallery. With time, addresses and names do change, so a compilation of this sort cannot, despite all efforts, be absolutely precise.*

ALABAMA

BIRMINGHAM

Maralyn Wilson Gallery
2010 Cahaba Rd.
Birmingham, AL 35223
205-879-0582

The Side Show
2005 11th Ave. S.
Birmingham, AL 35205
205-933-1807

ARIZONA

PHOENIX

Lambert Miller Gallery
24 N. Second St.
Phoenix, AZ 85004
602-271-4329

SCOTTSDALE

Beyond Horizons
7162 E. Stetson Drive
Scottsdale, AZ 85251
602-994-3359

The Hand and the Spirit Crafts
Gallery, Inc.
4222 N. Marshall Way
Scottsdale, AZ 85251
602-949-1262

Kate Eliot
PO Box 5447
Scottsdale, AZ 85261

Mind's Eye Crafts
4200 N. Marshall Way
Scottsdale, AZ 85251
602-941-2494

CALIFORNIA

BERKELEY

The Gift Horse
2926 Domingo Ave.
Berkeley, CA 94705
415-843-7264

Zosaku
2110-B Vine St.
Berkeley, CA 94709
415-549-3373

BEVERLY HILLS

Louis Newman Galleries
322 N. Beverly Drive
Beverly Hills, CA 90210
213-278-6311

CAPITOLA VILLAGE

Camelean Designs
107 Capitola Ave.
Capitola Village, CA 95010
408-476-7001

CARMEL

Concepts Gallery
6th and Mission Sts.
Carmel, CA 93921
408-624-0661

Walter/White Fine Arts
7th and San Carlos Sts.
Carmel, CA 93921
408-624-4957

DAVENPORT

David Boye Knives
17 San Vincente St.
Davenport, CA 95017
408-426-6046

LA JOLLA

Gallery Eight
7464 Girard Ave.
La Jolla, CA 92037
714-454-9781

LOS ANGELES

The Craft and Folk Art
Museum
5814 Wilshire Blvd.
Los Angeles, CA 90036
213-937-5544

Del Mano Gallery
11981 San Vicente Blvd.
Los Angeles, CA 90049
213-476-8508

Garth Clark Gallery
5820 Wilshire Blvd.
Los Angeles, CA 90036
213-939-2189

Ivor Kurland Gallery
8742A Melrose Ave.
Los Angeles, CA 90069
213-659-7098

Jacqueline Anhalt Gallery
748½ N. La Cienaga Blvd.
Los Angeles, CA 90069
213-657-4038

Janus Gallery
800 Melrose Ave.
Los Angeles, CA 90046
213-658-6084

Mandell Art Services
(consultant)
400 S. Westgate Ave.
Los Angeles, CA 90049
213-471-2733

Marcia Rodell Gallery
11714 San Vicente Blvd.
Los Angeles, CA 90049
213-820-8972

MENDOCINO

Gallery Fair
Kasten and Ukiah Sts.
Mendocino, CA 95460
707-937-5121

MILL VALLEY

Fireworks
4 El Paso
Mill Valley, CA 94941
707-795-8493

OJAI

Running Ridge Gallery
310 E. Ojai Ave.
Ojai, CA 93023
805-646-1525

PALO ALTO

Los Robles Galleries
167 Hamilton Ave.
Palo Alto, CA 94301
415-327-3838

SAN ANSELMO

The Great Acorn Co. Inc.
800 San Anselmo Ave.
San Anselmo, CA 94960
415-454-2990

SAN FRANCISCO

The Allrich Gallery
251 Post St.
San Francisco, CA 94108
415-398-8896

Braunstein Gallery
254 Sutter St.
San Francisco, CA 94108
415-392-5532

Cole-Wheatman Interiors
1933 Union St.
San Francisco, CA 94123
415-346-8300

Compositions
2801 Leavenworth St.
San Francisco, CA 94133
415-441-0629

Contemporary Artisans
Gallery
530 Bush St.
San Francisco, CA 94108
415-981-4443

The De Young Museum Shop
Golden Gate Park
San Francisco, CA 94118
415-558-2887

Extravagance
The Showplace   299
2 Henry Adams St.
San Francisco, CA 94103
415-864-2237

Light Opera
102 Ghirardelli Square
San Francisco, CA 94109
415-775-7665

Made In USA
2801 Leavenworth St.
San Francisco, CA 94133
415-885-4030

Meyer, Breier, Weiss
Fort Mason Center Bldg. A
San Francisco, CA 94123
415-928-2119

Miller-Brown Gallery
55 Hayes St.
San Francisco, CA 94102
415-861-2028

The Quay Gallery
254 Sutter St.
San Francisco, CA 94108
415-421-1958

Union Street Goldsmiths
1763 Union St.
San Francisco, CA 94123
415-776-8048

SANTA BARBARA

Elizabeth Fortner Gallery
1114 State St.
Santa Barbara, CA 93101
805-966-2613

Ruth Walters of Santa Barbara
916C State St.
Santa Barbara, CA 93101
805-963-0827

SANTA MONICA

A Singular Place
2718 Main St.
Santa Monica, CA 90405
213-399-1018

COLORADO

ASPEN

Gallery 10, Inc.
525 East Cooper Ave.
Aspen, CO 81611
303-925-9044

AURORA

James Robischon-Blue Door
II Gallery
3150-G South Peoria St.
Aurora, CO 80014
303-695-0123

DENVER

Panache
1071 Old South Gaylord St.
Denver, CO 80209
303-778-0519

The Sebastian Moore Gallery
1411 Market St.
Denver, CO 80202
303-534-5659

VAIL

A Place on Earth
568 W. Lionshead Mall
Vail, CO 81657
303-476-1118

CONNECTICUT

BROOKFIELD

Brookfield Craft Center
(April-December)
Whistonier Rd.

Brookfield, CT 06804
203-775-1040

GREENWICH

The Elements Gallery
14 Liberty Way
Greenwich, CT 06830
203-661-0014

GUILFORD

Guilford Handcrafts Center
Rt. 77 Box 221
Guilford, CT 06437
203-453-5947

NEW HAVEN

Creative Arts Workshop
80 Audubon St.
New Haven, CT 06511
203-562-4927

NEW MILFORD

The Silo
Hunt Hill Farm
Upland Rd.
New Milford, CT 06776
203-355-0300

DELAWARE

REHOBETH BEACH

Tide Line Gallery
41 Rehobeth Ave.
Rehobeth Beach, DE 19971
302-227-4444

WILMINGTON

Artisans III
7125 Market Street Mall
Wilmington, DE 19801
302-656-7370

Delaware Art Museum
2301 Kentmere Pkwy.
Wilmington, DE 19806
302-571-9590

DISTRICT OF COLUMBIA

The American Hand
2906 M St. NW
Washington, DC 20007
202-965-3273

Anton Gallery
415 E. Capitol St. SE
Washington, DC 20003
202-546-7330

Appalachian Spring
1655 Wisconsin Ave. NW
Washington, DC 20007
202-337-5780

Craftsmen of Chelsea Court
1311 Connecticut Ave. NW
Washington, DC 20036
202-466-3142

Fendrick Gallery Inc.
3059 M St. NW
Washington, DC 20007
202-338-4544

Jackie Chalkley Gallery
3301 New Mexico Ave. NW
Washington, DC 20016
202-686-8882

Mimosa Inc.
3301 New Mexico Ave. NW
Washington, DC 20016
202-363-8380

Sherley Koteen (consultant)
2604 Tilden Pl. NW
Washington, DC 20008
202-363-2271

Smull's
1606 20th St. NW
Washington, DC 20009
202-232-8282

FLORIDA

BAY HARBOR ISLAND

Galerie 99
1088 Kane Concourse
Bay Harbor Island, FL 33154
305-865-5823

BOCA RATON

The Artisans, A Fine Crafts
Gallery
2200 Glades Rd.
Boca Raton, FL 33431
305-368-1882

MIAMI

Barbara Gilman Gallery
270 NE 39th St.
Miami, FL 33137
305-573-4898

La Verne Galleries
3925 N. Miami Ave.
Miami, FL 33137
305-576-0408

The Twenty-four Collection
2399 NE Second Ave.

Miami, FL 33137
305-576-2423

PALM BEACH

Carani
150 Worth Ave.
Palm Beach, FL 33480
305-655-6462

Holsten Galleries
206 Worth Ave.
Palm Beach, FL 33480
305-833-3403

SOUTH MIAMI

Netsky Gallery
5759 Sunset Dr.
South Miami, FL 33143
305-662-2453

Ophelia Art To Wear
5794 Sunset Drive
South Miami, FL 33143
305-665-3986

GEORGIA

ATLANTA

American Art Inc.
56 E. Andrews Dr. NW
Atlanta, GA 30305
404-231-0535

Eve Mannes Gallery
288 E. Paces Ferry Rd. NE
Atlanta, GA 30305
404-237-8477

Form & Function
1 Rhodes Center NW
Atlanta, GA 30309
404-874-9718

Great American Gallery
1925 Peachtree Rd. NE
Atlanta, GA 30309
404-351-8210

Heath Gallery, Inc.
416 E. Paces Ferry Rd.
Atlanta, GA 30305
404-262-6407

Image South Gallery
1931 Peachtree Rd. NE
Atlanta, GA 30309
404-351-3179

The Signature Shop and
Gallery
3267 Roswell Rd. NW
Atlanta, GA 30305
404-237-4426

HAWAII

HONOLULU

Following Sea
1441 Kapiolani Blvd.
Honolulu, HI 96814
808-946-6167

Rare Discovery Collectibles
1050 Ala Moama Blvd.
Honolulu, HI 96814
808-524-4811

ILLINOIS

CHICAGO

Barbara Balkin Gallery
425 N. Clark St.
Chicago, IL 60610
312-321-9010

Betsy Rosenfield Gallery Inc.
212 W. Superior St.
Chicago, IL 60610
312-787-8020

Exhibit A
233 E. Ontario St.
Chicago, IL 60611
312-944-1748

The Randolph Street Gallery
756 N. Milwaukee Ave.
Chicago, IL 60622
312-666-7737

A Show of Hands Inc.
43 E. Walton Pl.
Chicago, IL 60611
312-943-3413

EVANSTON

Mindscape Gallery
1521 Sherman Ave.
Evanston, IL 60201
312-864-2660

WILMETTE

The Artisan Shop and Gallery
1515 Sheridan Rd.
Plaza del Lago

INDIANA

INDIANAPOLIS

Editions Limited Gallery
The Fashion Mall
8702 Keystone Crossing
Indianapolis, IN 46240
317-848-7878

Wilmette, IL 60091
312-251-3775

KANSAS

SHAWNEE MISSION

Morgan Gallery
5006 Stateline Rd.
Shawnee Mission, KA 66205
913-236-7796

KENTUCKY

BEREA

Benchmark Gallery
I-75 and Jane Street
Box 422
Berea, KY 40403
606-986-9413

LOUISVILLE

Artspace
2001-2007 Frankfort Ave.
Louisville, KY

LOUISIANA

BATON ROUGE

The Crafts Gallery
3074 College Dr.
Baton Rouge, LA 70808
504-928-1810

NEW ORLEANS

The Loom Room
623 Royal St.
New Orleans, LA 70130
504-522-7101

MAINE

BAR HARBOR

Caleb's Sunrise
115 Main St.
Bar Harbor, ME 04609
207-288-3102

BOOTHBAY HARBOR

Abacus Gallery
8 McKown St.
Boothbay Harbor, ME 04538
207-633-2166

OGUNQUIT

Maple Hill Gallery
Perkins Cove
Ogunquit, ME 03907
207-646-2134

PORTLAND

Handcrafters Gallery
44 Exchange St.
Portland, ME 04101
207-772-4880

MARYLAND

ANNAPOLIS

Pottery 'N Things
One State Circle
Annapolis, MD 21401
301-268-8778

BALTIMORE

Barstons Gallery
523 N. Charles St.
Baltimore, MD 21201
301-727-6866

By Design Gallery
1619 Sulgrave Ave.
Mt. Washington Village
Baltimore, MD 21209
301-578-0066

The Calico Cat, Inc.
2137 Gwynn Oak Ave.
Baltimore, MD 21207
301-944-2450

Meredith Contemporary Art
805 N. Charles St.
Baltimore, MD 21201
301-837-3575

Off Broadway
1634 E. Baltimore St.
Baltimore, MD 21231
301-327-4777, 276-1634

Tomlinson Craft Collection
711 W. 40th St.
Baltimore, MD 21211
301-338-1572

BETHESDA

The Glass Gallery
4931 Elm St.
Bethesda, MD 20814
301-657-3478

KENSINGTON

Plum Gallery
3762 Howard Ave.
Kensington, MD 20895
301-933-0222

LUTHERVILLE

Craft Concepts
Green Spring Station
Falls and Joppa Rds.
Lutherville, MD 21093
301-823-2533

MASSACHUSETTS

BOSTON

The Glass Veranda
36 Newbury St.
Boston, MA 02116

Impressions Gallery
275 Dartmouth St.
Boston, MA 02116
617-262-0783

J.A. Parker Co.
353-S Faneuil Hall
  Marketplace
Boston, MA 02109
617-523-0128

Thomas Segal Gallery
73 Newbury St.
Boston, MA 02116
617-266-3500

Signature Gallery
One Dock Square, North St.
Boston, MA 02109
617-227-4885

The Society of Arts and Crafts
175 Newbury St.
Boston, MA 02116
617-266-1810

BREWSTER

The Spectrum of American
  Artists & Craftsmen Inc.
369 Old King's Highway
Brewster, MA 02631
617-385-3322

BROOKLINE

Marion-Ruth Gifts
1385 Beacon St.
Brookline, MA 02146
617-734-6620

Wild Goose Chase
1429 Beacon St.
Brookline, MA 02146
617-738-8020

CAMBRIDGE

Mobilia Gallery
348 Huron Ave.
Cambridge, MA 02138
617-876-2109

Ten Arrow Gallery
10 Arrow St.
Cambridge, MA 02138
617-876-1117

Van Buren-Brazelton-Cutting
290 Concord Ave.
Cambridge, MA 02138
617-354-0304

CHESTNUT HILL

Quadrum Gallery
The Mall at Chestnut Hill
Chestnut Hill, MA 02167
617-965-5555

DEERFIELD

Historic Deerfield Museum
  Store
Deerfield, MA 01342
413-774-5581

HADLEY

Skera Contemporary Crafts
123 Russell St.
Hadley, MA 01035
413-586-4563

LENOX

Yamato House
104 Main St.
Lenox, MA 01240
413-637-3380

NANTUCKET

The Cockeyed Dove
18 Broad St.
Nantucket, MA 02554
617-228-1665

The Lion's Paw
Zero Main St.
Nantucket, MA 02554
617-228-3837

Nantucket Looms
16 Main St.
Nantucket, MA 02554
617-228-1908

NEWTON CENTER

Jubilation
91 Union St.
Newton Center, MA 02159
617-965-0488

NORTH HATFIELD

Baracca Gallery
197 Pantry Rd.
North Hatfield, MA 01066
413-247-5262

NORTHAMPTON

Pinch Pottery
150 Main St.
Northampton, MA 01060
413-586-4509

ORLEANS

The Artful Hand
Main St. Square
Orleans, MA 02653
617-255-2969

PITTSFIELD

Hancock Shaker Village
PO Box 898-01202
Pittsfield, MA 01201
413-443-0188

STOCKBRIDGE

Holsten Galleries
Elm St.
Stockbridge, MA 01262
413-298-3044

WELLESLEY

Joel Bagnal Goldsmiths
591 Washington St.
Wellesley, MA 02188
617-235-8266

WELLFLEET

Secrest Craftsmen's Barn
3 W. Main St.
Wellfleet, MA 02667
617-349-6688

WILLIAMSTOWN

The Potter's Wheel
Rt. 43
Williamstown, MA 01267
413-458-9523

WORCESTER

The Worcester Craft Center
25 Sagamore Rd.
Worcester, MA 01605
617-753-8183

MICHIGAN

ANN ARBOR

Selo/Shevel Gallery
329 S. Main St.
Ann Arbor, MI 48104
313-761-6263

BIRMINGHAM

Carol Hooberman Gallery
155 S. Bates

Birmingham, MI 48011
313-647-3666

Little Gallery
915 E. Maple Rd.
Birmingham, MI 48011
313-644-5566

Robert L. Kidd Associates
  Galleries
107 Townsend St.
Birmingham, MI 48010
313-642-3838

The Yaw Gallery
550 N. Woodward Ave.
Birmingham, MI 48011
313-647-5470

DETROIT

Detroit Gallery of
  Contemporary Crafts
301 Fisher Building
Detroit, MI 48202
313-873-7888

Pewabic Pottery
10125 E. Jefferson
Detroit, MI 48214
313-822-0954

EAST LANSING

Freeman Gallery
3046 Lake Lansing Rd.
East Lansing, MI 48823
517-332-5656

FARMINGTON HILLS

Plum Tree Pottery
30435 W. Ten Mile Rd.
Farmington Hills, MI 48024
313-476-4875

LATHRUP VILLAGE

Habatat Galleries
28235 Southfield Rd.
Lathrup Village, MI 48076
313-552-0515

MINNESOTA

MINNEAPOLIS

By Design
Lumber Exchange Bldg.
10 South Fifth St.
Minneapolis, MN 55402
612-333-2204

Textile Arts Alliance
1721 Mount Curve Ave.

Minneapolis, MN 55403
612-377-5688

Vermillion Editions Ltd.
400 First Avenue N.
Minneapolis, MN 55401
612-338-6808

ROCHESTER

Callaway Galleries
1 SW First Ave.
Rochester, MN 55901
507-289-6532

MISSOURI

ST. LOUIS

B.Z. Wagman Gallery
34 North Brentwood
St. Louis, MO 63104
314-721-0250

The Gallery at Craft Alliance
6640 Delmar Blvd.
St. Louis, MO 63130
314-725-1151

The Greenberg Gallery
44 Maryland Plaza
St. Louis, MO 63108
314-361-7600

Okun-Thomas Gallery
1221 South Brentwood
St. Louis, MO 63117
314-725-7887

MONTANA

BOZEMAN

Artifacts Gallery
308 E. Main St.
PO Box 1989
Bozeman, MT 59715
406-586-3755

NEBRASKA

OMAHA

Craftsmen's Gallery
511 S. Eleventh St.
Omaha, NE 68102
402-346-8887

NEW HAMPSHIRE

CONCORD

League of New Hampshire
Craftsmen
205 N. Main St.

Concord, NH 03301
603-224-3375

Concord Arts & Crafts
36 N. Main St.
Concord, NH 03301
603-228-8171

CONWAY

League of New Hampshire
Craftsmen, Conway
Main St.
Route 16, Box 751
North Conway, NH 03860
603-356-2441

EXETER

Exeter Craft Center
61 Water St.
Exeter, NH 03833
603-778-8282

FRANCONIA

League of New Hampshire
Craftsmen, Franconia
(summer only)
The Glaessel Bldg.
Box 428
Franconia, NH 03580
603-823-9521

HANOVER

League of New Hampshire
Craftsmen, Hanover
13 Lebanon St.
Hanover, NH 03755
603-643-5050

MANCHESTER

The Currier Gallery of Art
192 Orange St.
Manchester, NH 03104
603-669-6144

Manchester Institute of Arts
and Sciences
148 Concord St.
Manchester, NH 03104
603-623-0313

MEREDITH

Meredith-Laconia Arts &
Crafts (summer only)
Route 3
Meredith, NH 03253
603-279-7920

NASHUA

Nashua League of Craftsmen
147 Main St.

Nashua, NH 03060
603-882-4171

PETERBOROUGH

Sharon Arts Center
Route 123, Box 361
Peterborough, NH 03458
603-924-7257

SANDWICH

Sandwich Home Industries
Main St.
Center Sandwich, NH 03227
603-284-6831

SOUTH WOLFE

The Schoolhouse Shop
Wolfeboro Arts and Crafts
Association
Route 28
South Wolfe, NH 03894
603-569-3489

NEW JERSEY

FAIR LAWN

Kornbluth Gallery
7-21 Fair Lawn Ave.
Fair Lawn, NJ 07410
201-791-3374

HADDONFIELD

By Hand Fine Crafts Gallery
142 Kings Highway East
Haddonfield, NJ 08033
609-429-2550

LAYTON

Peter's Valley Store Gallery
Rt. 615
Layton, NJ 07851
201-948-5202

MONTCLAIR

Dexterity Ltd.
26 Church St.
Montclair, NJ 07042
201-746-5370

SCOTCH PLAINS

Beautiful Things Factory
1838 E. Second St.
Scotch Plains, NJ 07076
201-322-1817

TENAFLY

America House Gallery of
Contemporary Crafts
24 Washington St.

Tenafly, NJ 07670
201-569-2526

NEW MEXICO

ALBUQUERQUE

Mariposa Gallery
113 Romero St. NW
Old Town
Albuquerque, NM 87104
505-842-9097

SANTA FE

The Eason Gallery
338 E. De Vargas St.
Santa Fe, NM 87501
505-982-9573

Enthios Gallery
1111 Paseo de Peralta
Santa Fe, NM 87501
505-988-1505

NEW YORK

ALBANY

Forms and Foliage Ltd.
Wolf Road Park
Albany, NY 12205
518-458-1313

BINGHAMTON

The Goldsmith
81 State St.
Binghamton, NY 13901

BRIDGEHAMPTON

Elaine Benson Gallery
Montauk Highway
Bridgehampton, NY 11932
515-537-3233

BROOKLYN

The Clay Pot
162 Seventh Ave.
Brooklyn, NY 11215
212-788-6564

Meuniers
140 Montague St.
Brooklyn, NY 11201
212-855-7835

BUFFALO

Nina Freudenheim Gallery
560 Franklin St.
Buffalo, NY 14202
716-881-1555

Morgan Galleries
311 Bryant St.

Buffalo, NY 14222
716-885-0526

CORNING

Corning Museum of Glass
Corning Glass Center
Corning, NY 14830
607-937-5371

EAST HAMPTON

Appalachian Art
26 Montauk Highway
East Hampton, NY 11937
516-324-5353

Engel Pottery Inc.
1 Main St.
East Hampton, NY 11937
516-324-6462

The Pritam & Eames Gallery
29 Race Lane
East Hampton, NY 11937
516-324-7111

FISHERS ISLAND

Pandion Gallery
Fishers Island, NY 06390
516-788-7406

FLORIDA

Pot-pourri Contemporary
Crafts Gallery
85 N. Main St.
Florida, NY 10921
914-651-7418

HARTSDALE

Alan Brown Gallery
210 East Hartsdale
Hartsdale, NY 10530
914-723-0040

HUNTINGTON

Basket Gallery
288 New York Ave.
Huntington, NY 11743
516-427-4205

ITHACA

People's Pottery
150 The Ithaca Commons
Ithaca, NY 14850
607-277-3597

KINGSTON

Shattuck Pottery
RD3 Box 249B
Kingston, NY 12401
914-331-7687

MAMARONECK

Of Cabbages and Kings
587 E. Boston Post Rd.
Mamaroneck, NY 10543
914-698-0445

NEW PALTZ

Handmade
6 North Front St.
New Paltz, NY 12561
914-255-6277

NEW YORK CITY

Alexander F. Milliken Gallery
98 Prince St.
New York, NY 10012
212-966-7800

BFM Gallery
(through designers and
architects)
150 E. 58th St.
New York, NY 10155
212-755-1243

Charles Cowles Gallery
420 W. Broadway
New York, NY 10012
212-925-3500

Condeso Lawler Gallery
119 W. 25th St.
New York, NY 10001
212-741-2377

Contemporary Porcelain
105 Sullivan St.
New York, NY 10012
212-966-6392

Convergence Gallery
484 Broome St.
New York, NY 10013
212-226-0028

The Elements Gallery
90 Hudson St.
New York, NY 10013
212-226-5910

Andre Emmerich Gallery
41 E. 57th St.
New York, NY 10022
212-752-0124

Aaron Faber Inc.
666 Fifth Ave.
New York, NY 10103
212-586-8411

Fine Art Acquisitions Ltd.
40 W. 57th St.

New York, NY 10019
212-489-7830

Gordon Foster Antiques
1326A Third Ave.
New York, NY 10021
212-744-4922

Gallery 10
379 W. Broadway
New York, NY 10012
212-226-3183

Gallery 10
21 Greenwich Ave.
New York, NY 10014
212-929-9411

The Glass Store Inc.
1242 Madison Ave.
New York, NY 10028
212-289-1970

The Hadler-Rodriguez
Galleries
38 E. 57th St.
New York, NY 10022
212-752-7734

Heller Gallery
965 Madison Ave.
New York, NY 10021
212-988-7116

Heller Gallery
71 Greene St.
New York, NY 10012
212-966-5948

Incorporated Gallery
1200 Madison Ave.
New York, NY 10028
212-831-4466

Jorice
1057 Second Ave.
New York, NY 10022
212-752-0129

Julie: Artisans' Gallery
687 Madison Ave.
New York, NY 10021
212-688-2345

Luten, Clary & Stern
(through designers and
architects)
1059 Third Ave.
New York, NY 10021

Max Protetch Gallery
37 W. 57th St.
New York, NY 10019
212-838-7436

Modern Master Tapestries Inc.
11 E. 57th St.
New York, NY 10022
212-838-0412

Pindar Gallery
127 Greene St.
New York, NY 10012
212-533-4881

Sointu Modern Design Store
20 E. 69th St.
New York, NY 10021
212-570-9449

Surroundings
460 W. Broadway
New York, NY 10012
212-475-8153

The Theo Portnoy Gallery
56 W. 57th St.
New York, NY 10019
212-757-0461

Tiffany & Co.
727 Fifth Ave.
New York, NY 10022
212-755-8000

The Workbench Inc.
470 Park Ave. South
New York, NY 10016
212-481-5454

PITTSFORD

The Three Crowns
3850 Monroe Ave.
Pittsford, NY 14534
716-586-5160

PORT JEFFERSON

Trackside Emporium
14 East Broadway
Port Jefferson, NY 11777
516-473-8222

ROCHESTER

The Creator's Hands
336 Arnett Blvd.
Rochester, NY 14619
716-235-8550

The Gallery of Contemporary
Metalsmithing
800 Powers Bldg.
16 Main St. West
Rochester, NY 14614
716-546-1224

Hopper's Gallery
647 South Ave.

Rochester, NY 14620
716-546-3202

Memorial Art Gallery
490 University Ave.
Rochester, NY 14607
716-275-3081

Rochester Museum and
Science Center
657 East Ave.
PO Box 1480
Rochester, NY 14603
716-271-4320

Shelter Goods
680 Monroe Ave.
Rochester, NY 14607
716-473-2145

RIVERHEAD

Elegant Extras
31 E. Main St.
Riverhead, NY 11901
516-727-7413

SCARSDALE

The Craftsman's Gallery
16 Chase Rd.
Scarsdale, NY 10583
914-725-4644

SOUTHAMPTON

The Gayle Willson Gallery
42B Job's Lane
Southampton, NY 11968
516-283-7430

Works Gallery
14 Job's Lane
Southampton, NY 11968
516-283-5093

SYRACUSE

The Everson Museum Sales
Gallery
401 Harrison St.
Syracuse, NY 13202
315-474-6064

Hanover Gallery
401 Irving Ave.
Syracuse, NY 13210
315-474-0476

WHITE PLAINS

Westlake Gallery Ltd.
210 E. Post Rd.
White Plains, NY 10601
914-682-8123

WOODSTOCK

Clouds Gallery
1 Mill Hill Road
Woodstock, NY 12498
914-679-8155

The Gilded Carriage
95 Tinker St.
Woodstock, NY 12498
914-679-2607

NORTH CAROLINA

ASHEVILLE

Allanstand Craft Shop at
the Folk Art Center
PO Box 9545
Asheville, NC 28815
704-298-7928

New Morning Gallery
7 Boston Way
Asheville, NC 28803
704-274-2831

BAKERSVILLE

Larson Pottery Showroom
Rt. 3, Box 80
Bakersville, NC 28705
704-688-3104

CHAPEL HILL

Cameron Craft Gallery
University Mall
Chapel Hill, NC 27514
919-942-5554

GREENSBORO

Green Hill Art Gallery
200 N. Davie St.
Greensboro, NC 27401
919-373-4515

KITTY HAWK

Duck Blind Ltd.
Box 222
Kitty Hawk, NC 27949
919-261-2009

WINSTON-SALEM

The Crafts Shop
300 S. Main St.
Winston-Salem, NC 27101
919-723-4125

Southeastern Center for
Contemporary Art (SECCA)
750 Marguerite Dr.
Winston-Salem, NC 27106
919-725-1904

OHIO

CINCINNATI

The Private Collection Inc.
21 E. Fifth St.
Cincinnati, OH 45202
513-381-1667

Vertu
320 W. 4th St.
Cincinnati, OH 45202
513-621-5047

CLEVELAND

DBR Gallery
13225 Shaker Square
Cleveland, OH 44120
216-491-8062

The New Gallery of
Contemporary Art
11427 Bellflower Road
Cleveland, OH 44106
216-421-8671

COLUMBUS

Ohio Designer Craftsmen
Gallery
1981 Riverside Dr.
Columbus, OH 43221
614-486-7119

NOVART
2083 E. 14th St.
Cleveland, OH 44115
216-241-4935

Sylvia Ullman American
Crafts Gallery
13010 Woodland Ave.
Cleveland, OH 44120
216-231-2008

TOLEDO

Collector's Corner, Toledo
Museum of Art
2445 Monroe St.
Toledo, OH 43697
419-255-8000

OKLAHOMA

TULSA

Arts Signature
Performing Arts Center
Gallery
Third St. at Cincinnati Ave.
Tulsa, OK 74103
918-582-7532

OREGON

PORTLAND

Contemporary Crafts Gallery
3934 SW Corbett Ave.
Portland, OR 97201
503-223-2654

The Fountain Gallery of Art
117 NW 21st Ave.
Portland, OR 97209
503-228-8476

Oregon School of Arts and
Crafts
8245 SW Barnes Rd.
Portland, OR 97225
503-297-5544

Patrie Tapestries
314 SW Ninth St., Room 5
Portland, OR 97205
503-224-9916

The Real Mother Goose
901 SW Yamhill St.
Portland, OR 97205
503-223-9510

PENNSYLVANIA

BRYN MAWR

The Store
861 Lancester Ave.
Bryn Mawr, PA 19010
215-525-1285

ELKINS PARK

Gallery 500
Church and Old York Rds.
Elkins Park, PA 19117
215-572-1203

NEW HOPE

The James Martin Gallery
36 N. Main St.
New Hope, PA 18938
215-862-2459

PHILADELPHIA

The Clay Studio Gallery
49 North Second St.
Philadelphia, PA 19106
215-925-3453

The Fabric Workshop
1133 Arch St.
Philadelphia, PA 19107
215-568-0858

Helen Drutt Gallery
305 Cherry St.
Philadelphia, PA 19106
215-735-1625

Past Present Future
243 S. 17th St.
Philadelphia, PA 19103
215-735-4549

Richard Kagan Studio and
Gallery
326 South St.
Philadelphia, PA 19147
215-925-2370

Sign of the Swan Craft
Gallery
8433 Germantown Ave.
Chestnut Hill
Philadelphia, PA 19118
215-242-5300

Swan Gallery
132 S. 18th St.
Philadelphia, PA 19103
215-242-5300

Webster/Wallnuts Gallery
2018 Locust St.
Philadelphia, PA 19103
215-732-8850

The Works Gallery
319 South St.
Philadelphia, PA 19147
215-922-7775

PITTSBURGH

The Clay Place
5600 Walnut St.
Pittsburgh, PA 15232
412-441-3799

SPRING HOUSE

Artisans Three
The Village Center
Spring House, PA 19477
215-643-4504

VERONA

The Store
719 Allegheny River Blvd.
Verona, PA 15147
412-828-6121

RHODE ISLAND

PROVIDENCE

Lily Iselin Gallery
218 Wickenden St.
Providence, RI 02903
401-272-9769

SOUTH CAROLINA

HILTON HEAD

Artistic Sass/Primary Art
14 Greenwood Dr.
Hilton Head Island, SC 29928
803-785-8442

TENNESSEE

CHATTANOOGA

The Armory
1936 Dayton Blvd.
Chattanooga, TN 37415
615-870-1163

The Plum Nelly Shop
1201 Hixson Pike
Chattanooga, TN 37405
615-266-0585

GATLINBURG

Gazebo
529 Parkway
Gatlinburg, TN 37738
615-436-4064

NASHVILLE

The American Artisan
4231 Harding Road
Nashville, TN 37205
615-298-4691

TEXAS

DALLAS

At Home
4309 Oak Lawn Ave.
Dallas, TX 75219
214-528-0440

The Frontroom
6617 Snider Plaza
Dallas, TX 75205
214-369-8338

Human Arts
2800 Routh St.
Dallas, TX 75201
214-748-3948

Mattingly-Baker Gallery
3000 McKinney Ave.
Dallas, TX 75204
214-526-0031

Neiman-Marcus
American Artforms Galleries
Main and Irvay Streets
Dallas, TX 75201
214- 741-6911
Also in Neiman-Marcus stores
in the following cities:
Beverly Hills and San
Francisco, California, Atlanta,
Georgia, Chicago, Illinois, and
Houston, Texas

FORT WORTH

Handcrafters Inc.
237 Hulen Mall
Fort Worth, TX 76132
817-292-8820

HOUSTON

Eve France
2043 W. Gray
Houston, TX 77019
713-526-9991

The Hadler-Rodriguez
Galleries
20 Pinedale
Houston, TX 77006
713-520-6329

Hanson Galleries
The Town & Country Mall
Houston, TX 77024
713-977-1242

Perception Galleries
1724 Bissonet
Houston, TX 77005
713-527-0303

SAN ANTONIO

Objects Gallery
4010 Broadway
San Antonio, TX 78209
512-826-8996

Southwest Craft Center
La Villita Galleria
420 Paseo de la Villita
San Antonio, TX 78205
512-222-0926

UTAH

SALT LAKE CITY

Salt Lake Art Center
20 South West Temple
Salt Lake City, UT 84101
801-328-4201

VERMONT

MIDDLEBURY

Vermont State Craft Center
at Frog Hollow
Frog Hollow Rd.
Middlebury, VT 05753
802-388-3177

STOWE

Stowe Pottery
Mountain Rd.
Stowe, VT 05672
802-253-4693

VIRGINIA

ALEXANDRIA

Full Circle
317 Cameron St.
Alexandria, VA 22314
703-683-4500

ANNANDALE

Dawson's Small Arms of the
World
7215 Columbia Pike
Annandale, VA 22003
703-256-5115

ARLINGTON

Elizabeth Michaels
(consultant)
3619 S. 7th St.
Arlington, VA 22204
703-892-6227

CHARLOTTESVILLE

Signet Gallery
212 Fifth St. NE
Charlottesville, VA 22901
804-296-6463

LEESBURG

Whistle Walk Crafts Gallery
7 S. King St.
Leesburg, VA 22075
703-777-4017

RICHMOND

Lewis/Schaal Gallery
3135 W. Cary St.
Richmond, VA 23221
804-355-0377

VIRGINIA BEACH

The Decker Studio
3198 Pacific Ave.
Virginia Beach, VA 23451
804-422-4244

WASHINGTON

SEATTLE

Foster/White Gallery
311½ Occidental Ave. S.
Seattle, WA 98104
206-622-2833

Linda Farris Gallery
322 Second Ave. S.
Seattle, WA 98104
206-623-1110

Northwest Craft Center and
Gallery
Seattle Center
Seattle, WA 98109
206-624-7563

Traver Sutton Gallery
2219 Fourth Ave.
Seattle, WA 98121
206-622-4234

WEST VIRGINIA

HUNTINGTON

Huntington Galleries
Park Hills
Huntington, WV 25701
304-529-2701

WISCONSIN

FISH CREEK

Edgewood Orchard Galleries

Fish Creek, WI 54212
414-868-3579

MILWAUKEE

D. Erlien Gallery
5623 N. Lake Dr.
Milwaukee, WI 53217
414-963-0888

SHEBOYGAN

John Michael Kohler Art
Center
608 New York Ave.
Sheboygan, WI 53081
414-458-6144

WYOMING

JACKSON

Artwest Gallery
220 S. Glenwood St.
PO Box 1248
Jackson, WY 83001
307-733-6379

GLOSSARY

CLAY

Ash glaze. A distinctive glaze that after firing has a mottled, runny appearance, created by adding ash to the liquid glaze before firing.

Bisque firing. The first firing necessary to harden the clay so that glaze will adhere. After glazing, the piece is fired at least once more.

Celadon glaze. A very pale green glaze, one of the oldest glaze colors found on the earliest Chinese porcelains and very popular today.

China. A generic term for all porcelain dinnerware, but more widely used to refer to commercially manufactured porcelain than to handmade porcelain.

Coiling. A hand-building method in which long ropes of clay are spiraled into walls of a spherical form. The seams between successive coils may be smoothed after the form is complete and before firing.

Colored clay. Clay with pigment added before forming.

Crackle glaze. A decorative technique that produces a network of fine, hairline cracks within the glaze. Cracks develop in the glaze only and do not affect the strength of the pot itself.

Earthenware. An opaque, porous clay body that is fired at relatively low temperatures (under 1100° C). The fired clay may be white, tan, or red. Earthenware is chosen by potters who desire bright glaze colors.

Flameware. A clay body specially formulated to achieve a low rate of thermal expansion, which allows the user to put the clay directly over a range heating unit without danger of breakage.

Glaze. A liquid applied to bisque fired clay, which hardens to a nonporous, glasslike surface after firing. Glazes may be either glossy or matte.

Hand-building. Any method of shaping clay without the aid of a mechanical device. The coil and slab are the most commonly used hand-building methods.

High-fired. Refers to clay bodies fired at temperatures high enough to make the fired clay vitreous, or impervious to liquids.

Kiln. A furnace built of heat-resistant materials for firing ceramics.

Leather-hard. In ceramic work, the term used for the final stage of drying before bisque firing when the clay is firm and no longer damp.

Low-fired. Refers to clay bodies such as earthenware that can be fired at low temperatures that will not affect bright glaze colors.

Luster glaze. Metallic and iridescent glazes; they are always applied over another glaze and are thus not usually dishwasher safe.

Nerikomi. Japanese technique of achieving marbleized and striated patterns within the clay body. Colored clay bodies are stacked in layers to form a loaf or cylinder, which is then folded and twisted to distort the straight lines of the colored layers. After distortion, the loaf is sliced crosswise and the thin slices pressed into a mold to form the walls of a clay vessel.

Ovenware. Indicates that a clay vessel may be safely used as a baking or roasting dish, but should not be used over the direct heat of a surface unit or in a broiler.

Porcelain. A white, sometimes translucent clay body that is fired at high temperatures (1300° C and above), becoming vitreous, or glasslike, with firing.

Pottery. A generic term for all ceramic objects.

Press molded. A hand-building technique in which wet clay is pressed into a plaster mold.

Raku. A Japanese firing method in which a pot is taken from the kiln while red-hot and put immediately into a combustible material, such as sawdust, leaves, straw, or shredded paper. The pot is hot enough to burn these materials, creating black smoke to blacken the pot. The quick cooling of the pot also causes the glaze to crackle, or develop fine hairline cracks that absorb smoke.

Resist. A decorative technique of masking designated areas with wax so that they will not be glazed.

Salt glaze. A glaze with a distinctive texture resembling orange peel, achieved by adding salt to the kiln during firing.

Slab built. A hand-building technique in which a potter constructs a form with flat sheets of clay, held together with slip.

Slip. Clay in a liquid state, used for casting, decoration, and as an adhesive.

Slip-cast. A forming method in which liquid clay is poured into a plaster mold; the mold absorbs water from the clay, leaving clay that must dry until firm before being removed from the mold.

Stoneware. A clay body fired at temperatures of 1200° C and above. Somewhat gritty in feeling and limited to natural earthen colors of gray to rust, it is prized for its durability and in baking vessels, for its even heat distribution.

Terra cotta. Red earthenware, low-fired and porous.

Underglaze. Decoration that is applied directly to the clay surface before glazing and firing. Such decoration is protected by the glasslike glaze from fading and wear.

Wheel thrown. A forming method in which a potter uses only his hands to shape a round, symmetrical piece on a revolving wheel.

White earthenware. Porous, low-fired clay body that is white in color.

Wood firing. A method of firing in which wood is the fuel for the kiln.

FIBER (including basketry)

Batik. Liquified wax, starch, resin, or clay is applied to cloth in a desired pattern to prevent these areas from absorbing color when dipped into a dye bath. After the dyeing, the wax is completely removed, revealing a pattern that is the original color of the cloth.

Coiling. A construction method based on a spiral and used to create a spherical container or vessel. As a continuous coil spirals upward, each successive layer is stitched to the one beneath to secure the structure permanently. Basket makers use pine needles and a number of other natural materials as well as yarns to created coiled vessels.

Felting. A method of creating wool fabric without weaving. Individual wool fibers have overlapping scales, as does human hair. When moisture and heat are applied, these scales open up, and when rubbed against each other, the scales catch on one another, permanently interlocking the fibers. The amount of friction and pressure that must be applied by the craftsman makes this a physically demanding process, but it has an advantage over weaving in that the size of the finished piece is not limited to the width of a loom.

Ikat. Before weaving, small bundles of warp yarns are tie-dyed in a desired pattern. When the individual yarns are threaded onto the loom, the dyed areas do not fall in a straight hard-edge line, but create a varied softer, dye line. Differs from tie-dyed cloth in that the yarns are dyed before being woven.

Knotting. Tying together yarns, cords, or threads using any one or many standard knot configurations. Allows the fiber artist to create three-dimensional fiber sculptures of unlimited size by working off the loom.

Off-loom. Refers to a number of fiber construction techniques that make it possible to create an expanse of fabric or sculptural hanging, literally without using a loom: knotting, wrapping, coiling, plaiting, knitting and crocheting. Off-loom techniques allow greater scale than a loom and three-dimensional constructions rather than a flat wall hanging. Fiber artists often combine off-loom techniques, such as wrapping, with loom weaving to achieve greater textural effects.

Photo-silkscreening. A light sensitive photo emulsion is coated over a pre-cut stencil or screen and ink or dye is passed through the screen to produce a positive print.

Plaiting. A construction technique of interweaving three or more yarns, threads, or cords. The most common example is plaiting hair into pigtails. Fiber artists use more complex plaiting methods to construct both baskets and wall hangings.

Reed. A round basket-weaving material cut in lengths up to several yards long from the center of imported rattan. It is made pliable by soaking in water.

Resist. A process of using liquid wax on cloth or yarn to prevent dyes from penetrating designated areas, thereby creating a resist pattern of undyed areas. Batik is the most widely known method of resist dyeing.

Splint. A strip of wood of uniform width and thin enough to be pliable when wet, used to make a woven basket. May be used with reed, wild vines, or other splints to weave a basket. Although the strip of wood is accurately called a splint, the finished baskets, particularly those of traditional folk design, are often called ''split-oak'' baskets.

Tapestry. Technically, a woven fabric in which the weft yarns (the horizontal yarns on the loom) completely cover the warp yarns (the vertical yarns on the loom), with the result that the design is created solely by the weft yarns. Characteristically, it is a very flat, tightly woven piece. The capability of reproducing fine detail makes it popular among fiber artists who want to depict representational imagery.

Trapunto. A quilting technique in which the design is outlined with running stitches and then additional padding or batting is added to create low-relief designs.

Twill. A loom-woven pattern that is distinguished by parallel diagonal lines.

Warp. The threads or yarns that run lengthwise in fabric or hangings woven on a loom. These are the yarns that are actually threaded through the many heddles of the loom and are stretched taut during weaving.

Weaving. A construction method distinguished by interlocking of materials at right angles to each other. The materials may be warp and weft yarns for fabric or wall hangings or they may be splints, reed, or vines for woven baskets.

Weft. Yarns that run selvage to selvage in making fabric or woven hangings. Once the loom is threaded with warp yarns, the weft yarns are laid in with a shuttle going over and under the warp in a desired pattern.

Wrapping. To completely or partially cover yarns or other materials by winding yarn tightly around a core. Wrapping is used both to add strength and rigidity to the core material and for purely aesthetic reasons.

GLASS

Casting. A forming technique of pouring molten glass into a mold.

Freeblown. Glass objects that are shaped without molds, such as those used by commercial glass makers to achieve exacting consistency in a set of goblets, for instance. Also called ''offhand.''

Gather. The relatively small amount of molten glass picked up on the end of the blow pipe at any one time, taken directly from the furnace. Even for a large piece, glass is added gradually in successive gathers rather than taken up in one large gather.

Handblown glass. Objects formed by inflating a gather of glass by blowing from the mouth through a hollow tube (blow pipe) held in the hands.

Hot glass. Glass taken directly from a furnace and shaped while still in a molten state. The term is used among craftsmen to distinguish this technique from stained glass and from cold working, such as cutting and polishing of a blown form.

Latticinio. A Renaissance decorative technique of embedding rods of colored glass within clear or translucent glass objects. It is traditionally characterized by a spiraled design, often with many parallel spirals.

Marver. A flat sheet of steel used in shaping and decorating handblown glass. The glass artist may rotate the molten glass at the end of the blow pipe over the marver to flatten the sides, or he may lay out a pattern of glass rods on the marver and by passing the molten glass form over these rods, transfer the pattern to the molten glass.

Off-hand. Used interchangeably with ''freeblown'' to designate objects shaped solely by the blow pipe and hand tools. The result may be a functional goblet, vase, or bowl, or a sculptural form.

Sandblasting. A decorative process used to achieve a matte or frosted surface on glass. A pattern can be created by masking certain areas of the glass, which will remain glossy and clear. This is a mechanized process in which the sand is driven by wind onto the cold glass surface.

Slumped. A method used to shape thick plate glass. It is heated until it softens to a point at which it can be shaped in a mold.

Stained glass. Cold, flat sheets of colored glass are cut in desired shapes and held together in a desired composition by lead strips.

Studio glass. A term that has emerged within the past twenty years to distinguish glass objects, both functional and sculptural, that are created by an individual artist working in his studio. In contrast, commercially handblown glass is designed on a drafting board and executed by a team of glass blowers for a mass market.

METAL

Annealing. A process of heating metal to soften it so that it can be shaped with a hammer and anvil. A piece is annealed with each course in order to keep it malleable.

Bouging. Hammering with a leather or wooden mallet to remove irregularities or distortions created in stretching or raising. Must be done with each course.

Chasing. Adding decorative textures to metal by hammering pointed but noncutting tools to form a pattern. Work is done on the front surface only.

Constructed. Formed in separate pieces entirely by hand and then joined by hand processes such as soldering, riveting, and hinging.

Course. A complete cycle of forging (either raising or stretching), bouging, and annealing. Even a very simple metal bowl will require at least five courses; more complex pieces may require as many as forty courses.

Electroforming. A method of producing hollowware, which begins with a wax mold. In an electrochemical bath, metal is deposited in a thin sheet on the surface of the mold. The wax is melted and removed, leaving the metal shell.

Electroplating. An electrolytic process of applying a very thin layer of a more expensive metal to a second, usually a base or nonprecious metal.

Enameling. A process of fusing fine glass particles to metal.

Fabrication. A construction method in which parts are formed separately and then put together in finished form. One example is a metal teapot for which the spout, handle, and lid were shaped and finished before being assembled.

Fine silver. The purest form of silver, at 99 percent, compared with sterling silver, which is 95 percent silver.

Flatware. Refers to all metal forms such as knives, forks, spoons, and plates that are more or less flat.

Forging. A broad term for the process of shaping metal with a hammer and an anvil or metal stake, including stretching and raising.

Hollowware. Any metal form that is hollow, including vessel forms such as vases, goblets, teapots, and other container forms such as boxes.

Mokumé. A Japanese process recently popularized by American craftsmen in which a variety of different-colored metals are layered and fused together, creating a distinctive pattern that looks like wood graining.

Oxidizing. A decorative process of coating metals with chemical oxides to darken the metal.

Planishing. A finished process of using a smaller hammer to remove heavier, uneven hammer marks made in raising or stretching. Planishing marks are sometimes left as surface decoration.

Raising. A forming technique by which a flat sheet of metal is hammered in repeated courses to produce a seamless hollow vessel. Distinguished from stretching by being done only on the outside of the form.

Repoussé. A decorative technique to create a bas relief design. Metal is always worked from the reverse side, pushed out with hammers and punch tools.

Spinning. A technique for creating symmetrical hollowware by gradually forcing sheet metal against a metal or wooden form which is turning on a lathe.

Shibuishi. A Japanese process in which an alloy is created from three parts copper and twenty parts silver. When dipped into a chemical dyeing solution, the colors of the original metals are altered to achieve a subtle gray color.

Stretching. A process of shaping metal by hammering it against a metal anvil or stake, thus thinning it. Distinguished from raising because hammering is always done on the inside surface of the object. Since work must be done from the inside, stretching is commonly used for shallow or horizontal forms such as large bowls rather than enclosed vase or urn shapes.

WOOD

Beading. A narrow, half-round trim or molding.

Bevel. To cut at an inclined or sloping edge rather than at a 90° angle, used decoratively on the outside edges of wood furniture.

Burl. A knobby, abnormal outgrowth on a tree and the distinctively grained wood from that growth; used in turned wood bowls and decorative boxes by craftsmen and as veneered surface by commercial furniture makers.

Dovetail joint. A traditional method of joining two pieces of wood in furniture construction. Distinguished by a fan-shaped tenon that forms a tight, interlocking joint when fitted into a corresponding mortise. In traditional woodworking, the joint is used without glue or nails to allow for natural expansion of the wood.

Hardwoods. The wood of a broadleaf tree. The most popular hardwoods for furniture construction are oak, cherry, walnut, mahogany, and exotic woods such as ebony, padauk, purpleheart, and zebrawood.

Inlay. A decorative process in which small pieces of wood are recessed within a larger solid piece of wood. The inlaid wood is usually chosen for its contrasting color or grain in order to create a distinctive pattern.

Joinery. To construct furniture or cabinetry with interlocking joints.

Laminating. Bonding together multiple layers of wood; used to achieve greater strength and thickness as well as for decorative purposes.

Marquetry. A form of inlay. The term usually refers to more elaborate patterns of inlay using variously colored woods.

Mortise. A cavity cut into the end of a piece of wood and shaped to receive a corresponding tenon to form a tightly interlocking joint.

Peg construction. A round wooden pin that intersects two pieces of wood to join them together securely. The peg may be a separate third piece of wood or it may be a carved extension of one of the pieces. A hole the size of the peg must be drilled into the pieces of wood to be joined, and the peg is usually hammered in to ensure a snug fit.

Softwood. The wood of conifers, or trees with needles. Pine is one of the few softwoods suitable for furniture construction.

Spalted. Decaying wood of dead trees that has developed natural variations in color and darkened grain lines in the process of decay. Popular among woodworkers for turned bowls.

Tenon. A projection carved at the end of a piece of wood in a shape to correspond with a receptive cavity or mortise on a second piece of wood. Fitted together, they form a tightly interlocking joint.

Turned wood. Wood shaped on a lathe with cutting tools. It is used for vessel forms, such as bowls and vases, and for decorative effects on table and chair legs and wooden candlesticks.

SELECTED BIBLIOGRAPHY

GENERAL

Emery, Olivia H. *Craftsman Lifestyle: The Gentle Revolution.* Pasadena, CA: California Design Publications.

Hall, Julie. *Tradition and Change: The New American Craftsman.* New York: E. P. Dutton, 1977.

Lucie-Smith, Edward. *The Story of Craft: The Craftsman's Role in Society.* Ithaca, NY: Cornell University Press, 1981.

Yanagi, Soetsu. *The Unknown Craftsman.* Adapted by Bernard Leach. New York: Kodansha International/USA, 1972.

CLAY

Axel, Jan, and McCready, Karen. *Porcelain: Traditions and New Visions.* New York: Watson-Guptill Publications, 1981.

Berensohn, Paulus. *Finding One's Way With Clay: Pinched Pottery and the Color of Clay.* New York: Simon and Schuster, 1972.

Birks, Tony. *Art of the Modern Potter.* New York: Van Nostrand Reinhold Co., 1976.

Birks, Tony. *The Potters Companion.* New York: E. P. Dutton, 1974.

Clark, Garth. *American Potters: The Work of 20 Modern Masters.* New York: Watson-Guptill Publications, 1981.

Clark, Garth, and Hughto, Margie. *A Century of Ceramics in the United States.* New York: E. P. Dutton, 1979.

Leach, Bernard. *The Potters Challenge.* New York: E. P. Dutton, 1975.

Nelson, Glenn C. *Ceramics: A Potters Handbook.* New York: Holt, Rinehart & Winston, 1971.

Rawson, Phillip. *The Appreciation of the Arts/6: Ceramics.* New York: Oxford University Press, 1971.

Speight, Charlotte F. *Hands in Clay: An Introduction to Ceramics.* Sherman Oaks, CA: Alfred Publishing Co. Inc., 1979.

Wechsler, Susan. *Low-Fire Ceramics: A New Direction in American Clay.* New York: Watson-Guptill Publications, 1981.

Woody, Elsbeth. *Pottery on the Wheel.* New York: Farrar, Strauss & Giroux, 1975.

Woody, Elsbeth. *Handbuilding Ceramic Forms.* New York: Farrar, Strauss & Giroux, 1979.

FIBER

Black, Mary E. *New Key to Weaving: A Textbook of Handweaving for the Beginning Weaver.* New York: Macmillan Publishing Co., 1961.

Chase, Pattie. *The Contemporary Quilt: New American Quilts & Fabric Art.* New York: E. P. Dutton, 1978.

Constantine, Mildred, and Larsen, Jack Lenor. *Beyond Craft: The Art Fabric.* New York: Van Nostrand Reinhold Co., 1973.

Constantine, Mildred, and Larsen, Jack Lenor. *The Art Fabric: Mainstream.* New York: Van Nostrand Reinhold Co., 1981.

Fiberarts Magazine, ed. *The Fiberarts Design Book.* New York: Hastings House, 1980.

Gordon, Beverly. *Feltmaking.* New York: Watson-Guptill Publications, 1980.

Gutcheon, Beth. *The Perfect Patchwork Primer.* New York: David McKay Co. Inc., 1973.

Hart, Carol, and Hart, Dan. *Natural Basketry.* New York: Watson-Guptill Publications, 1976.

Harvey, Virginia. *The Techniques of Basketry.* New York: Van Nostrand Reinhold Co., 1974.

Held, Shirley E. *Weaving: A Handbook for Fiber Craftsmen.* New York: Holt, Rinehart & Winston, 1973.

Larsen, Jack Lenor. *The Dyers' Art: Ikat, Plangi, Batik.* New York: Van Nostrand Reinhold Co., 1976.

Marein, Shirley. *Off the Loom: Creating with Fiber.* New York: Viking Press, 1972.

Meilach, Donna Z. *A Modern Approach to Basketry with Fibers and Grasses.* New York: Crown Publishers, 1974.

Regensteiner, Else. *The Art of Weaving.* New York: Van Nostrand Reinhold Co., 1970.

Regensteiner, Else. *Weaver's Study Course: Ideas and Techniques.* New York: Van Nostrand Reinhold Co., 1975.

Rossbach, Ed. *Baskets as Textile Art.* New York: Van Nostrand Reinhold Co., 1973.

Rossbach, Ed. *The New Basketry.* New York: Van Nostrand Reinhold Co., 1976.

GLASS

Elskus, Albinas. *The Art of Painting on Glass.* New York: Charles Scribner's Sons, 1980.

Flavell, Ray, and Smale, Claude. *Studio Glassmaking.* New York: Van Nostrand Reinhold Co., 1974.

Kulasiewicz, Frank. *Glassblowing: The Technique of Free-Blown Glass.* New York: Watson-Guptill Publications, 1974.

Littleton, Harvey. *Glassblowing: A Search for Form.* New York: Van Nostrand Reinhold Co., 1971.

METAL

Loyen, Frances. *The Thames & Hudson Manual of Silversmithing.* New York: Thames & Hudson, 1980.

Steakley, Douglas. *Hollowware Techniques.* New York: Watson-Guptill Publications, 1979.

PAPER

Heller, Jules. *Papermaking.* New York: Watson-Guptill Publications, 1978.

Studley, Vance. *The Art & Craft of Handmade Paper.* New York: Van Nostrand Reinhold Co., 1977.

WOOD

Fine Woodworking Magazine, eds. *Fine Woodworking Design Book Two.* Newtown, CT: The Taunton Press, 1979.

Fine Woodworking Magazine, eds. *Fine Woodworking Techniques.* Newtown, CT: The Taunton Press, 1978.

Frid, Tage. *Tage Frid Teaches Woodworking: Joinery, Tools and Techniques.* Newtown, CT: The Taunton Press, 1979.

Frid, Tage. *Tage Frid Teaches Woodworking: Shaping, Veneering, Finishing.* Newton, CT: The Taunton Press, 1981.

Joyce, Ernest. *The Encyclopedia of Furniture Making.* New York: Sterling Publishing Co., 1979.

Meilach, Donna Z. *Woodworking: The New Wave.* New York: Crown Publishers, 1981.

CRAFT MAGAZINES AND NEWSPAPERS

(a), annual; (/a), issues per year; (bi-a), biannual; (bi-m), bimonthly; (m), monthly; (q), quarterly; (*), periodical received as a benefit of membership.

American Ceramics (q)
15 W. 44th St.
New York, NY 10036

American Craft (* bi-m)
American Craft Council
401 Park Ave. South
New York, NY 10016

Ceramics Monthly (10/a)
Professional Publications

Box 12448
Columbus, OH 43212

Fiberarts (bi-m)
50 College St.
Asheville, NC 28801

Fine Woodworking (bi-m)
The Taunton Press
Box 355
Newtown, CT 06470

Glass Studio (m)
Box 23383
Portland, OR 97223

Journal of Glass Studies (a)
Corning Museum of Glass
Corning, NY 14830

Metalsmith (* q)
Society of North American Goldsmiths
(SNAG)

2849 St. Ann Dr.
Green Bay, WI 54301

New Work (bi-m)
Experimental Glass Workshop
c/o Richard Yelle
24 Spring St.
New York, NY 10012

Stained Glass (* q)
Stained Glass Association of America
1125 Wilmington Ave.
St. Louis, MO 63111

INDEX

ACKNOWLEDGMENTS

A book of this scope cannot be compiled without the talents and efforts of many different people. For all those who have willingly shared their time and expertise, I am very grateful. I would like especially to express my gratitude to Lena Tabori, who conceived this book, and to Marsha Melnick, my editor, whose sound advice and invaluable direction helped it take shape.

Numerous craftsmen and gallery owners shared information with me, and I want to acknowledge a few individuals who were of particular help: Sarah Bodine of *Metalsmith* magazine, who led me to some of the best work being done in metal, and Douglas Steakley, who helped me understand modern techniques of metalsmithing; Douglas and Michael Heller for their counsel on glass; Warren and Bebe Johnson of Pritam & Eames Gallery for their advice as well as for allowing us to photograph in their gallery; Kay Eddy of The Elements Gallery for her help in finding homes of collectors; John Cram of The New Morning Gallery, Ed Nash of The American Hand, and Nicholas Rodriguez of Hadler-Rodriguez Galleries for helping me to locate good work; and Carol Sedestrom and the entire staff of American Craft Enterprises for allowing us to photograph at the Baltimore Winter Market.

Those who opened their homes to us for photography made possible a first-hand look at contemporary crafts in home settings, a very real contribution to this book that I greatly appreciate. They include Judy and Pat Coady, Ken Deavers, Kay and George Eddy, Barbara and Daniel Fendrick, Sandra and Louis Grotta, Sherley and Bernard Koteen, Jack Lenor Larsen, Nancy and Harvey Leeds, Helene Margolies, Drewry and Christoph Nostitz, Sandy and Fred Roth, Lena Tabori, Don Thomas and Jorge Cao, and Julia and Carter Walker.

David Arky, Joseph Kugielsky, and Breton Littlehales deserve recognition as the photographers who shot in these homes, and Jonathan Wallen who photographed at the Baltimore Winter Market.

I would like to thank Christy Ballou and Marya Dalrymple, who spent many hours over the past two years contacting craftsmen and carefully cataloging over 6000 slides; Chuck Boyce, who compiled the extensive directory of Craftsmen and Galleries; and Marian Lange, whose good judgment and persuasive demeanor greatly increased the variety and quality of work we considered.

In addition, I want to thank those members of my family, John Pearson and Jean Hitch, and my friends, Jennie Cashdollar and Joanne Polster, who provided their time, transportation, and homes during research and photography trips. Special thanks to Dick Pearson whose help made it possible for me to concentrate all my efforts on this book.

And finally, to all the craftsmen who submitted work for consideration, I am grateful for their efforts.